Transcendence
and Understanding

Transcendence and Understanding

Gadamer and Modern Orthodox Hermeneutics in Dialogue

Zdenko Š. Širka

Foreword by Assaad Elias Kattan

PICKWICK Publications · Eugene, Oregon

TRANSCENDENCE AND UNDERSTANDING
Gadamer and Modern Orthodox Hermeneutics in Dialogue

Copyright © 2020 Zdenko Š. Širka. All rights reserved. Except for brief quotations in critical publications or reviews, no part of this book may be reproduced in any manner without prior written permission from the publisher. Write: Permissions, Wipf and Stock Publishers, 199 W. 8th Ave., Suite 3, Eugene, OR 97401.

Pickwick Publications
An Imprint of Wipf and Stock Publishers
199 W. 8th Ave., Suite 3
Eugene, OR 97401

www.wipfandstock.com

PAPERBACK ISBN: 978-1-5326-7807-3
HARDCOVER ISBN: 978-1-5326-7808-0
EBOOK ISBN: 978-1-5326-7809-7

Cataloguing-in-Publication data:

Names: Širka, Zdenko Š., author. | Kattan, Assaad Elias, foreword

Title: Transcendence and understanding : Gadamer and modern orthoodxy hermeneutics in dialogue / by Zdenko Š. Širka ; foreword by Assaad Elias Kattan.

Description: Eugene, OR : Pickwick Publications, 2020 | Includes bibliographical references and index.

Identifiers: ISBN 978-1-5326-7807-3 (paperback) | ISBN 978-1-5326-7808-0 (hardcover) | ISBN 978-1-5326-7809-7 (ebook)

Subjects: LCSH: Gadamer Hans-Georg—1900-2002. | Orthodox Eastern Church—Doctrines. | Transcendence of God. | Transcendence (Philosophy). | Hermeneutics—Religious aspects—Orthodox Eastern Church. | Hermeneutics—Religious aspects—Christianity—History.

Classification: BT124.5 .S56 2020 (print) | BT124.5 .S56 (ebook)

Manufactured in the U.S.A.   MARCH 2, 2020

Scripture quotations are from the New Revised Standard Version Bible, copyright © 1989 National Council of the Churches of Christ in the United States of America. Used by permission. All rights reserved worldwide.

This book is the result of research project no. 17-00987S "Transformations of Tradition: Implications for Contemporary Ecumenical Theology," funded by the Czech Science Foundation.

This book is dedicated to our twins, Jakub and Hana.

The conversation that we are is one that never ends. No word is the last word, just as there is no first word.

HANS-GEORG GADAMER

Contents

Foreword by Assaad Elias Kattan | ix
Preface | xi
List of Abbreviations | xiii
Introduction | xv

1. Sources of Gadamer's Hermeneutics | 1
2. Development of Gadamer's Hermeneutical Project | 22
3. Reception and Critical Evaluation | 36
4. Horizons of Human Understanding and Transcendence in Gadamer's Hermeneutical School | 55
5. The Contributions of Gadamerian Hermeneutics | 81
6. The Emergence of Modern Orthodox Hermeneutics | 93
7. Sources of Orthodox Hermeneutics Revisited | 109
8. The Move beyond the Neo-patristic Synthesis | 128
9. Human Understanding and Transcendence in Current Orthodox Hermeneutics | 147
10. The Role of Interpretative Community | 166

    Conclusion | 178

Bibliography | 191
Index of Names | 209

Foreword

THE present book emerged from a doctoral dissertation submitted in 2015. Zdenko Širka picks up therein a query that has long been floating, as it were, in theological circles, yet rarely attended to in detail and in a meticulous fashion. Is it possible to bring into a seminal dialogue Hans-Georg Gadamer's hermeneutical program and those insights that may be gleaned from what Orthodox theologians have written about hermeneutics during the twentieth century? To be sure, this is today a crucial question for Orthodox theology. In fact, the debate over hermeneutics among the Orthodox has witnessed throughout the recent years a noticeable revival closely related to the fact that hermeneutics is increasingly perceived as a modern *locus* par excellence whose relevance has hardly been diminished, let alone discounted, by postmodernity. Orthodox theology seems today to have no task more urgent than to grapple with the numerous challenges raised by modernity, from criticism as an all-encompassing *method* through democracy and human rights to feminism and gender issues. If hermeneutics appears, at first glance, to be the less visible on this voluminous agenda, it remains nevertheless the more crucial in virtue of its relatedness to the foundational principles of theology, that is, to understanding and interpretation.

It comes as no surprise that the question of how to negotiate hermeneutics is raised in this book by a Protestant theologian. For since its inception by Friedrich Schleiermacher in the nineteenth century as an academic theological discipline, hermeneutics has been more often than not a Protestant concern. Even Paul Ricoeur, a French philosopher whose thought is fully pervaded by hermeneutical inquiry, was a Protestant. It is nevertheless highly intriguing to notice that, in this book, a Protestant scholar ventures into a critical appraisal of how and to which extent *Orthodox* theology engages hermeneutics. This proves to be not only an expression of scholarly committed ecumenism in times when ecumenical competence is no longer self-evident when it comes to scholarship, but also an extremely promising sign of intellectual osmosis between Orthodoxy and Protestantism. It goes without saying that, in order to yield fruits, such an osmosis needs to abide by the rules of critical thinking as an underlying principle of mutual learning without which no real dialogue is possible.

Within this perspective, Zdenko Širka's *Transcendence and Understanding* is a most welcome book on an extremely timely subject. A reading journey through it, open as hermeneutical inquiry itself, will be amply rewarded.

—Assaad Elias Kattan
University of Münster

Preface

This book is a shortened and rewritten version of my dissertation, defended at the Charles University (Prague, Czech Republic), but in many ways it is much more than that. In one sense it can be considered a final stop, as it brings many answers to questions that emerged during my theological studies in Bratislava two decades ago. These questions made me travel all around Europe as an academic nomad, spending innumerable hours in countless European libraries, as well as sitting and listening to lectures on the most diverse subjects at various universities.

My questions were basic, the most important of which were: How can a human being know and talk about God? What does it mean to be a Christian in the world? Why does the image of God vary in diverse confessions? To what extent does our personal identity and history influence the way we see the world and the one who transforms the world?

My pursuit passed through three stages. It is a credit to my first teacher, Günther Gassmann (recently deceased), who told me: "*Zdenko, you must study hermeneutics to get your answers.*" Needless to say, I had no idea what hermeneutics was and had to begin at the beginning.

The second stage of my pursuit was the discovery of the work of Hans-Georg Gadamer, which had an enlightening and liberating effect on me and, as I hear from my students, his ideas continue to attract seekers.

The third stage began at the moment when Ivana Noble showed me a book written by an Orthodox theologian, John Breck. She commented, "*You might like it.*" I did, and my further involvement with Orthodoxy and Orthodox theology built a theological pillar that backed-up Gadamer's thoughts.

Hence, I present a book in hermeneutics concerning a dialogue between Gadamer and modern Orthodox hermeneutics, which closes the circle for me and shows that Gassmann and Noble were right.

On the other hand, the book is not yet a final stop, but another starting point as, in my humble opinion, it only opens further possibilities and points toward likely venues where doors still must be opened, by me or someone else. Among Orthodox scholars there is growing interest both in hermeneutical questions and Gadamer, but at the same time there is uncertainty over the limits of dialogue. Even so, I believe that the track is correct and I am certain that they must read more Gadamer to find their answers.

There are many people who accompanied me during my long journey and unselfishly provided me the motivation and support to continue. I am grateful to each of them. The first I must thank is Prof. Ivana Noble, who always directed me along the right path, helped me with her enormous knowledge, as well as giving much advice and thoughts. My sincere thanks further extends to those who only walked with me on parts of that voyage, yet immensely influenced or supported my research and its result: Prof. Eberhard Jüngel, who enabled an ecumenical scholarship in Tübingen in order to pursue my hermeneutical study at its very beginnings; the staff of the International Baptist Theological Seminary and Doc. Parush Parushev, who provided an academic surrounding where I could grow as a person and an academic worker; the staff of the Institute of Ecumenical Studies and Jabok College, where I was able to share the results of my research with fellow students and gain teaching experience; the librarians of various European universities where I conducted my research over the years; the leadership of the Protestant Theological Faculty that provided me the academic background to continue my research, as well as the many colleagues with whom I discussed results and problems of my research at various conferences, workshops and seminars. I cannot forget Nancy Lively for her repeated editing of this text and for the life-energy she shares with me. All are among those who directed and influenced the path of my research and the direction of my life.

This book is a result of the research project "Transformations of Tradition: Implications for Contemporary Ecumenical Theology" funded by the Czech Science Foundation and without their financial support I would never have been able to put on paper the outcomes of my decade-long research.

Most of all, my appreciation goes to my wife, Ivanka, for her unselfish support, boundless patience and the unconditional love she has shown me over the years. I dedicate this book to her, and to our new-born twins, Jakub and Hana.

List of Abbreviations

GW   Hans-Georg Gadamer. *Gesammelte Werke.* 10 vols. Tübingen: Mohr Siebeck, 1985–95.

WM   Hans-Georg Gadamer. *Wahrheit und Methode.* 6th ed. Tübingen: Mohr Siebeck, 1990.

TM   Hans-Georg Gadamer. *Truth and Method.* 2nd ed. Translated by Joel Weinsheimer and Donald G. Marshall. London: Continuum, 2004.

GS   Wilhelm Dilthey. *Gesammelte Schriften.* 12 vols. Leipzig: Teubner, 1922–36.

Introduction

THE epigraph of this book, as used above, expresses several issues which are key to this publication: insistence on dialogue as the essential feature of human beings, the dynamic structure of our existence, insistence on the infinity of the perennial dialogue, the absence of a final answer and definite knowledge, and the necessity of the other who helps to overcome the solely individual approach. Here, conversation is elevated to the position where participants and their context are themselves neither the beginning nor the end. This lays a foundation for the main questions of the book: How can we mediate not only the content of the understanding of who we are in relation to each other, to the world in which we live and to God, but also the comprehension of the process of understanding across various historical periods and different cultures, called here the horizons of human understanding? How can what is transcendent, as active and enabling the cooperation, be testified within the horizons of human understanding without becoming created *by* the people as what reaches beyond them? How can the transcendent be mediated as the transcendent? How can the balance between historical mediation and the silence that dismisses mediation be preserved? How does the transcendence of the transcendent impact both the content and the process of understanding? What authority has mediation and those who mediate the transcendent?

The purpose of this book is to bring into the conversation both Western and Orthodox hermeneutical schools. In order to investigate the differences between approaches in understanding, transcendence will be explored by two approaches. One is represented by Hans-Georg Gadamer and his followers, such as Wolfhart Pannenberg, Edward Schillebeeckx, David Tracy, Kevin Vanhoozer, and others, who had formative impacts on current Western hermeneutics. The other school, modern Orthodox hermeneutics, is represented by figures such as John Breck, Assaad Kattan,

Theodore Stylianopoulos, and others, less focused around a single person, yet demonstrating common distinct attributes.

Gadamer is not only understood as a separate intellectual; the discussion about him includes the effective history and continuation of his work in the West in the last third of the twentieth century (a shift from Gadamer's to Gadamerian hermeneutics). In a similar manner, Orthodox hermeneutics is not personalized either, but epitomized by concrete current voices. Therefore, the first five chapters will deal with Gadamer and his hermeneutical school and the last five will deal with modern and postmodern Orthodox hermeneutics.

While analyzing Gadamerian hermeneutics, the first part of the book shows its strength in investigating transcendence as it appears horizontally in historically and culturally conditioned mediations, as well as in giving focus to the historical character of our being in language, which includes new evolving situations, but does not dismiss the classics. Gadamer contributes to this debate with his relational character of understanding, where the hermeneutical process is described horizontally as a dialogue (or play), in which "what is beyond" (called *Sache*) is a result of cooperation and relation, and appears within the human horizon as a result of human participation. Gadamer calls this shift from a finite and limited subject to the ungraspable, inexpressible and incontrollable power that reaches beyond them, a mystery or a miracle of language.[1]

As we will see, this is one of the reasons for the argument that Gadamer's intentions need to be further developed by theologians and, as the book points out, would benefit from a closer investigation of the participatory relationship between the immanent and the transcendent as we find it in Orthodox theology.

In the first part of this book concerning Gadamer and his hermeneutical school, we will first point out the ancient roots of Gadamer's holism, where his thoughts about the horizon of understanding found inspiration. These also show which, how and why some of the aspects underlined by his predecessors were absorbed and adapted within his own hermeneutics.

His interest in Greek philosophy originated in his early years and was crucial for his hermeneutics, especially the concepts of dialogue (from Plato) and of practical wisdom (from Aristotle). Plato will be mentioned because, through his dialogues, Gadamerian hermeneutics developed as dialectical with an emphasis on dialogue and conversation. Aristotle's articulation of practical knowledge *phronē̄sis*, in a different approach,

---

1. See the following article that critically deals with the miracle of language: Vanhoozer, "Discourse on Matter," 5–37.

showed the true nature of the process of understanding, not from the perspective of a subject that grasps the object, but as an experience through which prejudice or habits, passed on in a tradition, encounter the strange and new.

Further it will be pointed out why and how Gadamer was aware of various modern representatives of hermeneutics. Only those who contributed to the discussion concerning the horizons of human understanding and transcendence will be thoroughly mentioned, beginning with the character of our being in language as developed in a discussion with Friedrich Schleiermacher, according to whom everything presupposed in hermeneutics is but language.

Wilhelm Dilthey repeatedly claimed that man is a historical being and, opposite to Schleiermacher, he moves to historicality and more strongly develops the project of historical reason, which influenced Gadamer. Martin Heidegger will be mentioned because he re-oriented understanding into the way in which humans exist and relate with the world.

After the explanation of where and how the notions of dialogue, history, universality, language and prejudice, important for the discussion of human horizons and transcendence, entered into the Gadamerian hermeneutical school, the second chapter will draw on the three periods of Gadamer's work. Here it will be shown how his concept of the horizons of human understanding and transcendence developed from his early works, oriented on the question of the understanding of human sciences versus natural sciences, until the period he began his projects with transcendence, described as a "religious turn." Gadamer's work attempted to free the area of human responsibility, recover human finitude and underline the dialogue that allows seeing and hearing the other.

Very soon after its publication, his main book, *Truth and Method*, was recognized as one of the most important contributions to current philosophy, but in the same period Gadamer's hermeneutics became subject to extensive criticism and discussion. This will be described in chapter 3, where how Gadamer's thoughts have been accepted and how they changed through this reception will be displayed, in both philosophical and theological areas. The discussions with Jürgen Habermas and Paul Ricoeur will be meticulously described. Further in the chapter, the main voice will be given to theological thinkers, who critically received Gadamer's hermeneutics in their various fields of interest. These will be divided according to the character of their analysis and elements they discussed: discussion about the transcendental elements in Gadamer's hermeneutics, its traditional character, the concept of history and Gadamer's notion of conversation.

Further, in the chapter 4 of this volume, there will be a move to a detailed analysis of the horizons of human understanding and transcendence in Gadamer's hermeneutical school. Special attention will be paid to the historical character of our understanding and its elements, such as history, prejudice, authority and tradition. Additionally, it will point to the forms of understanding that are born out of the merging of horizons, as is illustrated in the concepts of dialogue, application and play. Following that, transcendence will be presented as an aspect of our being in language, as is illustrated in the concepts of language, incarnation and aesthetic experience.

Chapter 5 offers a summary approach to the horizons of human understanding and transcendence will be offered there. It will be shown which aspects of Gadamer's hermeneutics remain beneficial for theological hermeneutics and where further complements from other sources would be additionally beneficial.

Further, in the second part of the book, beginning with chapter 6, an analysis of modern Orthodox hermeneutics is offered. Modern Orthodox hermeneutics is relational and its representatives bring a strong sense of belonging to both community and tradition as its main elements. "What is beyond" is revealed here rather than created and always transcends both this world and human nature. Transcendence is not the result of cooperation between humans and history, but mainly comes to this relationship from the outside, as the Holy Spirit, and makes the world divine. The problem is that vertically understood transcendence divinizes too much and leaves not enough space for the human element, suspicion and otherness. There is a lack of a criterion of validity to evaluate these elements and to differentiate between tradition and customs, between the voices of people and the call of the Holy Spirit.

The reason for bringing Gadamer's hermeneutical school into this dialogue is the need to strengthen the historical dimension of tradition, to take more seriously into account the role of humans as a complement to the eschatological dimension. Preserving both approaches and indicating how they complement one another helps to achieve a balance between symbolic speech (the testimony, the liturgical celebration) of the in-breaking of the transcendent, and the silence where mediation does not substitute for transcendence.

In order to hermeneutically grasp the question of the human understanding of transcendence and in order to build a proper stand for a hermeneutical discussion about the understanding process between Gadamer and Orthodox theology, attention is first paid, in chapter 6, to the struggles and inspirational sources having a formative impact on Orthodox hermeneutics. In order to understand the specific contributors to Orthodox hermeneutics, it is necessary to place the concept of modern and postmodern Orthodox hermeneutics as it has historically evolved. Hence, in this chapter we draw an analysis and overview of various ways in which hermeneutic theory entered and developed in the Orthodox context, first in reference to the meeting in Athens in 1936, second in reference to the neo-patristic renewal in Greece in the sixties, third in reference to the seventies, when a discussion about hermeneutics continued more explicitly in the context of biblical studies and fourth in reference to the current redefinition of the relation between exegesis and hermeneutics, and to the critical reception of neo-patristic ideas.

Subsequently with these periods, modern hermeneutics within the Orthodox context developed in three directions: as patristic hermeneutics, as biblical hermeneutics, and as a hermeneutical theology.

While focusing on the movement of the return to the Fathers, a problem of negative identity formation as a key to what Orthodox hermeneutics should be and will be explored in chapter 7. In this chapter, I will aim to achieve two things. First, I will deal in more detail with Georges Florovsky and Christos Yannaras and their concepts as expressive of two ways of dealing with the Orthodox sources, Russian emigrant and Greek. Their concepts are different and come from different times and places, but they still display common features when they show why and how the patristic period became normative for Orthodoxy. This section about modern hermeneutics among Russian émigrés and Greeks will be followed with a section about the problems which arise out of this discussion.

These are two: patristic captivity and captivity in an anti-Western attitude.[2] The analysis of the Greek and Russian waves serves to find the reasons for where and why these captivities appeared. Namely, neo-patristic movements liberated Orthodox spirituality and monasticism, but ended up in a too radical contrast and this is addressed by the current generation of theologians who endeavor for an openness and dialogue.

The phrase "patristic captivity" is taken from Timothy Noble and inspired me because of its hermeneutical implications. In his interpretation, patristic captivity contributes to the expressions of Orthodox identity and, more importantly, both captivities show the very apparent presence of a hermeneutic criterion and of implicit hermeneutics based on a very clear theological methodology.

---

2. The phrase *patristic captivity* was introduced by Timothy Noble in the concluding panel discussion of the International Scientific Conference Symbolic Mediation of Wholeness in Western Orthodoxy, organized by the Protestant Theological faculty of Charles University, May 25, 2014.

Chapter 8 will further contain the critical reception of the work with the sources, as well as alternative and positive work with them. Both critical and alternative work overcome the negative identity formation, which is explored here first through the critique of Orthodox theologians and those who deal with the Orthodox tradition, Pantelis Kalaitzidis, Aristotle Papanikolaou, Brandon Gallaher, Assaad Elias Kattan and Ivana Noble. These representatives aim to avoid negative building of identity and negative self-identification that misses renewal and innovation. Negative identity formation is further complemented and as well overcome by alternative work with the sources, which also shows the influence of non-Orthodox authors. It will be presented in the systematic rehabilitation of patristic methodology and hermeneutics as is visible in the work of John Breck and Theodore Stylianopoulos.

Chapter 9 discusses Orthodox hermeneutics in terms of a strong sense of belonging to a community and, at the same time, discusses seeing transcendence as something that principally comes into relationships from the outside. This perspective was achieved by the critical reception and alternative work with the sources.

The focus will first be on the reception of Gadamer's thoughts in the Orthodox world. The reception of Gadamer's thinking and his hermeneutical concepts is a very important part of my argument as this is the point where two worlds begin to interact. The reception of Gadamer by Andrew Louth, Assaad Kattan and Nicolae Turcan will be presented. The themes addressed in this section will form a basis for the rest of chapters 9 and 10.

Namely, in Gadamer there is a focus that the reconstruction of the historical context includes the personality of the one who understands, which is the church. Gadamer's work therefore brings the recovery of tradition, understood as the continuity of a human communication of an experience, not as something that limits, but is the context in which one is allowed to be free. The concept of genuine conversation shows that the church must accept the validity of tradition, not simply in a sense of acknowledging it, but to listen to what it says to us. Gadamer also addresses the fact that interpretation is not an attempt to reconstruct the original historical context, but rather a matter of listening across the historic gulf that is filled with tradition and which brings the interpreted object to the interpretative community. Gadamer's concept of the temporal distance is especially inspiring, as it presupposes that the act of understanding is not achievable without fore-understanding and that the interpreter is part of the act of interpretation.

At the same time, the fusion of horizons that underlies an interpreter's involvement in the interpretative act might contribute to a healthy and fruitful discussion among the Orthodox over the limits of tradition. These thoughts of Gadamer complement modern Orthodox hermeneutics and will be the basis for its issues on Scripture and Tradition and contemplation over science, which is dealt with in chapter 9 and, for discussion about the interpretative community and on its liturgical dimension, is dealt with in chapter 10.

The relation between them will be manifested as the hermeneutical circle, which means that Scripture and Tradition are not in contrast or in too close cooperation, but are in the form of a circle, meaning that they influence one another and cannot be divided. Tradition and Scripture build the core of Orthodox hermeneutics with another concept, which is a community of believers, often called "ecclesial reading" or a "liturgical reading." These themes reassess the radical clash between the divine and human in our perception of revelation of the transcendence and include the elements of the participation and historicity of the interpretative community.

In conclusion, it will first be shown that Orthodox hermeneutics can enrich Western, Gadamerian hermeneutics by the emphasis Orthodoxy places on eschatology, mediation of the transcendent as transcendent, balance between communitarian and personal understanding, supremacy of active and revealed mystery and participation of the community through liturgy.

Further it will be shown that Gadamer's hermeneutical school can enrich Orthodox hermeneutics by compacting the historical aspect of tradition rooted in language as a complement to the eschatological tradition, then by giving alternative criteria for discernment of what is a good interpretation of the classics, for helping to move beyond the polarity of tradition and innovation, for the relational character of understanding where the hermeneutical process is described as a dialogue, as well as for accepting the plurality of the mediations of transcendent in historically conditioned situations.

The book argues that preserving both approaches and specifying how they supplement each other helps to show the limits of encountering the transcendent reality that can be testified by human language, but not reduced to it.

This study is one of the first works that systematically presents the work of Hans-Georg Gadamer in dialogue with modern Orthodox hermeneutics. Moreover, it is also one of the first publications that systematically presents the development of various forms of hermeneutics in current and modern Orthodox theology.[3] My initial aim and the motivation behind the whole

---

3. See also my two previous articles: Širka, "Experience with Hermeneutics," 58–89; Širka, "Gadamer's Concept of Aesthetic Experience," 378–407.

project is to summarize what has been agreed so far in the dialogue between Gadamer's hermeneutics and modern Orthodox hermeneutics, as well as to bring new building material into the growing Orthodox reception of Gadamer and initiate further discussion on the topics where this reception might continue. I also hope to initiate deeper dialogue between Western and Eastern thinking on the ground of hermeneutics. Namely, this relatively marginal dialogue between Western and Orthodox hermeneutical schools touches the relation between the human and divine elements and attempts to achieve a balance between the authority of symbolic speech and silence, when and where transcendence cannot be replaced by mediation.

There are three main goals I aim to achieve in this book. My first is to show how Gadamer, in his process of understanding, grasps and reaches the "what is beyond" and how transcendence is described in his model, as well as to provide a critique and reception of this account. My further goal is to show how modern Orthodoxy defines the process of understanding and how it describes the revelation of transcendence, while providing a critique of this account. My third goal is to point to the strengths and weaknesses of these two accounts, as well to point out how these positions can complement one another. Methodically, a threefold structure will be used in presenting each partner to this dialogue: sources and roots of the approach, its development and critical presentation of the problem. In the first part I will search for the roots of Gadamer's understanding of transcendence and present the development of his thought. I will proceed similarly in the second part, where I will explain various sources of the modern development of hermeneutics in Orthodox theology and place a special focus on its various understandings in the current Orthodox context. Equipped with information gathered about the main problems, authors and influences, I will provide a critical account of Orthodox hermeneutical theory in relation to its understanding of the revelation of God.

1

Sources of Gadamer's Hermeneutics

THIS chapter explains the backstory of Gadamer's concepts and the intellectual context behind his thinking. During his life he maintained close ties to many twentieth-century philosophical and theological schools of thought: the Neo-Kantianism of Paul Natorp and Nikolai Hartmann in Marburg, Edmund Husserl's and Max Scheller's phenomenology, Martin Heidegger's and Rudolf Bultmann's existentialism in Marburg. He encouraged discussions with the school of ideology critique (Jürgen Habermas), as well as Jacques Derrida's deconstructionism, Richard Rorty's pragmatism, and many others.

Gadamer's interests also lay in the ancient philosophical schools, as he began his career as a philologist, oriented toward Greek thinking. Nevertheless, he also interacted with modern thinkers, such as René Descartes, Immanuel Kant, Georg Hegel, and Friedrich Schleiermacher.

In this chapter, I begin with Gadamer's intellectual bibliography and then point to the several ancient and several modern influences that bring into focus the elements of his horizon of human understanding. Ancient influences are the models of dialogue and practical wisdom, which developed as the conversational and revelatory aspects of hermeneutics. Modern influences important to his thinking are universality based upon the language of Schleiermacher that became the mark of Gadamer's hermeneutics. The historicism of Dilthey, in Gadamer's hermeneutics, evolved into the historicity of the interpreter and understanding, as a part of what was being developed by Heidegger In Gadamer's writings that took a form that prioritizes the *identity* of the one who interprets.

These motifs are the primary topic of this publication, as they lay the foundation for how the *content* of understanding who we are in relation to the world and to God is mediated in historically and culturally conditioned situations, as well as *how* this is testified to within the horizons of human understanding.

Gadamer's Intellectual Biography

This intellectual biography of Hans-Georg Gadamer will introduce (i) the main works and moments of his academic life, (ii) the period covered by his work, including its development and (iii), a discussion of his relation with the Christian faith.

Gadamer was born in Marburg in a German academic family originally from Silesia (today Poland) and growing up in Breslau (Wroclaw). His father, Johannes Gadamer, was a chemistry professor, as well as a strict and authoritarian person. His mother died very early and his brother, an epileptic, was institutionalized in his teens.

Religion played an important role in this family, as Gadamer's mother, Johanna Gadamer, had a strong holier-than-thou faith and from whom Gadamer received, as he says, a "vaguely religious disposition."[1] However, this disposition never flowered into faith.[2]

When his father became the rector of the University of Marburg, Gadamer began studying philosophy and classical philology there. He became acquainted with Nicolai Hartmann, Max Sheller and Rudolf Bultmann. The University was, at that time, a center of northern neo-Kantianism and from out of this milieu came Gadamer's doctoral thesis. *The Essence of Desire in Plato's Dialogues* (*Das Wesen der Lust nach den platonischen Dialogen*) was written in 1921 under the supervision of Paul Natorp.[3]

These years were very dramatic for Gadamer. He completed his doctorate (1921), got married (1923), became independent of his father, had

---

1. Gadamer expressed himself this way in a conversation with Jean Grondin in July 1989. His mother died when he was four and Gadamer remembered her as a person with strong religious and pietistic inclinations. Grondin, *Hans-Georg Gadamer—eine Biographie*, 19.

2. Gadamer often recalled that he attended worship services in Breslau every Sunday with his brother Willi (1898–1944), and there was a pastor who started every sermon with words from Mark's Gospel: "I believe; help my unbelief!" This contrast between belief and unbelief discloses much about Gadamer's faith as a seeker. See Grondin, *Hans-Georg Gadamer—eine Biographie*, 23.

3. The manuscript of this dissertation remains unpublished and is lost, maybe even because Gadamer himself was never satisfied with it and never returned to it.

financial problems related to the great inflation of 1923 which reduced the value of his trust fund and contracted polio, placing him under a month-long quarantine. During this stressful period, he read Heidegger's unpublished essay on Aristotle,[4] which caused a reversal in his intellectual life.[5]

Therefore, he spent the summer semester of 1923 at Freiburg, where he attended Heidegger's seminars and Husserl's lectures. Gadamer followed Heidegger back to Marburg, and became one of his students, along with others such as Leo Strauss, Jakob Klein, Gerhard Krüger and Karl Löwith).[6] Also during this period he published his first article in the commemoration for Natorp's seventieth birthday.[7] It illustrated the influence of Heidegger that allowed him to achieve a distance from "Natorp's comprehensive system design and the naive objectivism of Hartmann's research of categories."[8] The result of the Heidegger relationship was Gadamer's post-doctoral dissertation on Plato's dialogue *Philebos*, titled *Plato's Dialectical Ethics* (*Platos dialogische Ethik*, 1929).[9]

During the Nazi period Gadamer avoided politics, as it was far more productive to be discreet.[10] After his dissertation was published in 1931, over a long period he published but one monograph, titled *Volk and History in Herder's Thought* (*Volk und Geschichte im Denken Herders*, 1942).

Upon receiving temporary teaching positions in Kiel and Marburg, he became a professor in Leipzig in 1938, but due to administrative duties he could no longer adjust his research with his lectures. His writings during this period were mostly on Greek philosophy and German idealism, and he shared the results of his studies only with his students. During those times, he worked on Aristotle's physics as well as a certain project on Plato.[11]

---

4. Heidegger, "Phenomenological Interpretations with Respect to Aristotle," 355–93.

5. "affected me like an electric shock" (Gadamer, *Philosophical Apprenticeships*, 47).

6. After a year, Heidegger showed disappointment with Gadamer's progress, and for this reason Gadamer returned to the study of classical philology under Paul Friedländer. When Friedländer wanted to ask Gadamer to do a habilitation in classical philology, Heidegger, to much surprise, asked Gadamer first. Concerning this see Gadamer, *Philosophische Lehrjahre*, 43.

7. Gadamer, "Systemidee in der Philosophie," 55–75.

8. *GW* 2:483. If not stated otherwise, and if a reference to English translation is missing, all translations from German to English are mine.

9. Gadamer wrote his habilitation in 1929 and published it in 1931, it is now included in *GW* 5:5–163; the English version was translated by Robert Wallace and published in 1991.

10. "sich unauffällig zu verhalten" (*GW* 2:490).

11. This project was interrupted; see *GW* 2:489.

After a short period as rector in Leipzig (1946–1947) and while teaching in Frankfurt (1947–1949), he accepted the call from Heidelberg to occupy the chair that had been Karl Jasper's (1949). With this, a new era began in his life and he remained at Heidelberg University until his retirement in 1968, living in the nearby town of Ziegelhausen until his death.

At the University of Heidelberg, he was able free his mind from school-politics, conduct research and teach. At that time Gadamer was a passionate teacher, enjoying teaching and conversation, but with problems writing. He says that writing "remained for long a right pain, because I had always a damn feeling Heidegger watched me over my shoulder."[12]

But he much enjoyed going to the *agora*, to be among and to discuss with the people he met, as well as encountering others and being surprised by them. Gadamer was a master of shorter essays, a writer of occasional pieces, an essayist, with a lucid writing style enriched by many examples and stories, all of which made his works accessible to a wider audience.[13] He became very well known throughout Germany and attracted people of talent to join him at Heidelberg.

For example, he recognized Habermas's talent and invited him to teach in Heidelberg, where he remained from 1961 to 1964. Many foreign students arrived as well to learn philosophy in Heidelberg, including Gianni Vattimo from Italy, Valerio Verra and Emilio Lledó from Spain. What Gadamer offered them was hermeneutical practice, as "hermeneutics is primarily a practice, the art of understanding and making comprehensible."[14]

For a long time Gadamer was devoted to his students and failed to write anything groundbreaking. But all was poised to change, when in 1957 he accepted an invitation to give the *Cardinal Mercier lectures* at the University of Louvain. These lectures were published as a small book in French under the title *La problème de la conscience historique* (1963). It articulated the main points of the later *Truth and Method* (*Wahrheit und Methode*, 1960), his most important book, articulating the main effects of his Heidelberg era. The motivation to prepare this book came from among his students who

---

12. *GW* 2:491. Although, Heidegger was one of those who encouraged Gadamer to write a book. He repeated several times: "Gadamer finally has to write a book!" (Grondin, *Hans-Georg Gadamer—eine Biographie*, 300).

13. Moreover, he was not using very rigid terms and terminology, but was not imprecise, quite the opposite. He recalled also Leibniz and his "I approve everything I read." Leibniz, the librarian, probably understood this in a sense that everything has a reason if one takes others and their reasons into account. Gadamer understood this sentence as a hermeneutic one, as acknowledging one's own finitude and openness for others. *GW* 2:492.

14. "Hermeneutik ist vor allem eine Praxis, die Kunst des Verstehens und des Verständlichenmachens" (*GW* 2:493–94).

asked him to write out his thinking and present what he had been doing in his classes.[15]

Truth and Method, said Gadamer, was "nothing else than trying to give information about the style of my studies and my teaching theoretically."[16] He wrote that the first ten years in Heidelberg he strove to avoid all administrative duties and congresses as far as possible in order to work on his publication, following Horace's motto that *all good needs nine years to ripen if it is about to become any good.*[17] The resulting book, published in 1960, is based on a manuscript finished during the winter semester of 1958/59.[18]

Gadamer's retirement in 1968 enabled him to collect his essays in four volumes of *Short Essays* (*Kleine Schriften*), which were later superseded by ten volumes of his *Collected Works* (*Gesammelte Werke*). *Truth and Method* appeared in six succeeding editions,[19] but often overlooked is that the second volume of *Collected Works*, which contains *Preliminary Stage* (*Vorstufe*) and *Developments* (*Weiterentwicklungen*), is also titled *Truth and Method*, without a subtitle. The first and second volumes obviously belong together.[20] With his second volume, Gadamer showed the need to take into account his early as well later works, since the importance of *Truth and Method* at that time overshadowed his other writing.[21]

After his retirement, Gadamer was invited to teach in world universities in the United States, Canada, throughout Europe, South America, and Africa. He referred to these years as his *second youth*[22] and during this term hermeneutics became known worldwide. As a tireless world traveler he lectured wherever he was invited and those lectures were separately

---

15. Gadamer mentioned this several times, for example in a dialogue with Misgeld and Nicholson. See Misgeld and Nicholson, *Hans-Georg Gadamer on Education*, 63.

16. *GW* 2:492.

17. Gadamer, *Philosophische Lehrjahre*, 180–81.

18. Generally, it is accepted that Gadamer had a sabbatical WS 1958/59 (see for example Tietz, *Hans-Georg Gadamer*, 27). Grondin also mentions the letter from July 29, 1958 to the Ministry of Culture, where Gadamer asked for this sabbatical semester (Grondin, *Hans-Georg Gadamer—eine Biographie*, 319), but Gadamer in denies having it (Gadamer, *Philosophische Lehrjahre*, 181).

19. The second, third, and fifth editions were revised, the fifth (1986) was included in the *Collected Works* as its first volume.

20. Hans-Georg Gadamer talks about this connection himself in *GW* 2:4. This is further proved by a common register for two volumes.

21. Similarly writes also Grondin: "If you want to understand and even read WM, you have to consult the work after, but also before WM. The composition of WM did not stop in 1960. It is still going on" (Grondin, *Der Sinn der Hermeneutik*, 23).

22. Gadamer, *Philosophical Apprenticeships*, 158.

published.²³ Then followed his further works on Georg Hegel (1971), Martin Heidegger (1983), Paul Celan (1973), and the collections *The Beginning of Philosophy* (*Der Anfang der Philosophie*, 1997), *The Beginning of Knowledge* (*Der Anfang des Wissens*, 1999), and the final *Hermeneutic Outlines* (*Hermeneutische Entwürfe*, 2000).

At this point it is important to mention a second issue of this intellectual biography, namely the time-frame during which Gadamer worked. As has already been pointed out, his work is documented in the *Collected Works*, as well as in those books published during the last third of the twentieth century.

I suggest that his academic work should be divided into three periods, which helps one truly grasp the entire range of Gadamer's hermeneutical method. The first or early period, covers the years 1921–1959 and, although it is the longest period, it is the least productive. Here belong his short essays from this early period, works on Greek philosophy, including his Louvain lectures and the first draft of *Truth and Method*, known as *Urfassung*.

The second period begins with the completion of *Truth and Method*, published in 1960. This particularly includes its second edition, especially its foreword, which was his reaction to discussions with Emilio Betti and Jürgen Habermas.

The third period of Gadamer's work would include his lectures, essays and books published after 1965 until his death in 2002, as well as those interviews he gave toward the end of his life. This later period shows a turn in philosophy by Gadamer, illustrated by his emphasis in the area of transcendence. This is the result of various intellectual discussions he held and of the positive reception of his thinking in various areas, including theology. During this period hermeneutics became a main concept in European thinking and, with it, the Gadamerian hermeneutical school emerged.

Regarding his religious background, the last issue of this intellectual biography, Gadamer was by confession a Protestant with a Lutheran youth upbringing. He acknowledged Protestantism as an important influence on his thinking.²⁴ He never managed to accept faith in a Christian sense and remained only upon the doorstep of the church. One might identify him as

---

23. All published by Suhrkamp: *Die Vernunft Im Zeitalter der Wissenschaft* (1976), *Poetica* (1977), *Lob Der Theorie* (1983), *Die Vielfalt Europas. Erbe und Zukunft* (1985), *Das Erbe Europas* (1989), *Über Die Veborgenheit der Gesundheit* (1993).

24. He did not consider himself to be as religious as his teacher Martin Heidegger considered himself to be. Gadamer gives the impression that he might have done that only in order to distance himself from Heidegger's Catholicism. See *GW* 8:126.

a *nominal Protestant*,[25] or view his hermeneutics as *disguised Christianity*,[26] but calling him an agnostic is quite the more appropriate.[27]

The usual way of interpreting Gadamer's relation to theology regards him as a *secular thinker* and points out that words such as *Gott* (God) and *Göttliche* (divine) appear in only four titles of his essays.[28] Further, Christian concepts are used only as *arguments* in order to explain his view of the hermeneutical process.[29] Nevertheless, Gadamer was always interested in theology and owed it a great deal for his writing on *concepts* of understanding. His discussion of Christian theology in *Truth and Method* shows that religious topics played a much more important role than Greek philosophy. Topics such as the *I–Thou* relation, *kairos*, application in homiletics and biblical exegesis, incarnation, and a sympathetic reading of Augustine or Aquinas are only the primary examples of Gadamer's theological discussions. The three most important theologians and thinkers of that age were his teachers or colleagues: Karl Barth, Martin Heidegger and Rudolf Bultmann.[30]

This intellectual biography shows the interrelation of Gadamer's academic life during the early, main and late periods of his hermeneutical thinking. Those included the emergence of his hermeneutical school, and of the religious concepts that, combined, led toward his thoughts on the horizons of human understanding and transcendence.

---

25. Grondin, "Gadamer and Bultmann," 123.

26. This approach underlines that for Gadamer philosophy is conversation of the soul with itself, and knowing is a matter of divine grace; Gadamer shows how to "find a way to teach us how to hear the voice—how to converse with God, how to live in a world in which 'what is' has asked us a question and awaits our reply" (Tingley, "Gadamer and Light of the Word," 42).

27. "He was agnostic because for him religion underscored the impossibility of ever reaching complete understanding" (Eberhard, "Gadamer and Theology," 286). Similarly, Chris Lawn argues that the best choice is to call him agnostic, as Gadamer does not deny a God and its existence, but leaves it as an open question. See Lawn and Keane, *The Gadamer Dictionary*, 61. On the topic see also a book: Lammi, *Gadamer and the Question of the Divine*.

28. "Der Gott des innersten Gefühls" (*GW* 9:162); "Über das Göttliche im frühen Denken des Griechen" (*GW* 6:154); "Kant und die Gottesfrage" (*GW* 4:349); "Sein Geist Gott" (*GW* 3:320).

29. "I am not a theologian." Excerpt of 1984 interview conducted by Erwin Koller in Hans-Georg Gadamer, *Ich glaube nicht and die Systeme der Philosophie*, Schweizer Fernsehen DRS, 2000, videocassette.

30. He spent a lot of time especially with Bultmann, because he participated in his famous "Bultmannian Graeca" (every Thursday at 19:00) for fifteen years, where they read Greek classics.

The following pages will refer to these and more, explaining in detail the account on which these interrelations are based.

Ancient Inspiration: Plato and Aristotle

Gadamer always emphasized the importance of reading past texts in their own context as a way to understand the tradition in which we participate; therefore, it is not surprising that three volumes of his *Collected Works* (out of ten) deal with Greek philosophy. Gadamer's recovery of Greek philosophy is not of side interest and should neither be understood as a withdrawal from current philosophy, nor a simple application of Greek ideas.[31] He especially returns to Plato and Aristotle when he attempts to overcome and correct the misdirection of modern philosophy. This is in regard to the notion of dialogue in Plato and the notion of practical knowledge *phronēsis*, which I will describe in the next section.

Let us begin with Plato (ca. 428–347 BCE, the philosopher in ancient Greece), who was an important metaphorical partner in Gadamer's hermeneutical discourse.[32] Gadamer learned two main things from him: first, that understanding is always a part of a dialogue and second, that the finitude of understanding becomes obvious in the self-revealing nature of the content of understanding. The art of dialogue is *underlined* as it presents notions of humility, finitude and not-knowing, rather than pretending to have knowledge.

For Gadamer, Plato is not a metaphysical thinker and he challenges the interpretation of Plato as a "two worlds" thinker. He also opposes Aristotle's reading of Plato as wrong, since Aristotle ignored Plato's open-ended concept of human existence and his sense for light, in which and through which things are revealed.[33] The turn to something transcendent for both Plato

---

31. As Dostal rightly claims, the matter is not "mere repetitions or a simple return to ancients" (Dostal, "Gadamer's Platonism," 45).

32. Gadamer is considered the most prominent Platonist of the twentieth century. Gadamer considered himself a lifelong student of Plato (*GW* 2:506). Some of the fruits of Gadamer's efforts are now available in English, see the volume entitled *Dialogue and Dialectic: Eight Hermeneutical Studies on Plato*. Gadamer planned, but never wrote, big book on Plato that would show the positive contribution of Platonism and his relation to Heidegger. Gadamer wrote about it in the introduction to the second edition of *Platos Dialektische Ethik* (1967), now *GW* 5:15. Moreover, in the introduction to its third edition in 1982 he still spoke about a big Plato book (*GW* 5:160), but it seems that the studies in volume 7 of *Collected Works* ended up as his big Plato work, titled *Plato im Dialog*. Pöggeler called this volume a second peak point following the publication of *Truth and Method*. See Pöggeler, "Hermeneutik und Dekonstruktion," 85.

33. Gadamer argues against Aristotle's reading of Plato, by saying that Plato in

and Gadamer does not mean that the world of sensual needs is ignored, but rather that our appeal to the transcendent is needed. Gadamer's interpretation of Plato also disagrees with that of his teacher, Heidegger, who relied more on Aristotle than on Plato and for whom Plato is a metaphysical thinker and a starting point where the forgetfulness of being began.[34]

Gadamer's habilitation on Plato's dialogue titled *Philebos*[35] is actually a phenomenology of dialogue, projected as an excursus about the theory of dialectics.[36] He deals here with the topic of dialogue for the first time and attempts to grasp the main principles of Plato's dialectics deduced from Socrates's dialogues. Here it becomes clear that Gadamer is interested in the *way* in which philosophical questions are formulated, namely, through the discipline of dialogue, as an effective universal criterion of truth.[37] By the discipline of dialogue one must understand a structure in which those who search for understanding submit themselves to the power of dialogue and allow themselves to be led by it into the play of question and answer.

Gadamer's argument is that understanding is always a part of dialogue or, in other words, that understanding is dialogical. Socratic dialogue is seen as a means for communicating ideas, not in order to abolish the other, but to accommodate to it. Gadamer does not re-read dialogues as a heroic account of Socrates having argumentative battles with sophists regarding the relativity of their truth. He provides a different perspective on Plato, as one who does not own the truth and as one who, like a midwife, gives birth to the truth in dialogue. Words such as "dialogue" and "conversation" are not mere metaphors and they lie at the center of Gadamer's description of understanding, as "conversation that we ourselves are."[38] A true dialogue

---

Parmenides depicted only a web of ideas, a dialectical interweaving, and there was no ontological separation in Plato between two worlds. *GW* 6:113.

34. The most succinct critique of Plato by Heidegger is in the work *Platons Lehre von der Wahrheit* (1954, Bern), where Heidegger states, regarding Plato's cave allegory, that the sight of the disclosed truth is lost in the moment the emphasis is placed on the higher idea and Being; in that moment the revelation of truth (*alētheia*) is lost. Many of Heidegger's students, such as Walter Bröcker, Gerhard Krüger, Leo Strauss, and Georg Picht, did important work on Plato. On the topic see Arthos, "Gadamer's Dialogical Imperative," 169–176.

35. Originally, there was a second part planned, but Heidegger, who at that time wanted to return from Marburg to Freiburg, had been pushing Gadamer to finish writing. Only 50 years later did a second part appear, namely *Idea of Good between Plato and Aristoteles* (1978), now in *GW* 7:128–227.

36. See *GW* 5:14, where the word "dialectic" does not refer to Hegel's way of thinking, but to the dialogical in Plato's thinking. See also *GW* 7:123.

37. See *GW* 7:182.

38. *TM* 370 ("von dem Gespräch aus, das wir sind" (*WM* 382).

has many characteristics, one of which is incompleteness, since the dialogue is never planned or complete, and we never conduct or lead dialogue, but we fall into it.

The prefix *diá* (common for *dia*-lectics and *dia*-logue) that points to a motion, throughout, is very important, because it shows a certain unpredictability and uncertainty. Dialogue moves in ways that cannot be predicted and the participants are usually transformed by it. The main similarity between hermeneutics and dialogue is that the interpretation of a text also strives to achieve an agreement with the text about its subject matter, an agreement that includes recognizing the other and accepting the possibility that the reader may be addressed and corrected.

After I pointed out that Plato was important for Gadamer for the dialogical nature of his understanding, further analysis of his ancient sources continues with Aristotle's (384–322 BCE, Greek philosopher and scientist) articulation of practical knowledge *phronēsis* as one of the main pillars on which Gadamer builds his hermeneutical thought.[39]

Gadamer heard about *phronēsis* for the first time in the 1923 summer semester, when he attended a seminar with Heidegger in Freiburg on *Nicomachean Ethics*.[40] Whereas Aristotle's practical knowledge leads Gadamer to develop a dialogical hermeneutics, which refers to Plato's dialogical thinking, Heidegger in his critique of Plato claimed that we need to read the "dark" Plato from the perspective of "light" from Aristotle. Gadamer developed his own interpretation of *phronēsis* in a manuscript on practical knowledge, which was a critique of Heidegger's interpretation.[41]

---

39. Aristotle's exposition of *phronēsis* can be found in book 6 of *Nicomachean Ethics*. This book is a critique of Plato's conception of absolute Good as abstract and universal—how can the knowledge of universal Good help a doctor to heal his patient, if he studies health in general, but not the concrete health of a concrete person? (Et Nic, book I 1097a 6–15). Gadamer says that *phronēsis* is "the hermeneutic basic virtue itself" (GW 2:328).

40. Beside this "official" seminar, Heidegger also invited Gadamer for weekly readings of Aristotle in a smaller circle; these were personal meetings and not part of the official curriculum at the university (GW 2:485). For Gadamer this was the place where traditional logic suddenly changed into "the vitality of life-world reality" (GW 10:21).

41. *Praktisches Wissen.* (GW 5:230–248). Gadamer wrote this essay in 1930, but did not publish it during Heidegger's lifetime, because it contains the critique of Heidegger's conception of the "Eigentlichkeit der Existenz" (authenticity of existence). Unlike Heidegger, Gadamer always claimed that there was no difference between Plato and Aristotle; therefore, he had no problem with extending Aristotle's ethical reflection on Plato and interpreting Plato in the light of Aristotle's ethics. Stolzenberg calls this essay "the core and source of his own philosophical hermeneutics" (Stolzenberg, "Hermeneutik der praktischen Vernunft," 135). For more on Gadamer and *phronēsis* see: Schuchman, "Aristotle's Phronesis and Gadamer's Hermeneutics," 41–50; Figal, "Phronesis as Understanding," 236–48; Rese, "*Phronesis* als Modell der Hermeneutik," 127–50.

Gadamer was attracted to this concept, that contrasted the static objectivity of sciences, especially because it complements Plato. According to Plato, not even a moral man can know the good, and the ability of human wisdom always ends in not-knowing (*Unwissenheit*). Therefore, Gadamer uses Aristotle's practical theology as a model according to which the "interpretive sciences can be thought."[42]

The reason Gadamer acquired the concept of *phronēsis* is that it shows the true nature of the process of understanding, not from the perspective of a subject that grasps the object, but conceived as an application of the universal rule to a particular situation. Moreover, this is, for him, the core problem of hermeneutics—the relation between the universal and the particular. For him, understanding is a case of application of the universal to a concrete and special situation, where a text from the tradition is always understood under the historical circumstance of the interpreter.[43]

Therefore, the good to one who acts is only given when one confronts the situation, similar to the interpretation process. The interpreter does not find the sense of the text as something universal and separately existing, but one finds it only in the individual circumstance of understanding when one applies his previous understanding of the issues and his concrete situation to the text.

The chapter "Hermeneutical relevance of Aristotle" in *Truth and Method* is central to the book, and Gadamer shows there that understanding, similar to practical knowledge, is "not detached from a being that is becoming, but determined by it and determinative."[44] Practical knowledge is distinguished from other concepts of knowledge, theoretical and technical (*tehnē*).

Gadamer shows three differences between *phronēsis* and *tehnē* from Aristotle's thought: (i) we can learn *tehnē* and forget it, unlike moral knowledge. (ii) They differ regarding the nature of means and ends. Practical knowledge has no particular end, but aims at good living, while technical knowledge is a set of rules that are applied in a situation, as both a tool and a means. (iii) While *tehnē* has no relation to the personality of the craftsman, *phronēsis* is aware of it.[45]

Practical knowledge is therefore a certain form of knowledge of what is right for human behavior in various situations in the lives of individuals. It is an ability applied when one is drawn into a certain situation where he

---

42. *GW* 2:499.
43. *TM* 310 (*WM* 317).
44. *TM* 310 (*WM* 317).
45. See *TM* 315–20 (*WM* 322–29).

or she must find the best solution to act and behave in it, then deciding to do this or that. The reason for its need is that moral traditions and accumulated rules fail to help and guide us in these particular situations. Thus, an ethical situation is never disconnected from the person involved in it, but is always applied to a specific situation and its conditions. What is good is never known and given ahead or prior to the situation in which it exists.

In hermeneutical terms, the human good, a particular one, is only possible as a mediation of the universal moral knowledge involved in a particular situation. What must be achieved in this mediation is the *decision* for a certain action, but at the same time it must be *directed* toward the good that needs to be achieved. This reflection and finding the correct action is not a methodical and structured process that follows guidelines, and is not ruled or led by methods or principles. The knowledge that is needed for the action is always connected to the self-understanding of the subject. An individual inhabits a moral tradition, but tradition cannot give a precise guideline for how to act in a particular situation. Understanding therefore concerns a task of application.[46] Similar to *phronēsis*, understanding brings a feature of existence from where the interpreter is located, to the situation in which he is involved.

Schleiermacher's Universality of Hermeneutics

The horizon of human understanding in Gadamer's hermeneutical method is characterized by existing within the language, and by considering language as a medium of understanding. This is the direct influence of Friedrich Daniel Ernst Schleiermacher (1768–1834)[47] and his hermeneutical theory. Actually, the passage about the universality of hermeneutics based on language from *Truth and Method* is nothing but an extensive commentary on Schleiermacher's slogan: "Everything presupposed in hermeneutics is but language."[48]

Despite Schleiermacher's positive role for Gadamer's thinking, there were also two areas where he criticized Schleiermacher, the first being the "better understanding" in the sense of reproduction of the author's intent, and the second as the dominance of the psychological aspect of interpretation over the grammatical. It is this critique that evolved in the emergence

---

46. *TM* 313 (*WM* 320).

47. Known as the founder of a modern Protestant theology, and author of the first textbook of modern dogmatic *Der Christliche Glaube* (1821).

48. "Alles voraussetzende in der Hermeneutik ist nur Sprache" (*WM* 387). Gadamer quoted this from Kimmerle, *Schleiermacher*, 38.

of the most important elements of relation between the horizontal and vertical dimension of the understanding process in Gadamer's hermeneutics: universality of language, a balanced relation between the universal and individual, and the focus on production rather than reproduction of the subject matter.

Schleiermacher claimed to be the first to offer a scientific and systematically universal hermeneutics, in opposition to earlier "special (*spezielle*) hermeneutics."[49] In these instances hermeneutics was understood as an aid for theological, philological or literal sciences in situations where the text became incomprehensible.[50] The main achievement of Schleiermacher was that he devised general hermeneutics as a formal discipline that could be applied to all kinds of interpretation.

Gadamer began from this point and focused on the unity of two contradictory, but not mutually exclusive, poles about which Schleiermacher spoke, between a rational element and experience. This unity is not a harmonizing unity, but one based on the antithesis between understanding "from the center of the language" and understanding "from the center of the artist."[51] This aspect is first of all reflected in his dual definition of hermeneutics (according to Schleiermacher) as an art of understanding (*Kunst des Verstehens*),[52] but also as a technique (*Technik*) that involves objective criticism, manual skills and practical capabilities.

A unity based on antithesis is also reflected in the dual notion of language, which is defined as the expression of our inner thoughts, one that exteriorizes our interiority. On one hand, language is communal as it summarizes the universal rules and concepts of all linguistic expressions. On the other, language points to our individuality, which is present in spoken word/speech in a specific and particular time, space, context and motivation. These two moments are also present in Schleiermacher's urgency to interpret texts in two ways: grammatically and technically.[53] The latter has

---

49. "Hermeneutics as an art of understanding does not yet exist generally, but only several special hermeneutics" (Frank, *Schleiermacher*, 75).

50. Schleiermacher differentiates between *lax* and *strict* hermeneutical praxis: lax praxis grants that understanding is the rule and the hermeneutical strategy is needed only when approaching murky places; the strict praxis grants a real possibility of misunderstanding. Frank, *Schleiermacher*, 92.

51. Kimmerle, *Schleiermacher*, 37–38.

52. See Frank, *Schleiermacher*, 75.

53. *Grammatical* interpretation, according to Schleiermacher, grasps the meanings in a common usage and therefore focuses on over-individual literary and critical work with the text from the perspective of a universal system of language. (See Frank, *Schleiermacher*, 101–66) *Technical* interpretation on the other hand understands the speech and language as an expression of the particular individual witness, and its task

often been called psychological, or technical-psychological, and has been a matter of extensive critique of Schleiermacher due to the priority of the psychological over the grammatical aspect, which even Gadamer followed.

Prioritizing of subjective (technical/psychological) interpretation is a mark of Schleiermacher's later works, while the notes from before 1819 show a much stronger focus on the grammatical aspect. This observation is a result of Hans Kimmerle's new edition of Schleiermacher's hermeneutical lectures that also include his early notes from 1804, which were unknown.[54] Not until 1959, did Kimmerle examine all Schleiermacher's unpublished writings in the Berlin Library, and sorted them chronologically, in order to see the development of his thoughts. This later tendency to divide the previous unity between language and thought impacted the fact that the text became only an empirical expression pointing out the beyond-textual individuality of the author.

Although Schleiermacher still mentioned that the "thought and its expression are one and the same,"[55] he abandoned this concept and, with it, he also abandoned the unity between universal and individual, between general language rules and individual speech, identity of thinking and language, which had characterized his earlier thinking. In his essay on Schleiermacher, Gadamer comes to the conclusion that the research around Schleiermacher had missed Schleiermacher's main accomplishment,[56] as, quoting Schleiermacher: "Language is the only presupposition in hermeneutics, and everything that is to be found, including the other objective and subjective presuppositions, must be discovered in language."[57]

Besides the area of language related to the psychological aspect, Gadamer had problems with Schleiermacher's concept of reproduction of the author's intent. In order to avoid the possibility of false and wrong interpretation, Schleiermacher suggests a backward re-construction, seeking to re-create the individuality of the author by re-creating his mental processes, and so to understand the authors better than they understood themselves.

---

is to grasp what the exactly what words want to say, and so to grasp the individuality of the author. This interpretation has been often called psychological, or technical-psychological. See Frank, *Schleiermacher*, 167–237.

54. Until 1959, the only published edition of Schleiermacher's hermeneutics was an edition, which his friend and student Friedrich Lücke collected from the manuscripts and notes, and posthumously published in 1838. Manfred Frank in 1977 republished the Lücke edition from 1838, and I refer to this edition.

55. Kimmerle, *Schleiermacher*, 21.

56. *GW* 4:361.

57. Kimmerle, *Schleiermacher*, 38. English translation according to Kimmerle, *Hermeneutics*, 50. Cf. *WM* 387; *GW* 4:316–62.

This was actually Kant's axiom, used very often by Schleiermacher.[58] We can see that Schleiermacher in his restorative enterprise moves the attention from the objective meaning of the text to the analysis of the personal process, which means to reconstruct an *intuition* and overcome the methodical rules of *interpretation*.

This was a problem for Gadamer, this reproduction of the author's intention, uncovering an artist's uniqueness and moving into the psychology of genius. For Gadamer, understanding did not mean to understand *better* in the sense of superior *knowledge* and he sees as wrong this focus on language as a mere expression of the author's individuality.[59] Instead, he mentions something else: the productive aspect of understanding where a text *takes* the reader, and aims to bring reader/interpreter into the hermeneutical circle. These aspects, developed both in Gadamer's critique and the reception of Schleiermacher, are the main features in the discussion between the horizontal and vertical dimensions of understanding.

Dilthey's Historical Perspective

The work of Wilhelm Dilthey (1833–1911, a German philosopher and philologist) was also important for Gadamer and found an essential role in his *Truth and Method*. There are several reasons for this. First, as at that time the term hermeneutics was often connected with Dilthey's name, second due to the role of history in Dilthey's historicism and third, due to Dilthey's and Gadamer's distinction between human and natural sciences. The reception of Dilthey was already noticeable in Gadamer's early works,[60] but it would be an exaggeration to say, as Grondin claimed, that the "whole of Gadamer's work begins with Dilthey and to which his hermeneutics is the reply."[61] The role of history is important for Gadamer as it helps his analysis of how *what is transcendent* can be present under historically mediated conditions.

Dilthey's elaboration of history, which influenced Gadamer, lies in his analysis of human sciences. He saw human sciences endangered by the rise of natural sciences, which tended to be the only ones to own objective insights. Therefore, rather than to collapse all knowledge in one category of

---

58. Frank, *Schleiermacher*, 94. On the topic see: Bollnow, " Waß heißt einen Schriftsteller," 117–38.

59. See Gadamer's analysis in *TM* 184–95 (*WM* 188–201).

60. In "Das Problem der Geschichte in der neueren deutschen Philosophie" (1943), "Wahrheit in den Geisteswissenschaften" (1953), "Was ist Wahrheit" (1957), his lectures in Leuven (1957), even in his first draft of *Truth and Method* (*Urfassung*).

61. Grondin, *Philosophy of Gadamer*, 67.

science, Dilthey divided knowledge into two components: human sciences (*Geisteswissenschaften*, such as philosophy, theology, philology, economic or politics), and natural sciences (*Naturwissenschaften*, such as chemistry, physics or biology).

Both human and natural sciences reach their goal by descriptions of objective phenomenon, but the difference is that in human sciences these objects are expressions of the inner life (*dauernd fixierte Lebensäußerungen*),[62] which come from history and are created by the human mind. Human sciences contain the capability to understand the life of another person through *empathy*, where Dilthey talks about *transposition*.[63] This is not possible with natural sciences, where one can prove only non-human phenomena. Dilthey's aim was to create a methodology for objective interpretations of these expressions of inner life. Therefore, he developed hermeneutics as the foundational theory for the humanities, in order to prove that human sciences can be considered scientific *and* objective in a same manner as natural sciences.

Gadamer draws upon Dilthey's distinction between two interpretative practices: explanation (*Erklären*) and understanding (*Verstehen*), where *Verstehen* should be understood as an awareness of mental content (feelings, ideas) communicated in expressions, such as texts or art. *Erklären*, on the other hand, is the method of the natural sciences, which deal with the outer manifestations of things.[64] These expressions of experience are not mere emotions and feelings, but are manifestations of the inner life. Gadamer agrees with Dilthey that, when we reflect on these manifestations, we see that understanding is not final and determinate. Rather the opposite, it is indeterminate, needs to be repeated, is never ending and never final. The same with history, which is not final, but develops and is progressive. Both for Dilthey and Gadamer the account of life that can be understood is only accessed and understood through the many expressions of an inner life and results in a readiness to be surprised.

The expressions of lived experience are always connected with a hermeneutical circle, which for Dilthey means that human beings are irrevocably historical (i.e., historically conditioned). This means that, at the stage of lived experience, human understanding is always connected with interpretations from the past and this builds a platform upon which understanding happens. This circle is enabled by Dilthey's concept of historical reason,

---

62. *GS* 7:217.
63. *GS* 5:250.
64. "Sciences explain nature, humanities understand expressions of life" (*GS* 5:253).

according to which the human being is a historical being (*ein geschichtliches Wesen*).

The starting point for the humanities, according to Dilthey is therefore the historical experience.[65] The hermeneutical circle solves two problems for Dilthey: it shows that the human person is historically conditioned and it also shows the possibility of objectivity in historical understanding. For Gadamer, this is a problem as this is where historical consciousness turns into self-knowledge, as Dilthey does not answer why historical research should not turn into a philosophy of absolute idealism. Gadamer thinks it does.

Gadamer criticizes Dilthey on several levels and sees several contradictory tendencies in his work.[66] First, Dilthey never became fully aware of the positivist and Cartesian roots of his work, which left him split between positivism and romanticism.[67] According to Gadamer, in Dilthey's work the central *aporia* of hermeneutics is more strongly visible than in Schleiermacher. When Dilthey says that the goal of understanding is not to know what the text says, but the objective is to know the one who expresses his individuality in that text, this results in a shift of the emphasis from the epistemology of the text to the experience expressed in the text. In other words, Gadamer says that Dilthey did not manage to grasp the *truth* contained in the text, because he saw it only in "forms in which life is expressed" (*Ausdrucksformen des Lebens*).[68]

The reception of Dilthey in Gadamer's thinking includes an important aspect in that the human person is *historically* conditioned. As well, it includes a critique when the claim of immediate truth is abandoned in favor of a historical understanding of forms in which life is expressed.

Heidegger's Notion of Interpretative Being

In the previous sections, it was shown that Gadamer was influenced by Schleiermacher, with his notion of language and Dilthey, with his concept of historical being. Martin Heidegger (1889–1976, German philosopher) took a further step in his book *Being and Time* (*Sein und Zeit*, 1927), and in his revolutionary re-orientation of understanding as a way in which humans exist and relate with the world. By it, he directly influenced Gadamer's

---

65. "What man is, only history can tell" (*GS* 8:224).
66. For Dilthey's *aporias* see *TM* 214–35 (*WM* 222–35).
67. Gadamer points out this in his essay "Das Problem Diltheys" (*GW* 4:406–24).
68. *WM* 215. For Gadamer "Our understanding is not specifically concerned with its formal achievement as a work of art but with what it says to us" (*TM* 155).

hermeneutics, especially his concept of understanding as a mode of being, the structure of fore-understanding, thrownness, and dimension of being in language.

In this section, I will relate the relationship between Gadamer and Heidegger, and focus especially on the question of how far Gadamer's notion of individuality and transcendence is rooted in Heidegger's thinking. In order to explain this problem, the similarity and divergence between them will be pointed out and, finally, Heidegger's influence on Gadamer's developing of hermeneutics of transcendence will be analyzed.

The relation between Heidegger and Gadamer is at once the relationship of a teacher and student, as well as one of friendship.[69] Gadamer acknowledged his debt to Heidegger and stressed that, of all the thinkers he had met, Heidegger had the most influence on him.[70] After all, terms such as historical situatedness, finitude, facticity or pre-understanding, are from Heidegger, and *Truth and Method* could be perceived as an attempt to bring the later work of Heidegger closer to readers.[71]

Still, Gadamer never adopted many of Heidegger's terms and instead altered them: pre-understanding to prejudice, and hermeneutical philosophy to philosophical hermeneutics.[72] In conversation with Jean Grondin, Gadamer admits that he can be considered a follower of Heidegger, but

69. The main sources for the historical context are Gadamer's comments in his publications, since Heidegger's works do not reflect their relationship to such an extent. Gadamer's first encounter with Heidegger's name happened in 1921 at the seminar in Munich, when he met a student using a very unusual style of language. The student was "verheideggert" (Heidegger-struck), as they explained to Gadamer. Later in 1922, while Gadamer was seriously sick and spent many months in isolation at his parents' house, his supervisor Paul Natorp gave him the manuscript *Phänomenologische Interpretationen zu Aristoteles* to read. It was written by Martin Heidegger, at that time Husserl's young assistant. This manuscript is also called *Natorp-Bericht*, because it was part of the report based on which Heidegger had been applying for a teaching position in Marburg, although he had not published anything since 1916. This report has been for some time lost, but many years later found and published in 1989.

70. For Gadamer's work on Heidegger see the first seven essays in volume ten of his *Collected Works*, then essays in *Hermeneutische Entwürfe* (2000), which is a supplement to *Collected Works*, and a collection of expository essays on Heidegger collected in *Heideggers Wege* (1983), which contains richly instructive essays, full of personal anecdotes, which Gadamer uses when trying to make a point. English translation by John W. Stanley's 1994 *Heidegger's Ways*.

71. Already as early as the 1957 Louvain conferences, Gadamer appealed to Heidegger's hermeneutics of facticity, as visible in the title of the third conference: "Martin Heidegger and the significance of his hermeneutics of facticity for the human sciences."

72. In his letter from January 5, 1973 addressed to Otto Pöggeler, Heidegger writes: "The hermeneutic philosophy, alas, that's the thing of Gadamer" (cited in Pöggeler, *Heidegger und die hermeneutische Philosophie*, 395).

while Heidegger was driven by his life-long search after God, Gadamer himself did not have such a drive.[73]

The best way to define their relationship is to consider Heidegger as the beginning of Gadamer's concept of understanding, but not for his concept of hermeneutics.[74] According to Gadamer, the term hermeneutics, as he understands it is from the work of a younger Heidegger, for whom it was not a theory of methods, but became a theory of true experience;[75] In his *Truth and Method* Gadamer explored Heidegger's *Sein und Zeit* and underlined that "understanding is not a resigned ideal of human experience adopted in the old age of the spirit, as with Dilthey . . . it is, on the contrary, the original form of the realisation of *Dasein*, which is *being in-the-world*."[76]

Understanding is no longer a method, but a mode of being of life itself. From this it is a given that understanding is performed in a circular hermeneutical circle, as Heidegger writes: "any interpretation which is to contribute understanding, must already have understood what is to be interpreted."[77] Heidegger focused on the background of the interpretation present during our doing and wanting and talks about a *hermeneutical as*, when the world is being interpreted always as something, and it expresses our relation with the world at the basic level.

In his *Truth and Method* (the section entitled "Heidegger's fore-structure of understanding") Gadamer accepts Heidegger's analysis of human understanding (as expounded in *Sein und Zeit*), that every interpretation is grounded on a fore-understanding. He expands his structure of understanding on Heidegger's by making fore-understanding a part of the horizon of the reader. When doing this, Gadamer gives his theme a historical perspective, since prejudices are not something that the interpreter can own, but they still build our horizon, constitute our relation with the world, and are the platform on which we meet past traditions. He adopts Heidegger's implications of thrownness (*Geworfenheit*) in the world, which led him to reject a Cartesian subject–object model, and to underline the impact which the past has on the identity of the interpreter and to which extent it influences the current situation (let us call it the horizon) of the interpreter.

73. See Grondin, *Gadamer Lesebuch*, 293.

74. Visible especially in his essay "Text and Interpretation" (*GW* 2:330–60). Heidegger did not really care about Gadamer and out of all Gadamer's books, he mostly acknowledged the book on Paul Celan. See Gadamer, *Philosophical Apprenticeships*, 48–49.

75. See *GW* 2:446.

76. *TM* 250 (*GW* 1:264).

77. Martin Heidegger, "Understanding and Interpretation," translation according to Mueller-Vollmer, *Hermeneutics Reader*, 225.

In this area Gadamer follows Heidegger in the sense that he does not recognize the hermeneutical circle methodically, but as an ontological structural element in understanding. A pure methodological understanding of the hermeneutical circle, if at all possible, would focus on the interplay between text and interpreter, but it would be too static and would still be subjected to a subject–object dichotomy. Gadamer therefore describes understanding as the *movement* between tradition and interpreter, where an interpreter approaches the text with prejudices, which are already formed by the text.

So far, we have seen how Heidegger's concepts of thrownness and historicity influenced Gadamer's hermeneutics. The other important aspect is apparent when one talks about the nature of language, which brings me closer to the main question of this dissertation: how and where transcendence appears. The best known of Heidegger's statements about the relation between language and being from his famous *Letter on Humanism* (Über den Humanismus, 1946) says: "in thinking Being comes to language. Language is the house of Being. In its home man dwells."[78] In the same text, he says that language is the "house of the truth of Being"[79] and that "Being comes, lighting itself, to language. It is perpetually under way to language."[80]

These short sentences show that, for Heidegger, being and language are not identical, but also that he does not even strictly differentiate them. They cannot be identical, because language depends upon being and being lives in it; they cannot be strictly differentiated, because language cannot be without being. The metaphor of a house shows us that the language is the place for the revealing of being, which is always connected with a particular language. Heidegger puts language into a position which is independent of its usage, and this is a key to the mystery of being, because: "In its essence, language is neither expression nor an activity of man. Language speaks."[81]

Gadamer generally agrees with Heidegger's main idea. In an article devoted to Heidegger, he calls this "being at home in language" (*Zuhause sein im Wort*), our most intimate home. Words are not tools or signs pointing to somewhere, or paths leading somewhere, but are the space where we are at home.[82] Gadamer develops this further, in language being is not only disclosed (*a-letheia*), but being is present *in it*, "in the language that we

78. Heidegger, "Letter on Humanism," 193; Heidegger, "Über den Humanismus," 5.

79. Heidegger, "Letter on Humanism," 199; Heidegger, "Über den Humanismus," 9.

80. Heidegger, "Letter on Humanism," 239; Heidegger, "Über den Humanismus," 45.

81. Heidegger, "Language", 197. "Die Sprache spricht" (Heidegger, *Unterwegs zur Sprache*, 19).

82. See *GW* 3:329.

speak to each other, »being« is there,"[83] language is the world that we live in. Language is not only the house of being, but it is our home, language presents all the furniture and equipment in the house.[84] While for Heidegger language is house (*Haus*) for all, for Gadamer it is home (*Heimat*) for the individual.[85]

This chapter introduced the ancient and modern foundations of Gadamer's hermeneutics. The question was asked concerning how ancient and modern hermeneutics influenced Gadamer's thinking. We began with the concepts of dialogue and practical knowledge, followed by the modern sources of Gadamer's thinking, which also built a context for his thinking. Here the following areas were addressed: universality of language, historical outlook and the human being as one who interprets. All these elements shed light on Gadamer's understanding of the horizons of human understanding and of transcendence. In the next chapters we will speak about the development of Gadamer's hermeneutical method.

---

83. *GW* 8:40.

84. Gadamer, *Das Erbe Europas*, 172–73.

85. See also interview with Carsten Dutt, published in Dutt, *Hermeneutik—Ästhetik—Praktische Philosophie*, 39.

2

Development of Gadamer's Hermeneutical Project

IT was already pointed out that Gadamer's work should be divided into three periods. These are: the early period (1921–1959), middle period *Truth and Method* (1960–1965) and late period (1965–2002). Now it will be pointed out how this advance of Gadamer's hermeneutical method led to a religious turn in the late period and how this contributed to his understanding of horizons of human understanding and transcendence. In his case, one cannot talk about a huge change in thinking, but nonetheless the difference between these periods must be taken into account, as the relation between them is not of contradiction, but continuation.[1]

The first section dealing with the early works enables us to see the original context of the terms important for horizons of human understanding and transcendence, such as dialogue, history, language, prejudice or rehabilitation of the humanist tradition, the works in mind are from the thirties, forties and fifties. It was the first (unpublished) draft of *Truth and Method* (called *Urfassung*), which showed that the hermeneutical problem is deeply embedded in the discussion about the methodology of human and natural science and that is the setting of Gadamer's hermeneutical method.

---

1. The sources that make it possible to reconstruct the development are Gadamer's own autobiography *Philosophical Apprenticeships* (*Philosophische Lehrjahre*, 1977), Grondin's monumental biography, and Gadamer's various articles and interviews where he recalls the past or deals explicitly with the development of his thought; recommended are "Zwischen Phänomenologie und Dialektik" (1986, which is the intellectual biography, *GW* 2:3) and "Selbstdarstellung" (1975, more of a historical biography, *GW* 2:479).

This is also why the early works need to become part of the puzzle, as a quick look at the roots helps one to better understand the results. In this case, to understand the turn to transcendence in Gadamer's later period. Further, I will point to the shift observable in *Truth and Method*. I have especially in mind the move from hermeneutics of human sciences to universal hermeneutics. This shift is documented in the threefold division of *Truth and Method* and in its three steps (art, history, language), and also illustrated in the very title of the book.

The section related to the late works is the longest in this chapter and there is a reason for that. It is that the late works document the further progress of philosophical hermeneutics, which turned into applied and practical hermeneutics. This conveyed the relativization of several previous notions, such as the concept of limits of language versus the earlier universality of language. What is further documented is the turn to transcendental hermeneutics and to the notion of divine.

Early Works

A careful look at Gadamer's early works leads to the first observation. Several years before he wrote his main book, Gadamer dealt with quite a wide range of areas, which at that time still seemed disconnected. He himself was obviously aware that his essays from the period before 1960 formed a special group, so he compiled them in the second volume of his *Collected Works* (1986).

Let me at least mention the essay called "The Problem of History in the New German Philosophy" (1943),[2] where Gadamer works with terms such as historical reason, effective history, consciousness, which will become common much later, or the study entitled "Truth in the Human Sciences" (1953)[3] that showed a tendency toward what we call now Gadamerian hermeneutics, as Gadamer refers here to Socrates and Plato and advises a rehabilitation of seventeenth-century thinking (pre-Enlightenment).

It is hard to find a single attribute of his early works, but they are characterized by his interest in Greek philosophy centering on Plato.[4] One of the most important of Gadamer's works comes from the same period, under

---

2. "Das Problem der Geschichte in der neueren deutschen Philosophie" (*GW* 2:27–36). Heidegger's response when he read this article was: "And what about thrownness?" (*GW* 2:9).

3. "Wahrheit in den Geisteswissenschaften" (*GW* 2:37–43).

4. See *GW* 2:487.

the title *Practical Knowledge*,⁵ written in 1930 but published in 1985, which documents the development of practical philosophy and interest in practical knowledge *phronēsis*. The number of works written in this early period is rather low, although the period itself was long and lasted almost until his retirement. Therefore, the emerging concepts of dialogue and practical philosophy, a return to the pre-Enlightenment period, theological hermeneutics, focus on history, and critique of Western culture did not appear to be linked. One piece of the puzzle is missing, the *Urfassung*, the first draft of what later became *Truth and Method*. A short background is required.

There are three drafts of *Truth and Method*. In 1955, Gadamer wrote to Gerhard Krüger that he hoped to finish the book they had discussed for his fiftieth birthday in 1952.⁶ The result was the so-called *Urfassung*, the first draft, which is now in the repository of Heidelberg's university library.⁷ This draft was not known until 1980 and it is hard to date it, but it is approximately from 1956 and definitely dated before the 1957 Louvain lectures. Currently, only the first part is published.⁸

Gadamer was not satisfied with this text as it was not clear enough, and was too complicated and he writes, "as always I lacked the ability for simplifying and constructive unifying."⁹ Then there was the second draft, which we do not have and no one saw, but Gadamer spoke about it as being different from the first and this one is probably dated in 1957 or 1958.¹⁰ The third draft was finished during winter semester 1958/59, and published as a book.

The existence of the *Urfassung* is a very important element in the transition between the early period and *Truth and Method*, showing how Gadamer's thought developed. The draft is short and written in one breath, containing 80 pages and has neither a title, chapter titles nor chapters.¹¹

5. "Praktisches Wissen." (*GW* 5:230).

6. See Grondin, *Hans-Georg Gadamer—eine Biographie*, 318.

7. Handschriftabteilung Universitätsbibliothek Heidelberg. Sign. Heid HS 3913. Gadamer donated it as a gift, since from 11.02.1980 to 15.4.1980, the university library held a display about Gadamer. On this occasion he gave them the manuscript. The manuscript is not publicly accessible; it can be used only based on special permission. See more details in Grondin, *Der Sinn der Hermeneutik*, 3.

8. Gadamer, "Wahrheit und Methode. Anfang der Urfassung," 131–42. Problem with the *Urfassung* is that it is "complicated and vague" (Grondin, *Hans-Georg Gadamer—eine Biographie*, 318).

9. Words cited in Grondin, *Hans-Georg Gadamer—eine Biographie*, 318–19.

10. Mentioned only by Grondin. See Grondin, *Der Sinn der Hermeneutik*, 5.

11. I rely on these comments in my personal work with the manuscript and compare it critically with Grondin's articles published in *Dilthey Jahrbuch* (vol. 8), and in *Sinn der Hermeneutik*.

The manuscript is rooted in the problem of the methodological self-understanding of the human sciences in Wilhelm Dilthey, Johann Droysen and Hermann von Helmholtz. It arrives at the systematic central part through an analysis of the hermeneutical question in Schleiermacher and Heidegger.

At the end of *Urfassung* is an analysis of the Beautiful in Plato (as in the 1960 version), but surprisingly, the end returns to the problem of the human sciences. This is the first observation that, in manuscript, the aim of the whole project is to contribute to the discussion of human and natural science, although this is no longer so strongly visible in the printed book. *Urfassung* further relativizes the threefold division of *Truth and Method* into art, history and language.

Gadamer's main inspiration comes from Helmholtz's 1862 speech, where he speaks about instinctive feeling and artistic tact.[12] The second part of *Truth and Method* as published, builds upon the opposition of Hegel and Schleiermacher, but in *Urfassung* there is no mention of Hegel. The second part in *Urfassung* answers questions for the adequate self-understanding of the human sciences, therefore Gadamer uses there the effective history, fusion of horizons and prejudices—this is not so clear if one reads only the published book. Note that all these concepts, important for the analysis of human understanding and transcendence, were originally connected with different discussions than was later apparent, as Gadamer was still interested in the problem of human sciences and saw his own efforts as "geisteswissenschaftliche Hermeneutik."[13]

Urfassung also illustrates the shift from human-sciences-hermeneutics into philosophy. But this shift, as Grondin notes,[14] is not as visible in the published *Truth and Method* as in *Urfassung*, where the first line reads: "It is not only a need of logical self-explanation that links the humanities with philosophy."[15] Gadamer advises a turn into understanding philosophy based on hermeneutics, namely a philosophical hermeneutics, which does not operate with a special method, but with a rather different idea of experience and knowledge.

---

12. A speech when he started as vice-rector in Heidelberg. This aspect is not so strongly underlined in *Truth and Method* as in the *Urfassung*. See Helmholtz, "Ueber das Verhältnis," 159–85.

13. "Hermeneutics of the human sciences." Compare with *WM* 264, 286, 314, 316, 319, 330, 464.

14. Grondin, *Der Sinn der Hermeneutik*, 15.

15. "Es ist nicht nur ein Bedürfnis logischer Selbsterklärung, das die Geisteswissenschaften mit der Philosophie verbindet" (Gadamer, "Wahrheit und Methode. Der Anfang der Urfassung," 131).

Experience of Art, History, and Language

The next step in reconstructing the development of Gadamer's hermeneutical method will focus attention on his magnum opus, *Truth and Method* (1960). I will not offer here an expository overview, but continue the discussion begun on the previous pages and show the shift between the first and second period. This section will circle around two issues: (i) a discussion concerning the title of the book, and (ii) a discussion about the threefold division of his book. The discussion of the title will help to more closely approach the tension in Gadamer's thinking. That of the division of the book in three parts will help to approach his shift from methodology in the humanities toward the universality of understanding based on language.

The current title of the book *Truth and Method* is not the original, which was *Principles of Philosophical Hermeneutics*.[16] The conjunction "and" in the title should not be understood as a conjunction expressing connection or opposition between truth and method, but rather as a word that is applied to reflect the foundation of the relation. The conjunction could be very well changed to "or" and thus show tension between truth and method, but still not opposition. The word "method" in the title is ambiguous and ironic,[17] since the book handles neither various truth theories, nor methods of how to achieve truth. Gadamer never thematizes truth itself. Even more important, against the claim of method being the most reliable source of authority, Gadamer reclaims other aspects, such as tradition, art, and religion. The title of the book points to the move from the methodology in the humanities toward the universality of understanding.

The tension addressed here is the tension between the *Verfremdung* or *Entfremdung*, alienating distanciation, which destructs the more primary experience of *Zugehörigkeit*, participation. This antinomy is already visible in the title of Gadamer's work.[18] The debate between the alienating distanciation and the experience of belonging therefore circles three spheres,

---

16. "Grundzüge einer philosophischen Hermeneutik." The publisher considered the term "hermeneutics" unknown and advised him to change it. Gadamer then came up with the title *Verstehen und Geschehen*, but this was too similar to Bultmann's *Glauben und Vestehen*. The current title is the third version, inspired by Goethe's *Dichtung und Wahrheit* (Grondin, *Einführung zu Gadamer*, 17). For more on the history of the title see how Gadamer explains it in *GW* 2:493, or in the Grondin, *Hans-Georg Gadamer— eine Biographie*, 319.

17. It is called "ironic" in the Introduction of Dostal, *The Cambridge Companion to Gadamer*, 2.

18. Pointed to in Ricoeur's, "Philosophical Hermeneutics," 15. These terms repeatedly appear in the *Wahrheit und Methode*, for *Zugehörigkeit* see pages 114, 129, 131, 134, 165, 171, 266; for *Verfremdung/Entfremdung* see pages 19, 90, 168, 172, 390.

around which the hermeneutical experience is divided: aesthetic, historical, linguistic. In the field of aesthetics (experience of art) this antinomy occurs between the experience of being captured by the work of art and the pretension of the judgment of taste to impose its criteria on the object. In the second area (experience of history) this antinomy is presented by the experience of being a part and belonging to tradition, and the pretension to be free of all prejudices. In the part about language (experience of language) this antinomy is visible between the pretension to treat linguistic signs as tools and the mutual understanding which emphasizes that *we* are the dialogue.

Truth and Method is considered to be a heterogenic work and a quick look at the topics covered shows it to have independent studies that could otherwise stand separately. Gadamer himself delivered the impression that his work was simply a compilation, when he called his book a "theoretical outline that from different sides summarizes the studies on the unity of a philosophical whole."[19]

At the beginning of *Truth and Method*, he further relativizes the threefold division of the book by mentioning another three, *Philosophie, Kunst, Geschichte* (philosophy, art, history), but omits language.[20] The answer to the question of whether *Truth and Method* is homogeneous or heterogeneous is far more important than it seems, as not only is the coherency of Gadamer's hermeneutics is at stake, but the entire concept of a horizon of understanding. Art, history and language are not only the three *parts* of the book, but are the three basic *experiences* and encounters with the truth which ground the relation of the horizon of human understanding and transcendence.

The first part of *Truth and Method* (entitled "Problem of Methods") gives witness to the discussion about human sciences, which is also an emphasis of *Urfassung*. In order to oppose the hegemony of philosophical methodology, Gadamer first turned to non-methodical avenues and connected truth with art. Second, he opposed the way of thinking based on human subjective self-consciousness dissociated from objective reality. For him, the subject and object always create a unity and this unity (belongingness) is the primary experience that precedes every interpretation. Thirdly, Gadamer opposed Kant's aesthetic theory, which connected art with feeling and valued art as an emotional response to a painting or poem. Gadamer

---

19. *GW* 2:3.
20. *WM* 2. See discussion on this in Grondin, *Der Sinn der Hermeneutik*, 1–2.

called this into question, because it ignored the artwork itself and the truth claim it reveals.[21]

Further, in the second part of his book (named "The extension of the question of truth to understanding in the human sciences") Gadamer moved its attention to the way people conceive their past, focused on the link between past and present and argued that understanding is the awareness of the historical nature of our existence. This is important to remember for later discussion of the role of the historically mediated condition in relation to transcendence. Gadamer rejected truth as correspondence in the terms of *adequatio* (correspondence between human perception of world and the way the world is), since this claim distorts access to the way things really are. He rather offered the idea of the hermeneutical circle, with prejudices and human understanding as a dialogue with tradition.

The final matter is the ontological shift to hermeneutics guided by language, which explores language as the vehicle of understanding. This shift offered a platform where the discussion about the horizontal and vertical dimension could occur. It is the third part of *Truth and Method* where Gadamer presented his thoughts, "perhaps the most difficult because the least polished and most sketchy,"[22] full of imprecise formulations and contrasting the precise formulations in previous parts.[23] Up to this point, Gadamer demonstrated that understanding in the humanities cannot be limited to scientific methodology. The final step in his exposition is the concept of the nature of conversation in its *Sprachlichkeit*, linguisticality. All these lead to the book's central claim, "Being that can be understood is language,"[24] which implies that there is nothing understandable beyond the limits of language.[25]

---

21. The key to understanding these thoughts of Gadamer is Heidegger's work *Der Ursprung des Kunstwerkes*, especially the idea that truth is not reached by a method, but it is the truth that emerges and discloses, *a-letheia*.

22. Lawn and Keane, *The Gadamer Dictionary*, 147.

23. In a dialogue with Carsten Dutt, Gadamer admitted that during the following thirty years he had been explaining what he meant by ontology of language, and also admitted that he had "run out of breath" at the end of writing his book. Dutt, *Hermeneutik—Ästhetik—Praktische Philosophie*, 36. Grondin also mentions that Gadamer apologized several times for the third part of *Truth and Method*, saying that it was written in a hurry. Grondin, *Der Sinn der Hermeneutik*, 21.

24. "Sein das verstanden werden kann, ist die Sprache" (*WM* 478; *TM* 507). See also essays in a volume edited by Bubner, *Sein, das verstanden werden kann, ist Sprache*.

25. Gadamer's use of the concept of linguisticality is called his "most original thesis" (Kisiel, "Happening of Tradition," 365). It is called also "the pinnacle of Gadamer's achievement in *Truth and Method*" (Culpepper, "The Value of Hans-Georg Gadamer," 139).

In the final summary observation, one must note the central role that is given to language—language now *becomes* the medium in which a hermeneutical experience happens, as the middle ground in which understanding takes place. Gadamer's opinion is that language is the universal medium of understanding and therefore philosophical hermeneutics is the universal medium of understanding truth. Linguisticality, or more precisely, our constant embeddedness in language, is the ultimate basis for the universality of hermeneutics.[26]

Shift in the Later Period

Now special attention will be given to the topics and themes that occurred in the years following the publication of *Truth and Method*. This almost forty-year period (1965–2002) was his most fruitful period, both in terms of quality and quantity. On one hand, this period witnessed very intensive communications with various intellectuals, but on the other it provided a further development of Gadamer's theory. His works in the last third of the twentieth century manifested somewhat different hermeneutics than earlier[27] and its motto may be "that the Other might be right," as he said in the interview for *Spiegel* in 2000.[28] These aspects became even clearer after 1960.

It is proper to talk about the turn, or even several turns in his later period. First, there is the turn to applied hermeneutics, when Gadamer became more engaged with the practical areas of life (education, medicine, etc.); then the turn to language, especially to its boundaries. There is also the poetic turn with applications in poetic and religious texts and essays on Rilke, George and Celan. Finally, there is the religious turn that throws light on his entire work, but this theological and religious dimension of Gadamer's thought is as yet unremarked.[29] The religious turn will be placed under a

26. The universal phenomenon of linguisticality is described most succinctly in his essay "Man and Language" (*GW* 2:146), where he posits three essential features of being in language.

27. This fact is forgotten by many standard textbooks on Gadamer's hermeneutics, which focus mainly on *Truth and Method*.

28. "Ein Gespräch setzt voraus, dass der andere Recht haben könnte" (Sturm, "Rituale sind wichtig," 305).

29. Zimmermann talks about the third turn and Gadamer's late preoccupation with theology, even speculates that Gadamer in his late age became much closer to his teacher Heidegger, who he earlier often criticized as too religious. See Zimmermann, "Ignoramus," 320–22. In this important article, Zimmermann claims that religion and a feeling of transcendence are very important for Gadamer's hermeneutics, he bases his thoughts on the interview he had with Gadamer on February 26, 2002 (three weeks before Gadamer died).

microscope and be introduced by pointing to his turn to the application and limits of language. These present the main elements that build the horizon of human understanding and transcendence.

In the period after 1960, emphasis was placed on the various forms of practice and this is very often called a turn to applied hermeneutics. This term is used, thanks to the title of the translations of Gadamer's late essays *Hans-Georg Gadamer on Education, Poetry, and History: Applied Hermeneutics*.[30]

What kind of application is meant here? The editors of the volume stress that Gadamer's later works are not applications in the real sense of the word, as if his *Truth and Method* would provide theory and the later works its applications to various practical areas.[31] An application is namely an integral part of the hermeneutical process and is not separated from understanding and explanation, so the standard theory of an application scheme cannot be used in this case.

What must be accepted without any doubt is that, at a later stage, Gadamer became more engaged with the practical areas of life, such as education, medicine, language, role of the expert, religion, etc. Still, Gadamer himself underlines in the foreword to the second edition (1965) that this does not differ much from his intentions in *Truth and Method*. He says that his intent was not to investigate the theoretical foundation of work in these fields in order to put his findings to practical ends, his real concern was philosophical, "not what we do or what we ought to do, but what happens to us over and above our wanting and doing."[32]

However, in his later period he put application at the very heart of his project, where practical life is based on the same understanding process.[33] One area of application in Gadamer's later period was his focus on aesthetics and poetics and secondary sources use the term "poetic turn."[34] Applications in poetic and religious texts are collected in his *Relevance of the Beautiful* volume (1986).[35]

---

30. Edited by Misgeld and Nicholson. Another example is Gadamer, *Enigma of Health*, translated by Jason Gaiger and Nicholas Walker.

31. Misgeld and Nicholson, *Hans-Georg Gadamer on Education*, vii.

32. *GW* 2:438.

33. Essays published between 1976 and 1979 deal with practical philosophy or in other words, understanding hermeneutics as practical philosophy. Many of these essays were published in *Die Vernunft im Zeitalter der Wissenschaft* (1976).

34. Lawn, *Gadamer*, 95–97.

35. Edited by Robert Bernasconi in 1986. Introductory essay in this collection, "Remembrance of language," (xi–xxi) is a good overview of Gadamer's turn to poetry.

New interpretations of Gadamer's hermeneutics, which underline the turn in his later period also focus on aesthetic experience as an experience of transcendence. There are a few examples from the later period upon which it is possible to base a claim about Gadamer's turn to transcendence. The most sustained published reflections on religion are dialogues on the island of Capri with Italian philosopher Gianni Vattimo and French philosopher Jacques Derrida, published in a book *On Religion*.

Even more important is a late essay called "Aesthetic and Religious Experience" (1964/1978)[36] where Gadamer is oriented on the free offer of the Gospel. The task of proclaiming is not connected with the repetition of the message, but with the acceptance of the message; therefore, the proclamation of the message must be shared in a way that is accessible to people. Here, Gadamer shows the difference between proclamation and art—while understanding of art can be achieved, in Christian *kerygma* we are always shown what we *cannot* achieve.

Similarly, Gadamer writes in another of his late essays "To Thank and to Think of" (2000)[37] of his *search for the divine* in a speech about gratitude. He says that giving thanks to someone is always an act that cannot be reduced to a convention, and which always shows an excess, "an experience of transcendence, that is, it always exceeds our expectations on the basis by which we judge human relations."[38] Thankfulness reveals the hidden god "that now gains universal significance."[39] This universality is also recognized in his last interview with Riccardo Dottori, where Gadamer claims that philosophical hermeneutics is a search for transcendence and that a full recognition of transcendence as the limit of human knowledge plays an important role for mutual understanding.

In this dialogue Gadamer contrasts scientific epistemology, universally applied, and religion, wrongly marginalized as something private, detached from reason. But, he says, religion is part of a common heritage, part of culture's tradition. His emphasis on religion is consistent with his other works, against scientific methodology and for the experiences such as art.

Gadamer's religious turn was not a turn to confessional faith, but to world religions. As Gadamer says to Dottori:

---

36. "Ästhetische und religiöse Erfahrung" (*GW* 8:143–55; English translation published in the volume Bernasconi, *Relevance of the Beautiful*, 140–53).

37. "Danken und Gedenken," published in the volume *Hermeneutische Entwürfe*, 208–13.

38. Gadamer, "Danken und Gedenken," 210.

39. Gadamer, "Danken und Gedenken," 212.

> this means that what we must keep in mind here is that transcendence is not attainable anywhere. Transcendence is not simply believing in God, it is something incomprehensible . . . the *ignoramus* is the fundament of transcendence.[40]

In other words, the foundation of transcendence is a religiously experienced limit of human knowledge, *ignoramus*, of admitting our not-knowing. In this context the universality of hermeneutics based on language transforms into the universality of the hidden god and into the universality of not-knowing.

Transcendence, according to Gadamer is connected with the limits of human knowledge, as something that is greater than people are and involves abandoning dogmas and religion. There is more in this than pure opposition to dogmatism as, for him, transcendence must always be experienced. Conversation allowed by transcendence is defined as a genuine openness, and dogmatic theology must end in order to enter this kind of dialogue. It is, though, hard to imagine a Christian theologian accepting the possibility that the Trinity and Allah are one and the same.[41]

What Gadamer equates is religion and the experience of the limited human experience, as is illustrated by the Greek concept *páthei máthos*, learning through the experience of suffering.[42] What a person must learn through suffering is an insight into the limitations of humanity and to realize the barrier that separates man and divine. *Páthei máthos* does not only mean that we learn from our mistakes and get better knowledge of things through discontentment, it also shows why this is so. What we learn is the uncertainty of predictions and the futility of attempting to master the future, in his words:

> Thus experience is *experience of human finitude*. The truly experienced person is one who has taken this to heart, who knows that he is master neither of time nor the future. The experienced man knows that all foresight is limited and all plans uncertain.[43]

One might say that genuine experience teaches humans to *recover* the space that separates the human from the divine, and to *preserve* it. Out of this, several things are clear about Gadamer's religious hermeneutics: (i) the religious element is a form of experience which is *centrifugal*—we are brought

---

40. Dottori, *Century of Philosophy*, 78–79; Dottori, *Lektion des Jahrhunderts*, 85.

41. For more about Gadamer's views on religion and the potential impact on philosophy of religion, see Vessey, "Hans-Georg Gadamer," 645–55.

42. TM 351 (WM 362).

43. TM 352 (WM 363).

to what lies beyond, it happens against our wanting and doing, "hermeneutic experience is an experience *of passio of something revealing itself to us in those quiet moments of readings*",[44] (ii) but is also *centripetal*, individualizing within a particular circumstance.

During his final years, Gadamer was engaged with the question of how hermeneutics can address the need for dialogue between cultures and religions, therefore he talked about a conversation between cultures (*Weltgespräch*).[45] He was convinced that, if philosophy is to succeed in preparing the ground for global dialogue between cultures and religion, it is important that hermeneutics also incorporates religious transcendence. Especially in his dialogue with Dottori he suggested a pressing philosophical task to clear the ground for a world dialogue about transcendence, which is common to all religions. For Gadamer, it is either to *prepare this dialogue*, or to *perish*. For Gadamer the task of humanity is to search for this universal transcendence and to save itself from self-destruction: "if the four great world religions could reconcile themselves to acknowledging transcendence as the great unknown, then they might even be able to prevent the destruction of the earth's surface with gas and chemicals."[46]

However, Gadamer's notion of transcendence reveals several problems. What Gadamer says in his dialogue with Dottori about universal transcendence seems to affect the destruction of religion as such, a particular religion especially, should we focus too much on common universal religious experiences and ignore the qualitative differences of all religions. Yet for Gadamer there exists no other way to ensure dialogue, than to reduce all religions to a "common denominator: the experience of transcendence."[47]

Gadamer fails to acknowledge the truthfulness of particularity of religious faith, since he places the notion of transcendence as a common ground of humanity. My opinion is that he is unfaithful even to his fusion of horizons, because the fusion does not take into account the loss of particularity. Gadamer also fails to see that dogma and faith in religion are a matter of practice and a living faith, rather than a dead doctrine.

Still, this can also be considered a barrier for dialogue. Gadamer asks religions to leave their revelatory model, but he misses the fact that the universality of religion is connected with its particularity, and that

---

44. Davey, "Hermeneutics, Art and Transcendence," 377.

45. Dottori, *Century of Philosophy*, 73–74; Dottori, *Lektion des Jahrhunderts*, 79–80.

46. Dottori, *Century of Philosophy*, 129; Dottori, *Lektion des Jahrhunderts*, 139. Taylor claims that Gadamer's thoughts help with the challenge of understanding each other in a pluralistic spectrum. Taylor, "Understanding the Other," 279–81.

47. Zimmermann, "Ignoramus," 315.

interreligious dialogue cannot overcome this particularity.[48] While Christianity acknowledges a model of revelation in which reality is revealed from beyond being to us, Gadamer acknowledges a human mind that ascends toward transcendence. For him transcendence comes through others, as it involves an I–Thou relationship, but it is always grounded in *something* undefinable. What is missing is *Miteinandersein* (with one-another) being complemented with *Füreinanderdasein* (for one-another).[49]

As a last observation—is Gadamer's hermeneutics transcendental? For him, philosophy is conversation of the soul with itself and knowing is a matter of divine grace. This is visible in the motto of *Truth and Method* with Rilke's poem about the eternal partner and the great bridge-building of God. The question that must be asked therefore does not so much consider Gadamer's *personal* faith, but considers the way he *talks* and *describes* the notion of divine and transcendence.

His focus on transcendence can already be traced in *Truth and Method*, for example when he talks about the inner word in order to avoid subjectivism. This inner word is not a tool, but takes part in the subject matter (*Sache*), in a similar way as the eternal word is present in the incarnation of Christ.[50] There is no better thought in human history to explain this, only Christian incarnation states that the inner word is the same as the embodied one.

Therefore, Gadamer's religious turn expresses nothing new in his thinking, but is simply a more open acknowledgement of transcendence that was present in his thought from the beginning. As he says in an interview, "the sense of beyond is simply a fact of human history. It is useless to deny it."[51] In a sense, this turned confessional Christianity upside down. But Gadamer revised this, by saying it is an exaggeration to talk about it in this way, even missionary work must after all contain the inability to know the end and purpose. As he says in an interview: "it is human not to know, it is inhuman to turn this into a Church."[52]

---

48. Therefore, ends Zimmermann, if hermeneutics is to fulfill its task it is to be aware of its historical limitations. See Zimmermann, "Ethics of Philosophical Hermeneutics," 394.

49. Zimmermann, "Ethics of Philosophical Hermeneutics," 54.

50. See Wierciński, "Hermeneutic Retrieval," 1–23.

51. Zimmermann, "Ignoramus," 318. Zimmermann even speculates (320–21) that Gadamer in his later age became closer to Heidegger, who in Spiegel's interview "Only God can save us" has a similar position to Gadamer. The task of theology is to abandon religious convictions and agree on the universal concept of transcendence.

52. Zimmermann, "Ignoramus," 321.

After we discussed the move from hermeneutics of human sciences to universal hermeneutics; observable in Gadamer's early works and in the threefold partition of *Truth and Method*, and documented the further development of philosophical hermeneutics in the form of applied and practical hermeneutics, including the notion of transcendence, we continue with the critique and reception. Gadamer was in close contact with other thinkers throughout his life. We will speak about Jürgen Habermas and Paul Ricoeur.

3

Reception and Critical Evaluation

IN this chapter, attention will be given to philosophical critique and the theological usage of concepts from Gadamerian hermeneutics, in which I have chosen thinkers who addressed the issues relevant to our theme. I will introduce the heritage of Gadamer's hermeneutics by looking at a critique of his work with the dynamics of his life and, afterward, the reception of his ideas.

Very soon after *Truth and Method* was published, it was recognized as one of the most important books in current philosophy[1] and the concepts of hermeneutics became a common idiom for continental philosophy. Yet, at the same time, Gadamer's hermeneutics has been subject to extensive criticism and discussion. True, hermeneutics did not begin with Gadamer, but he was the first to articulate it in its universality and whose work enabled hermeneutics to expand into a wider cultural debate. On the one hand, this weakened hermeneutics in the real sense of the word, while on the other, hermeneutics continued to live in various projects and disciplines, even without being directly connected with Gadamer's project.[2]

The main debates in which Gadamer took part in the period 1960 to 2000 were with the critique of ideology of Jürgen Habermas, the neo-pragmatism of Richard Rorty, the deconstructionism of Jacques Derrida

---

1. Hans Albert rates the book as the Bible of present-day German philosophy in his letter to P. Feyerabend, February 20, 1967. Cited in Grondin, *Hans-Georg Gadamer—eine Biographie*, 320.

2. A nice example of the wide range of applications of hermeneutics is reflected in one of the latest collections of essays dedicated to Gadamer: Malpas and Zabala, *Consequences of Hermeneutics*.

and the postmodernism of Gianni Vattimo. But the first objections against Gadamer came from Emilio Betti,[3] Eric Donald Hirsch Jr.[4] and Hans Albert.[5] There were also "sympathetic" critics, who shared areas of concern and differences with Gadamer's hermeneutics, but at the same time, held in common a broad agreement concerning the essential features of hermeneutics.[6]

One example is Richard Bernstein, who in his book struggles with the question of truth and concludes that Gadamer fails to really succeed in charting a course between relativism and objectivism.[7] He believes that true meaning must be validated by a community of interpreters, but this is *exactly* the point that makes Gadamer's notion of truth problematic, since it lacks criteria for validation.[8] The next example is Joel Weinsheimer, who also delivers positive treatment of Gadamer's hermeneutic stance, but has concerns about the methods, as he argues that Gadamer puts forward many un-contended assumptions concerning natural sciences.[9] He understands that Gadamer's goal was a defense of art and humanistic knowledge, but thinks that natural sciences are less methodological and more hermeneutical than Gadamer sees them.[10]

Attention will be first given to Jürgen Habermas and two particular themes that appeared in the discussion between him and Gadamer, namely the rejection of the universality of the hermeneutic project and the refusal of the non-critical acceptance of conservative concepts.

---

3. Emilio Betti, Italian jurist, wanted to establish hermeneutics as a normative aesthetic doctrine with rules and principles, which would provide a guarantee for objectivity. See his works from 1955 to 1967, which are an open polemic against Gadamer: (i) his work in Italian *Teoria generale della interpetazione*, 1955; (ii) his work from 1962 *Die Hermeneutik als allgemeine Methodik der Geisteswissenschaften*; (iii) his review of *Truth and Method* from 1965; (iv) his *Allgemeine Auslegunglehre als Methodik der Wissenschaften*, 1967.

4. Eric Donald Hirsch, American literary critic, reduced hermeneutics to textual interpretation and argued that the author's intention is the ultimate determiner of meaning. His important books are *Validity in Interpretation* (1967) and *The Aims of Interpretation* (1976).

5. Hans Albert, German philosopher, in his *Traktat über kritische Vernunft* (1968) accuses hermeneutics of expanding the textual way of interpretation to questions about knowledge as such.

6. The word *sympathetic* is from Ringma, *Gadamer's Dialogical Hermeneutic*, 68.

7. Bernstein, *Beyond Objectivism and Relativism*, 168.

8. Bernstein, *Beyond Objectivism and Relativism*, 154.

9. Weinsheimer, *Gadamer's Hermeneutics*, 26.

10. Weinsheimer, *Gadamer's Hermeneutics*, 41.

Further, Paul Ricoeur supplements Gadamer's hermeneutics of tradition by suggesting a moment of distance as the condition for understanding, but at the same time in effect opposes Gadamer's notion of understanding as a presentation of subject matter. Finally, the floor will be given to various theologians who have continued the reception, critique and development of Gadamer's hermeneutical insights in their fields of interests.

Since Gadamer was not a theologian, he did not satisfactorily explore transcendence in relation to the divine. It is argued that, for this reason, Gadamer's hermeneutics needs to be (and is) further developed by various theologians and, as my thesis points out, would profit from a closer examination of the participatory relationship between the immanent and the transcendent.

Let us begin with Habermas.

Claim of Universality and Habermas's Critique

The debate between Gadamer and Jürgen Habermas (*1929) is one of the best-known confrontations, with its replies and counter-replies. At the same time, it is an example of a constructive debate that resulted both in mutual exchanges and transformations. My intention is not fully to describe the confrontation, as there are many other works that do this. Rather, I will concentrate on two particular themes that appeared in the discussion between them: the universality of linguisticality and the emphasis on tradition and authority. More precisely, to concentrate on what Habermas questioned: (i) he rejected the universality of the hermeneutic project, because Gadamer idealized the role of language, and (ii) opposed Gadamer's non-critical acceptance of conservative concepts, such as tradition, authority and prejudice.

The debate between Gadamer and Habermas began in 1967, when Habermas's article "Zur Logik der Sozialwissenschaften"[11] initiated the hermeneutic dispute and culminated in 1971 with a book entitled *Hermeneutik und Ideologiekritik*, where the exchange was collected with other contributions.[12] In confrontation with phenomenological, linguistic and

---

11. This essay is a *Literatur-Bericht*, in which Habermas discusses the prehistory, current discussion and the consequences of the methodical status of the social sciences, it was directed against the rehabilitation of prejudice, authority and tradition and the theory of historical-effective consciousness. This study was published in 1967 in *Philosophische Rundschau* under the title "Zur Logik der Sozialwissenschaften."

12. Habermas and Taubes, *Hermeneutik und Ideologiekritik*. This book also contains excerpts from Habermas's initial attack in 1967 "Zur Logik der Sozialwissenschaften" (in this volume published as "Zu Gadamers Wahrheit und Methode," 45–56). Habermas in this essay reacted to an essay "Die Universalität der hermeneutischen

hermeneutical opponents, Habermas argues for a linguistic theoretical basis for the social sciences. In this context, hermeneutics is considered an alternative to positivistic and neo-Wittgensteinian approaches. Overall, Habermas accepts Gadamer's hermeneutics and considers him alongside Ludwig Wittgenstein, but does not follow him blindly. He charges Gadamer with adopting a non-dialectical concept of the Enlightenment and being under the influence of Marburg neo-Kantianism.

First of all, Habermas rejects the universality of hermeneutics, because Gadamer idealized the role of language. Language is, for Gadamer, the medium that intermediates everything that comes about and he did not (at that time) accept the limits of language, whereas, for Habermas, the similar universal media are structures of labor, social power and domination.[13] For him, these build the context of our tradition, so the task of critical theory is to seek out this inauthentic power relation in language. Until this is done, the conversation is simply a utopian dream, because, what if the language is corrupt?[14] Since Gadamer failed to grasp the reality of a social life, the accusation of a linguistic idealism is an inevitable consequence.

Because, what if the consensus that forms tradition is *not* the product of discussion, but the *result* of force and coercion? According to Habermas, Gadamer overlooks the fact that consensus in understanding might be "systematically distorted" (*systematisch verzerrter Kommunikation*).[15] Habermas claims that Gadamer lacks the means to uncover or criticize socially determined distortions in communication.[16] He explicates the famous example of psychoanalysis which, as he thinks, provides a methodological model for critical social theories, as well as evidences the mechanism in

---

Problems" that Gadamer published the year before (1966, in *Philosophisches Jahrbuch* 73). The next year (1967) Gadamer published another essay "Rhetorik, Hermeneutik und Ideologiekritik" (first published in Gadamer, *Kleine Schriften* 1,113–30, also in *Hermeneutik und Ideologiekritik,* 57–82). Habermas responded (1970) in a long essay "Der Universalitätsanspruch der Hermeneutik" (first published in a Festschrift for Gadamer, also published in a *Hermeneutik und Ideologiekritik*, 121–59, translated in Bleicher, *Contemporary Hermeneutics*, 181–209). The 1971 volume *Hermeneutik und Ideologiekritik* also included Gadamer's "Replik" (first published in this volume). Gadamer's three essays are published in *GW* 2:219–75. See also Gadamer's introduction to (1972) third edition of *Truth and Method*, where Gadamer reacts to Habermas (*GW* 2:449–78, especially pages 452, 455, 457, 465–66, 467, 470–71).

13. See Habermas, "Zu Gadamers Wahrheit und Methode," 54.

14. "Language is *also* a medium of domination and social power" (Habermas, "Zu Gadamers Wahrheit und Methode," 52).

15. See Habermas, "Der Universalitätsanspruch der Hermeneutik," 147, 151, 154.

16. See Habermas, "Zu Gadamers Wahrheit und Methode," 53.

which we repress socially unacceptable motives and channel them into acceptable expressive forms.[17]

In return, Gadamer denies the limits that Habermas imposes to the ability of hermeneutics to deal with ideological factors. He attacked the analogy between psychoanalysis and critical social theory, and responded that relations of power, labor and dominion also build an objective framework.[18] With respect to Habermas's thoughts on labor and dominion, Gadamer denies that these factors are outside of hermeneutics. He responded by attempting to defend his claim on universality, and accused Habermas of defining its limits too narrowly.[19] Hermeneutics doesn't deal with the positions of individuals or groups in society, but with the assumptions which these positions *include*. Moreover, Gadamer continues that Habermas's contrast between linguistic tradition and the material conditions of labour and domination make no sense. If hermeneutic understanding extends to ideological content, then it is only because so-called extra-linguistic forces are part of tradition and are incorporated in it.[20]

The second area, where Habermas questions the main elements of the horizon of human understanding, lies the conservative and non-critical character of hermeneutics. Habermas criticizes Gadamer's attachment to romantic and conservative hermeneutics, which resolves around three key terms: tradition, authority and prejudice. While Gadamer works with the conservative conception of tradition, Habermas, contrastingly criticizes tradition from the social and ideological perspective and states that the concept of authority has been developed in the process of education and in the relationship between teacher and student.[21] Habermas argues that Gadamer fails to do justice to the power of reflection and therefore cannot grasp the opposition between reason on one hand and prejudice on the other.[22] According to Habermas, Gadamer defended the continuity between tradition and interpretation to the point where he'd lost sight of the effect of our consciousness on this tradition.[23]

Gadamer responds by mentioning authority that is not authoritarian, as he had in mind the *authentic* authority of a teacher or parent that provides legitimacy for the message he or she addresses, and which is recognized by

---

17. See Habermas, "Der Universalitätsanspruch der Hermeneutik," 136.
18. See Gadamer, "Rhetorik, Hermeneutik und Ideologiekritik," 69–72.
19. See Gadamer "Rhetorik, Hermeneutik und Ideologiekritik," 70–71.
20. See Gadamer "Rhetorik, Hermeneutik und Ideologiekritik," 72.
21. See Habermas, "Zu Gadamers Wahrheit und Methode," 48–49.
22. See Habermas "Zu Gadamers Wahrheit und Methode," 47–50.
23. See Habermas, "Der Universalitätsanspruch der Hermeneutik," 156.

the student who *acknowledges* the teacher's authority.[24] He traces the idealist illusion in Habermas's concept of reflection and accused him of overestimating the power of reflection—reflection can bring something, but not everything. Gadamer charges Habermas with the dogmatism of the Marxist critique of ideology, which works under the assumption that we understand *only* when we unmask false pretensions. Moreover, he claims authority is not always wrong, nor is reflection always good. Gadamer believes that Habermas's critique of the totalization of hermeneutics at the expense of critique is not sustainable.

It is not easy to evaluate their dialogue. One would say that the two partners were further apart at the end than at the beginning,[25] while others assume that their dialogue resulted in stalemate.[26] My opinion is that the debate ended in a mutual transformation of both partners, where each learned something from the other. For Habermas on one side, the psychoanalysis of the seventies was no longer at the center of his thought and under the influence of this debate he began to deal with the linguistic-theoretical fundamentals of the critical theory of society, which helped him to develop his theory of communicative *Handlung* (act). On the other side, Gadamer developed the critical potential of his hermeneutics and further focused on the boundaries and limits of language.[27]

In his later works Gadamer began to thematize the consequences of hermeneutics for practice and considered hermeneutical philosophy as the heir to the tradition of practical philosophy. Bernstein analyses this development and claims that Gadamer's shift is the result of his dialogical encounter with Habermas, when Gadamer increased his attempts to appropriate the concerns of his critics, and even "begins to sound more and more like Habermas."[28]

Distance as a Hermeneutical Condition and Ricoeur's Critique

The second critique presented here deals with one of Gadamer's French hermeneutical counterparts, Paul Ricoeur (1913–2005). It is important to talk about the difference between the hermeneutical projects of Ricoeur and Gadamer, because Ricoeur complements Gadamer's hermeneutics of tradition.

24. See Gadamer, "Rhetorik, Hermeneutik und Ideologiekritik," 73–74.
25. As does Kelly, "The Gadamer-Habermas Debate Revisited," 367.
26. As does Ringma, *Gadamer's Dialogical Hermeneutic*, 87.
27. See *GW* 2:254.
28. Bernstein, "What Is the Difference," 348.

He achieves this by refuting the concept of involvement in Gadamer's hermeneutics and postulates a moment of distance as the condition for understanding. Consequently, this leads to important questions concerning the relation of the horizontal and vertical dimensions in the horizon of human understanding and transcendence. Namely, the concept of the productive distanciation between the reader and the text. The autonomy of the text that Ricoeur suggests, in effect disputes Gadamer's notion of understanding as a presentation (*Darstellung*) of the *Sache* (subject matter) and the self-revelation of something beyond that strives for expression. Indeed, does this autonomy of the text, which opens a multiplicity of new appropriations through reading, abolish the self-revelation of what is transcendent?

Ricoeur and Gadamer offer two models for contemporary hermeneutics.[29] While Gadamer develops a dialogical model of interpretation, in which the text is a "Thou" with whom we are engaged in conversation, Ricoeur insists upon the reflective distance of the text as a linguistic object. Ricoeur sees a type of hermeneutics where life has always already (*immer schon*) interpreted itself and existence is a mode of interpretation,[30] as the shortcut to "direct" hermeneutics of existence and he proposes the long way (*la voie longue*).

According to this, existence is always mediated through an infinite number of interpretations of symbols.[31] For Gadamer, hermeneutics is a corrective to the methodological emphasis of the natural sciences, for Ricoeur, hermeneutics should have an epistemological function. For Ricoeur, hermeneutics cannot be conceived as an ontology, or as a universal theory of understanding, but must be limited to the interpretation of the text. Ricoeur admits "great proximity to the work" of Gadamer, but adds "it is indeed my concern to avoid the pitfall of an opposition between

---

29. Gadamer and Ricoeur met in 1957 in Leuven (where Gadamer lectured and presented his project of philosophical hermeneutics), and Ricoeur was one of the first to notice the importance of the book (in 1964). Their correspondence (published 2013) shows that they knew each other, spoke together very often and repeatedly met at various conferences and meetings, but the common clash between the French and German school was never overcome and their hermeneutical projects, both developed in the Sixties when they were both adults, never entered into the mutual dialogue. Besides, there was the story of the translation of Gadamer's book into French (which was finished only in 1996, the translation from 1974 was incomplete). See their recently published correspondence: Grondin, "Hans-Georg Gadamer, Paul Ricoeur," 51–93. For an Orthodox reading of Paul Ricoeur see the recent book written by Brian Butcher, *Liturgical Theology after Schmemann*.

30. See Heidegger, *Sein und Zeit*, 142–53.

31. See on this Grondin, "Ricoeur's Long Way of Hermeneutics," 149–59, see also Grondin, "Do Gadamer and Ricoeur," 43–64.

... understanding and explanation,"[32] even though his own hermeneutic seems to appear as an attempt to re-regionalize hermeneutics.[33] Ricoeur wants to shift the primary locus of hermeneutics and constitute a critical supplement to Gadamer's version.

The best sources for Ricoeur's analysis of Gadamer are his works, "Ethics and Culture" (1973), "Philosophical Hermeneutics and Theological Hermeneutics" (1975), *Human Sciences* (1981) and "Hermeneutics and the Critique of Ideology" (1986). They illustrate the need to overcome Gadamer's concept of participation between the subject and object (*Zugehörigkeit, appartenance*) by which he refutes an alienating distanciation (*Verfremdung, distantiation aliénante*).[34] Ricoeur repeatedly pointed to this issue as the point of divergence. The concept of distance discussed here, which deals with the relation between the reader and the text, must be distinguished from another (similar, but different) Gadamer concept of the temporal distance (*Zeitabstand*) that is occupied with a distance between author and the text, and is a guiding principle of Gadamer's hermeneutics.[35]

Gadamer speaks of alienation between subject and object as a scandal. An essential outcome of his work is the opposition between distancing and participation, which gives rise to unsustainable alternatives. On the one hand, distancing is the ontological presupposition that accepts as objective an approach in the human sciences as possible, yet implies the possibility of distance. On the other hand, this distance breaks and destroys the primordial relation of participation, by which human beings belong to historical reality. Thus, here are the alternatives: either we preserve the methodological attitude, but lose the ontological specificity of reality, or we keep the attitude of truth, but give up objectivity in the human sciences.

Gadamer advocates the dialogical model of interpretation where I and Thou are engaged in the conversation, Ricoeur, disagreeing, seeks to avoid choosing one of the alternatives and dissolves dichotomy. While Gadamer

32. Ricoeur, *Hermeneutics and the Human Science*, 36.

33. Ricoeur, "Philosophical Hermeneutics," 15.

34. See Ricoeur, "Ethics and Culture," 160; Ricoeur, "Hermeneutics and the Critique of Ideology," 328.

35. Gadamer develops the concept of temporal distance (*Zeitabstand*) in the context of his discussion on the history of effects, as a reaction to the Romantic claim to understanding the author better than he understood himself. Gadamer points to the distance between the author and the text and does not suspend the distance; moreover, he shows that this distance is a condition *sine qua non* of every understanding. This temporal distance is not an empty abyss needing to be overcome, but is filled with the continuity of tradition. That is, the present and past are both part of the continual tradition through which past operates in the present. Therefore Gadamer concludes that this in-between is the true locus of hermeneutics. See *TM* 297 (*WM* 300).

accepted the choice "either–or" and chooses one alternative, Ricoeur refuses to do this and he chooses a dominant problematic that allows him to escape the choice. This dominating problematic is that of the text; this is where the "fruitful notion of distanciation"[36] is introduced as the hermeneutical act of readers' appropriation of the text. Ricoeur elaborates the notion of text in light of the positive function of distance as the very "heart of the historicity of human experience."[37]

Therefore, Gadamer talks about the matter of the text that addresses us, but Ricoeur asks if this matter can be left to speak about without confronting the critical question of the way in which pre-understanding and prejudices are mixed?[38] He thinks that the hermeneutical experience, according to which the primary experience is of participation, discourages the recognition of critical approaches. Ricoeur states that the moment of distance is the very central one and here they agree, otherwise Gadamer's concept of fusion would not be possible. Ricoeur agrees with Gadamer that the horizon is not closed, but does *not* agree with him that it is a unique horizon. This situation is dichotomous and "prevents Gadamer from really recognizing the critical instance and hence rendering justice to the critique of ideology."[39] Ricoeur instead talks about the meeting of two distant horizons "the tension between the self and the other, between the near and the far, as is accomplished on a distant horizon."[40] This is the point where Ricoeur further develops Gadamer's thoughts and claims that distancing is a positive component and a condition of interpretation, since it belongs to it.

This relates to the biggest difference between them, which lies in the concept of linguistics. In his concept of the *long way* of hermeneutics, Ricoeur claims that belonging to tradition happens only through the interpretation of signs and texts. Text is defined as the "paradigm of the distanciation in all communication."[41] He refers here to Dilthey, who pointed to the expression of life in cultural signs that became autonomous from the author/creator, and who also focused on fixation in writing as the major cultural event for transmission of tradition.[42] Ricoeur sees fixation as a phenomenon of the

36. Ricoeur, "Hermeneutical Function of Distanciation," 130.
37. Ricoeur, "Hermeneutical Function of Distanciation," 130.
38. See Ricoeur, *Hermeneutics and the Human Science*, 90.
39. Ricoeur, "Hermeneutics and the Critique of Ideology," 328.
40. Ricoeur, "Ethics and Culture," 160.
41. Ricoeur, "Hermeneutical Function of Distanciation," 130.
42. "The moment of distanciation is implied by fixation in writing" (Ricoeur, "Hermeneutics and the Critique," 328).

autonomy of the text, a threefold autonomy: with regard to the reader, with regard to the initial context of discourse and autonomy with regard to the initial audience. Simply put, what the author originally meant in the text is no longer its meaning, as mediation by language is understood as mediation through text. This is similar to Schleiermacher, who wanted to perform a detailed examination of the text. But for Ricoeur the sense is disclosed, and it is in front of the text and not behind it. One no longer deals with the author, but with the text itself. Here Ricoeur follows Heidegger, when saying that the interpretation of a text is an activity of existential significance, but the modes of being do not open in a harmonious entering into the text (as in Gadamer), but are released in a critical interpretation of the text. Therefore, unlike Gadamer, Ricoeur welcomed modern methodologies as potentially helpful suggestions on the route toward a truly critical theory of hermeneutics. He admits that there is no distinct interpretative move that releases meaning, but there are many conflicting intentions and methods which *attempt* to appropriate a text. For the first time the text as a text is taken seriously in philosophical hermeneutics, as well as Ricoeur's concept of autonomy of text enabling a multiplicity of new appropriations of a text through reading.

How can we evaluate this debate between Gadamer and Ricoeur? Aylesworth's presentation of this debate puts Gadamer and Ricoeur in striking opposition. There are some overlapping themes, but differences exist in their views of text, dialogue, technology, subject and reflection.[43] Lawlor on the other hand, focuses primarily on finding unity between the authors that, according to him, lies in their attempt to recover a dialectical nature of understanding from the Greeks and Hegel.[44]

This is the moment on which one should build. For both of them interpretation lies in making something present: for Gadamer it is the presentation (*Darstellung*) of the subject matter, for Ricoeur it is the presentation of *l'intenté* that comes to presence. But the dialectical nature of universal and individual, of the relation between the historical character of our being in the language and what is beyond, is what makes Ricoeur an ally, not a critic.[45]

---

43. Aylesworth, "Dialogue, Text, Narrative," 63–91.

44. Lawlor, "Dialectical Unity of Hermeneutics," 82–92.

45. The editors of the volume: Mootz and Taylor, *Gadamer and Ricoeur* chose a similar approach.

Theological Evaluation of Gadamer's Hermeneutics

There were also theological thinkers who critically received Gadamer's hermeneutics in their various fields of interest and continued to build on his thoughts. The reason theological critical acceptance is important lies in the weakness of Gadamer's hermeneutical method mentioned earlier. Since Gadamer was not a theologian, he did not sufficiently survey what transcendence is in relation to the divine and transcendence appears for him as the acknowledgment of human finitude, which is autonomous to any eschatological moment. One could say that this seems to do little justice to Gadamer's project of a philosophical hermeneutics, for questions pertaining to the divine and to eschatology fall rather within the field of competence of theology. Thus, within his overarching hermeneutical framework, Gadamer is fully justified to bracket purely theological queries. This is fully legitimate to say, as theological questions were not in Gadamer's competence. However, this is not meant as a negative critique, as on the contrary it enables an open discussion between Gadamer and theology and explains the very reason why these gaps were filled and further developed by various theologians. A theological reception of Gadamer's hermeneutical method can be based on various concepts. At this moment, only those surveyed from the beginning are taken into account: historicity, language, tradition, prejudice and conversation.

The traditional character of Gadamer's hermeneutics deals primarily with the fusion of horizons and therefore this has been very often appropriated in theological discussions concerning the role of tradition in theology. Gadamer is an example of a thinker who rehabilitated tradition and pointed out the overlooked area that is the immersion of human beings in language and history.[46] The earliest Catholic treatment of Gadamer's notion of tradition is by Edward Schillebeeckx,[47] for whom Gadamer's hermeneutics is theoretical and provides no criterion for the correctness of theological interpretation.[48] Bernd Hilberath, the most thorough of all Catholic expositors of Gadamer,[49] provides an account of the subordination of tradi-

---

46. See Vanhoozer's article on the appropriation of tradition in theology. Vanhoozer, "Scripture and Tradition," 152–53.

47. In his lecture "Towards a Catholic use of Hermeneutics," delivered 1967. See Schillebeeckx, "Towards a Catholic Use of Hermeneutics," 1–50. Critically on a Catholic use of hermeneutics see also: Fischer, "Catholic Hermeneutics"; Carr, *Newman and Gadamer*; Carmichael, "Gadamerian Reading of Karl Rahner's."

48. For this see also in his other book: Schillebeeckx, *The Understanding of Faith*, 57.

49. His book is an encounter between theology and Gadamer's philosophy, and offers an encyclopaedic review of Gadamer's doctrines and their reception. See his book

tion to critique. He acknowledges two things Gadamer says: that the criteria for judging traditions are bequeathed by tradition, and that the proof for specific Christian traditions "is the task of theology, whose bonds with the past are unbreakable."[50] But he blames Gadamer for concentrating too exclusively on an abstract condition of understanding and refusing to offer theoretical validation for anything except tradition in general.[51] Nevertheless, while Hilberath laments the lack of epistemological criteria, he missed the value of Gadamer's concept of application that shows the unity of cognition and evaluation.

Paul Crowley is an example of a Catholic thinker who makes a positive application of Gadamer's concept of tradition and fusion of horizons. His thesis is that Gadamer's hermeneutics, with its principle of fusion of horizons, offers the key to a new approach to dogmatic development, a hermeneutical framework for discussion of dogmatic development.[52] The application of this principle shows how the message of revelation announced in the *kerygma* of faith can remain self-same and timeless even if it is understood within a new horizon. In the fusion of horizons, an exchange occurs in understanding of what is transmitted and received, as illustrated in the example of the relation of old and new, where the old understanding appears in the context of the new and the new returns to the old. This example shows how transmitted truth can remain itself even in a new situation and can explain new aspects of revealed truth in the Church's ongoing and historical experience of faith. So, Gadamer's fusion of horizons illustrates how new *aspects* of what is revealed can be possible without jeopardizing *what* is revealed.

Further theological development underscores that an understanding of the faith is defined as a process of a fusion of horizons occurring in the history of effects.[53] The Protestant theologian, Peter Stuhlmacher, sees that Gadamer emphasizes the historical effective consciousness of the interpreter, aware of his historical situation and by that he reveals the naivety of historicism according to which it is possible to search historical objects objectively without reflecting one's own situation. Stuhlmacher gives the example of the epistle to the Romans. It is without doubt this epistle had an immense influence on Western Christianity, but our interest in this book is

---

Hilberath, *Theologie zwischen Tradition und Kritik*, based on his 1977 dissertation.

50. Hilberath, *Theologie zwischen Tradition und Kritik*, 309–10.

51. See Hilberath, *Theologie zwischen Tradition und Kritik*, 293–94.

52. Crowley, *Dogmatic Development after Newman*, v.

53. "Dass Verstehen stets ein Prozess von Horizontverschmelzung darstellt und seinem Wesen nach zugleich ein wirkungsgeschichtlicher Vorgang ist" (Stuhlmacher, *Vom Verstehen des Neuen Testaments*, 197, see the whole section 197–201).

influenced by the history of effects (*Wirkungsgeschichte*) of this epistle. For Gadamer, understanding has a form of fusion of the horizons and the profit is the expanding and modification of the current horizon. But Stuhlmacher emphasizes the ability of the interpreter to apply his own historical situation, which is needed in order to admit the *otherness* of the text. Francis Schüssler Fiorenza continues in that understanding of not placing one's self into the shoes of others, but entails the fusion of horizons.[54] In the realm of theological education, Fiorenza says Gadamer's hermeneutics is significant, as it shows that religious tradition exists paradigmatically in the classics of that tradition that should not be relegated as past relics, but as something to which we belong. Theological education should point a student to the community of classics, so that his horizon is enlarged and he is able to grasp the relevance of tradition for current practice and the life of faith.

Now the focus will be on transcendental inspiration. The term *transcendental* for Gadamer's hermeneutics is not meant in the Kantian sense as a way in which we know objects even before we experience them, but is reminiscent of Kant's a-priori question as it seeks to disclose the possibilities of understanding. The transcendental character in Gadamer's hermeneutics is especially clear when one concentrates on how Gadamer describes the miracle of understanding. Kevin Vanhoozer points out that, for Gadamer, the event of understanding is what happens to us over and above our *willing* and the role of communicative agent is given to the subject matter (*Sache*), not to the author. Is the event of understanding then an active mastery or a passive happening? he asks.[55] Gadamer's preferred term to describe the way that matter beyond the text expresses itself, is miracle (*Wunder*): "miracle of 'an inner word' becoming an 'external word,' all the while remaining *itself*. Language is the self-presentation of Sache.[56] What comes into language is therefore different from the spoken word, it is the *Sache selbst* (the self-presentation of truth's content). For Gadamer understanding is not participation in the *Sache* itself, but in the conversation *about* it. Interpreting is less a subjective act than participation in an event of tradition, says Gadamer. It

---

54. He takes an example of Sophocle's Antigone, where one should not abstract from one's own situation, but rather appropriate the classic to the one's own life practice. Fiorenza, "Theory and Practice," 114.

55. In his article Vanhoozer, "Discourse on Matter," 7.

56. Vanhoozer, "Discourse on Matter," 29. See Gadamer's thought. "The greater miracle of language lies not in the fact that the Word becomes flesh and emerges in external being, but that that which emerges and externalizes itself in utterance is always already a word" (*TM* 456; *WM* 424).

means that, on one side, the event depends on tradition (communal aspect) but, on the other, it is always a situation of the individual and the event.[57]

The miracle of understanding remains a mystery for Gadamer. Understanding is not the methodological activity of a human subject; it is something that *Sache* does and the subject (person) "suffers." Moreover, exactly in this context, Gadamer invokes an analogy with the incarnation as a relation between human speech and thought. The miracle of understanding is a miracle of the *inner* word becoming the *external* word, while it *remains* what it is.

Despite Gadamer's appeal to the incarnation, the option that *Sache* swallows words implies, according to Vanhoozer, a rather unorthodox picture in which the inner word overwhelms its historical particularities. When searching for a christological heresy equivalent to Gadamer's position, Vanhoozer talks about the form of monophysitism associated with the extreme Alexandrian form in the early church, called Apollinarianism.[58] This position is (and was) heretical because it calls the true humanity of Jesus into question. Vanhoozer's proposal is that we must employ Christian categories not notionally but operationally, for the sake of understanding the miracle of understanding. Vanhoozer believes that Gadamer's account employs theological themes in a merely notional fashion. The only way Gadamer's description works, is in the interpretation of the Bible, where *Sache* is a grace, the Holy Spirit. Vanhoozer points out that in order for understanding to happen, the interpreter must exhibit certain virtues. Can those who exhibit righteousness engage in a conversation in which they will let something be told to them?[59] When Gadamer talks about effective historical consciousness, Vanhoozer suggests we should talk about pneumatic (i.e., spiritual) consciousness. Interpretative virtues (humility, openness) are gifts of the Spirit and it is the Spirit who does the ministry of *Sache* (subject matter).

Heinz-Günther Stobbe offers a different way to deal with the transcendental character, namely to put it in opposition to methodological analysis. Transcendental is when Gadamer seeks what happens in the interpretation that surpasses the will of the interpreter. This is wrong, thinks Stobbe, since only methodological reflection can help to distinguish between true and

---

57. An example is Acts 8, Philip and the eunuch from Ethiopia: Do you understand what you are reading? The matter is unclear, the author is silent. The answer is in tradition and this is the agent to which Philip refers. This is the hermeneutic crossroad. See the book Vanhoozer et al., *Hermeneutics at the Crossroads*.

58. This position emphasized the one divine nature of Jesus Christ where *logos* virtually takes the place of the human mind of Jesus.

59. See Vanhoozer, "Discourse on Matter," 32.

false prejudices.⁶⁰ Stobbe minds the lack of methodological guidelines, and thinks that the hermeneutical project ends in relativism rather than in objectivity.⁶¹

The next issue is the theology inspired by Gadamer's concept of history. By historical character, here is meant the concept of universal history, as theologian Wolfhart Pannenberg developed it in his reaction⁶² to Gadamer's book. He states that, when dealing with biblical texts, we must be aware of two gaps: (i) the gap between biblical texts and the events to which they point; this gap should be bridged over by historical study. (ii) The gap between first century Christianity and our present age; this is to be bridged by hermeneutics. Combining these two methods (historical study and hermeneutics) leads to a union, which Pannenberg calls universal-historical understanding.⁶³ Pannenberg goes further than Gadamer, and argues that these wider life-settings and epochs have their meaning only as parts of an even more comprehensive continuity of events. Therefore, the role of interpreter is not merely to reconstruct the texts as something merely past, but on the contrary, must be grasped in the continuity of meaning in which they stand, which connects them with the present age.⁶⁴

Pannenberg and Gadamer have a few things in common: (i) Pannenberg appreciates Gadamer's attempt to rid hermeneutics of all objectifying procedures; (ii) they agree that understanding is profoundly historical and (iii), Pannenberg recognizes a respect for the historical distance of the text from the contemporary interpreter. (iv) The horizon of understanding arises in the process of understanding and it is not assumed in advance, it is

---

60. Stobbe, *Hermeneutik*, 38. This book is an "extremely unsympathetic exposition of Gadamer." So Fischer, *"Catholic Hermeneutics,"* 694.

61. Stobbe, *Hermeneutik*, 47. In order to be fair, we must underline that Gadamer's thought *is* methodological, since his description of what happens in interpretation presupposes a certain methodological practice, although it does not get the priority transcendental reflection does.

62. Article "Hermeneutics and Universal History" (1963). Originally published as "Hermeneutik und Universalgeschichte" in *Zeitschrift für Theologie und Kirche*. A translation was made by George H. Kehm and is published in *Basic Questions in Theology*, 1:96–136. Gadamer did not write any consequentialessay in order to answer Pannenberg's comments. There are just a few remarks from his essays. In 1965, in the preface to the second edition of *Truth and Method*, Gadamer mentioned Pannenberg's article among the list of many other theologians who criticized his work and from whom he learned much, although he had not yet managed to make use of it. (*GW* 2:437). In *GW* 2:246 Gadamer sees Pannenberg's article as a "highly useful discussion of my book," and comments further (*GW* 2:247) that "there is no real dispute between Pannenberg and myself."

63. See Pannenberg, "Hermeneutics and Universal History," 97–98.

64. See Pannenberg, "Hermeneutics and Universal History," 100.

actually formed in a dialectical process of understanding;[65] and (v), there is also an agreement as regards the ultimate need for a fusion of horizons. A more comprehensive horizon must be projected that includes both the horizon of the text and the interpreter.

Disagreements arise around the term history. Gadamer recognizes a total historicity of man in the event of hermeneutical understanding, that is, man is always related to his historical traditions that arrive out of his past and influences his future. This is called the "historical nature of the interpreter," which requires that the understood is necessarily applied to his present situation. Pannenberg agrees with this, but further opposes Gadamer's observations regarding history as the overarching category with continuity of meaning between past events and present interpretation.

Pannenberg talks about provisional understanding—what we know and understand, we know and understand only provisionally. Any current understanding is never absolute and only the future experience of reality can show us what we have understood correctly and what we have misunderstood. Our understanding of the whole of reality is provisional because that "whole" is essentially historical, still in the process of being worked out, still becoming what it shall be. From this conclusion, Pannenberg is compelled to investigate an eschatological vision of the end of history, claimed to be anticipated in a provisional way in the history of Jesus of Nazareth. The comprehensive horizon that Pannenberg postulates is that of an eschatological kingdom of God.[66] The act of truly retaining the uniqueness of a text from the past, and yet, connecting this text with the present, requires the establishment of a historical continuity between the past and the present. Therefore, the end of history must be known, if there is to be a horizon comprehensive enough to contain the past as a past and yet to furnish a link to the present.[67] Such a universal history furnishes a mountain peak from which the meaning and continuity of history can be assessed.[68]

On the other hand, for Gadamer transcendence comes into sight as the acknowledgement of human finitude, free of any eschatological moment. Pannenberg insists that Gadamer's own hermeneutic moves him toward a conception of universal history.[69] But Gadamer's distaste for all such speculative philosophies of history and his own insistence upon human finitude,

---

65. Lauren Barthold in her 2010 book also proposes the dialectical aspect of Gadamer's hermeneutics.

66. See Pannenberg, "Hermeneutics and Universal History," 135.

67. See Pannenberg, "Hermeneutics and Universal History," 129.

68. Writes Halsey, "History, Language, and Hermeneutic," 283.

69. See Pannenberg, "Hermeneutics and Universal History," 129.

forces him to reject such universal histories. Pannenberg (with his idea of history as a totality presented from the perspective of the end) significantly seeks to use Hegel's modified conception of history. Instead of that, Gadamer asserts that the process of integration and appropriation of history is a never-ending one; there is no end (*telos*) of history, it never reaches completion nor does it progress *towards* completion. It is clear that in his rejection of a Hegelian end of history that Gadamer also rejects the permanence of a universal plan of history, such as found in classical salvation-historical patterns (for example, creation, sin, redemption, judgment, eternal life, eschatology).

In this manner, Gadamer's hermeneutics of history seems not to provide any connection between the search for truth and its full attainment in an eschatological state. For Gadamer there is no permanent understanding of the relationship between truth and the future, such as might be in a Christian salvation history in which the search for truth is eschatologically oriented towards union with the ground of truth, namely God.

Next, we move to the theology inspired by Gadamer's notion of conversation. When Thomas Guarino, in his study on revelation and foundationalism, seeks to address how to maintain the universality of revelation, but still to incorporate the "newly-presented horizons of otherness and difference,"[70] he traces three major strands of hermeneutic theory: reconstructive, phenomenological and radical. He places David Tracy with Gadamer as representatives of an ontological middle movement, more precisely, Tracy's theology as an appropriation of Gadamer's hermeneutics. The reason for this appropriation is that, where the Catholic position works with the theological emphasis on the notions of presence, identity, continuity, and integrity, the philosophical climate uses terms such as otherness, difference, or historicity. He is right, as Tracy follows Gadamer in many areas, such as a focus on interpretation, emphasis on radical finitude, rejection of Cartesianism and plurality of meanings. Nevertheless, Tracy does not let hermeneutics collapse into inappropriate relativism, so he searches for the criteria for the settlement of conflicting interpretation, and turns here to Habermas and Ricoeur. Tracy is committed to an open-ended process of reading biblical texts and of conversing about adequate methods of reading, does not seek to avoid a conflict of interpretations and encourages tackling the problem of plurality.[71]

---

70. Guarino, "Revelation and Foundationalism," 222.

71. Jeanrond says that we should agree with the pluralistic project of interpretation Tracy talks about, but we should also link it dialectically "to the development of principles and strategies of Christian action" (Jeanrond, "Biblical Criticism and Theology," 225).

This seems clear in the book *Plurality and Ambiguity* (1987), where Tracy pushes the importance of interpretation in theology and the need to reflect and interpret the very process of interpretation. "We need to reflect on what none of us can finally evade: the need to interpret in order to understand at all."[72] That is not a minor matter because when we act, judge, or experience, we are always practicing interpretation, as "To understand at all is to interpret."[73] When Tracy talks about the problem of interpretation, he doesn't explicitly mention who lies in the background of these thoughts. Gadamer is not mentioned at all. But in a footnote, he writes:

> In this and in the following sections, the work of Hans-Georg Gadamer on interpretation is prominent... The analysis I give of interpretation-as-conversation, although clearly indebted to Gadamer's pioneering work, is less directed than his to an ontology of understanding and more to developing an empirical model for the interpretation of texts, these two enterprises are not, I believe, divisive, but they are clearly distinct.[74]

Tracy takes the notions of classics, pre-understanding, game, interaction between text and interpreter from Gadamer, but his strongest emphasis is on the concept of conversation as interpretation. He is especially interested that "every classic needs continuing conversation by the community, continued by the history of effects."[75] The basis of Tracy's thesis, is that all "experience is interpretative and all interpretation is justly described as a peculiar form of conversation."[76] The analogy of a game is extremely helpful, as it shows that the game does not depend on the players (actually, self-conscious players are a danger for the game). It is also similar with conversation, which Tracy (from Gadamer) sees as influenced by questions, "in the back and forth movement of the conversation, you allow the logic of questioning to take over. You will go anywhere the question will go."[77] Conversation as questioning itself and a willingness to follow the question shows a reference to Gadamer.

There were many debates around *Truth and Method* that took part in the period from 1960 to 2000, but only those with Habermas and Ricoeur

---

72. Tracy, *Plurality and Ambiguity*, 8–9.

73. Tracy, *Plurality and Ambiguity*, 9.

74. Tracy, *Plurality and Ambiguity*, 115–16 n. 6. Actually, Gadamer repeatedly appears in his footnotes as one of the first references when talking about hermeneutical concepts: classics, pre-understanding, game, etc.

75. Tracy, "Is There Hope," 601.

76. Tracy, "Is There Hope," 602.

77. Tracy, "Is There Hope," 605, see also Tracy, *Plurality and Ambiguity*, 20.

were mentioned, as they posited important questions regarding the relation of horizontal and vertical dimensions in the horizon of human understanding and transcendence. Namely, the productive distanciation and the independence of the text, which Ricoeur proposed, disrupted Gadamer's notion of understanding as a presentation and self-revealing of the subject matter. Attention was given to theological voices who critically received and further developed some of Gadamer's hermeneutical insights. This investigation had a fourfold inspiration by the traditional, transcendental, historical and conversational character of Gadamer's hermeneutics.

4

Horizons of Human Understanding and Transcendence in Gadamer's Hermeneutical School

THIS portion of book thoroughly explores the horizons of human understanding and transcendence in Gadamer's hermeneutical school. It proceeds in three stages.

The first stage of this discussion pays attention to the historical features of understanding and their elements, as well as the roles of tradition, history, authority and prejudice will be scrutinized here. According to Gadamer, the act of understanding never happens in a hermeneutical vacuum and is always influenced by previous understanding. This circular movement within the tradition between prejudice and the current act of understanding, of which I will write in the third stage, Gadamer calls the fusion of horizons. This fusion is described as a dialogue, an application and play.

The next stage of my analysis will proceed from a discussion of the fusion of vertical and horizontal aspects of understanding, putting its emphasis on how transcendence has been approached in the Gadamerian hermeneutical school. Here it is important to highlight that the entire process of understanding occurs as an event of language and that the experience of people with their world is always based on language. The model of incarnation will be brought into discussion, in order to show the relation between word and thinking. In this sense, transcendence is not simply believing in God, but is a religiously experienced limit of human knowledge. In this perspective, the universality of hermeneutics grounded on language is transformed into the universality of not-knowing.

Let us begin with a poem. The relation between human understanding and transcendence first enters into discussion in the epigraph from Rilke's poem, which serves as the slogan of *Truth and Method*:

> Catch only what you've thrown yourself, all is
> mere skill and little gain;
> but when you're suddenly the catcher of a ball
> thrown by an eternal partner
> with accurate and measured swing
> towards you, to your center, in an arch
> from the great bridgebuilding of God:
> why catching then becomes a power—
> not yours, a world's.[1]

If we take this poem as a metaphor for man's relationship with God, it could be said that its message expresses the notion of theology, linked to the concept of divine revelation—theology as the catching of the ball thrown by an eternal partner. The ball as a symbol of the unpredictable pattern of movement is central. Is it the human being, compared to a ball, who is thrown (*geworfen*) through the air, or is it the human being itself who throws the ball?

It is clear that what addresses us, does so from beyond our wanting and doing and beyond our constructs. When we experience something that calls us to go *beyond* the limits of our possibilities, we experience the *limits* of our experience. This experience is an awareness that we participate in a process that has more sense than is communicated in a sentence and that is much larger than human beings.

The other question in this poem is, who is the eternal playfellow, the one that approaches and requests an answer and reaction from us? If we would *know* the answer, we would then become the *owners* of the knowledge and would not be capable of being captured by it. Gadamer attempts

---

1. The poem was published in Rilke's *Die Gedichte 1922 bis 1926*. It was written in Muzot on January 31, 1922, published in 1934. It is interesting to note that Rilke is mentioned in *Truth and Method* two more times (*WM* 110; *WM* 397 n. 2). In 1955 Gadamer used the material on Rilke (on which he had been working since 1930) and wrote an extensive review of Guardini's book, named "Rainer Maria Rilkes Deutung des Daseins" (*GW* 9:271–81). Gadamer agreed with Guardini that Rilke's poetry is a truly philosophical object for those living today, but still criticized him for applying a religious message to Rilke's words. On Guardini and Rilke also see his other essay in *GW* 9:313, "Rainer Maria Rilke nach 50 Jahren", 1976. A very important Gadamer's engagement with the late Rilke is his 1967 "Mythopoietische Umkehrung in Rilkes Duiniser Elegien" (*GW* 9:289).

to say that understanding is a power (*Vermögen*) that cannot be controlled. Although we are those who catch the ball, in the end we are those who are caught, it is the "grasping of what grips us."[2]

Is it a coincidence that the eternal playfellow has a feminine gender? After all, the correct translation of that line should be "thrown by an eternal girl-partner." It seems that all references to God (masculine, *der Gott*) are excluded, and it appears more probable that Gadamer has language in mind (feminine, *die Sprache*), which builds the world in which people live. Gadamer's view is that language is a universal medium in which and through which we live in the world. The hermeneutical experience takes place in language, but this experience cannot be abstracted or even formally distinguished from language.

This shows that a dialogue is needed, or even better, a game in which we are involved. This game is associated with the "arch in a great bridge," where the limits of our powers become obvious in the middle of the game. Human beings are owned by the world in which we live, our role is of reception—we *receive* the ball, we neither produce it, nor play an active role in the throwing of the ball.[3]

Historical Character of Understanding

While analyzing Gadamerian hermeneutics, this book explores transcendence as it appears horizontally in mediations, which are culturally and historically conditioned, while giving emphasis to the historical character of our being, which embraces newly evolving situations, but does not let go of the classics.

At the beginning, it must be said that hermeneutics, in our understanding, is a fundamental way in which human beings *are* in the world and *experience* it, so it should not be narrowed and restricted only to the interpretation of texts or historical events. This implies that one who understands

2. "*begreifen dessen, was uns ergreift*" (GW 2:108).

3. Jean Grondin, one of Gadamer's most famous students, from the very beginning stated that the matter of capturing "only what you've thrown yourself" refers to the Cartesian ideal of method of knowledge, which results in human beings becoming the masters and owners of the knowledge. See Grondin, *Einführung zu Gadamer*, 22–25. Words of Rilke's sonnet "Catch only what you've thrown yourself, all is mere skill and little gain," show that methodical knowledge does not lead anywhere. There might be result and gain, but from the perspective of "eternity" it is a "little gain." This is shown also in the motto of Gadamer's autobiography "*De nobis ipsis silemus*" which is a short version of words used by Immanuel Kant in his *Kritik der reinen Vernunft* (1787): "*De nobis ipsimus silemus: De re autem, quae agitur, petimus: ut homines eam non Opinionem, sed Opus esse cogitent*" (Kant, *Kritik der reinen Vernunft*, B II).

does not stand aside from the world and history, but is involved in the ongoing interaction, while both influencing and being influenced. This involvement means that the interpreter (viewer, reader) is not an autonomous subject, but is a radically historical and finite being. Since the interpreter is a historical being, understanding is also a historical act: "*Real historical thinking must take account of its own historicity.*"[4] Therefore, Gadamer's theory brings a recovery of the idea of historicity as a hermeneutical principle, where all events (past, present and future) build a tradition in which every interpreter stands in the moment as he executes the process of understanding. As he writes:

> In fact history does not belong to us; we belong to it. Long before we understand ourselves through the process of self-examination, we understand ourselves in a self-evident way in the family, society, and state in which we live. The focus of subjectivity is a distorting mirror. The self-awareness of the individual is only a flickering in the closed circuits of historical life. That is why the prejudices of the individual, far more than his judgments, constitute the historical reality of his being.[5]

This recovery of historicity is actually a critique of nineteenth-century historicism, whose representatives attempted to achieve *position-less*[6] understanding. For Gadamer, understanding is participation in the event of transmission, and interpreters cannot ever transcend their own historicity. There is no a-historical position that enables one to approach historicity objectively, but more precisely, through the effects in history it has already filtered its way into the mind of the reader.

This brings a different dimension of historicity, for which Gadamer uses the terms *Wirkungsgeschichte* (effective history) and *wirkungsgeschichtliches Bewusstsein*. *Wirkungsgeschichtliches Bewusstsein*, translated as "effective historical consciousness" or "historically effected consciousness."[7] It is the consciousness of an operating past in the present time.[8]

4. *TM* 299 (*WM* 305).

5. *TM* 278 (*WM* 281).

6. "positionslos." See Hammermeister, *Hans-Georg Gadamer*, 59.

7. There are various translations of this term, let me mention at least several: consciousness of standing within a still operant history, the consciousness in which history is ever at work, historically effective consciousness, authentically historical consciousness (Palmer, *Hermeneutics*, 191), awareness that one's own understanding is affected by history (Weinsheimer, *Gadamer's Hermeneutics*, 184). English translations of Gadamer's book use the "history of effect."

8. "The true historical object is not an object of all but a unity of the one and the other, a relationship that constitutes both the reality of history and the reality of

When Gadamer asserts that we always approach the past from a certain position, he implies that the past consists of two parts. The first is a historical event, the second is its effective history and both affect the interpreter, who stands in the present. Gadamer coins these two aspects (the reality of history and the realization of this history) in order to describe the process in which human beings both participate and interpret historical traditions.[9] This leads to two conclusions: (i) the reader cannot leave his own present position in order to approach the historical object objectively and (ii), that the historical phenomenon itself no longer exists neutrally in its own original context, but exists only in its effects during history.

This also admits that the reader, or the one who interprets, is not located in a fixed, neutral and isolated position, but exists as a part of history and, even more, exists as a part of the history of effects.[10] There is a nice example from David Hoy who says that we can now read Plato differently than Kant understood him, but we also read him differently because of Kant's reading of Plato.[11] Or, we can now read Paul differently than Luther did, but we also read Paul differently because of Luther's reading and interpretation of Paul. Reading authoritative texts of religious traditions always shows that our reading is invariably affected by the history of the text's effects on our consciousness.

Let us move one step further. When stating that the act of understanding takes place in the history of effects, this does not suspend the space between past and present. Moreover, the possibility to understand the otherness of the text is even conditioned by the *difference* created by its temporal distance (*Zeitabstand*), which is a "positive and productive condition enabling understanding."[12] Temporal distance is not an alienating historical distance or an empty abyss that simply separates us from the world of the text, or which must be bridged in order to reach a historical objectivity. This distance is not in the sense of emptiness, but is filled with "the continuity of custom and tradition."[13] The present and past are both part of the continual tradition through which the past operates in the present.

---

historical understanding" (*TM* 299; *WM* 305). The key word in these terms is *Wirkung*, an effect that history continues to operate even if no one realizes this (silent work of history). The word is similar to *wirken* (knit, weave, integrate), and to *verwirklichen* (realize, make real).

9. "Understanding is, essentially, a historically effected event" (*TM* 299; *WM* 305).
10. See *TM* 301 (*WM* 306).
11. See Hoy, *Critical Circle*, 42.
12. *TM* 297 (*WM* 302).
13. *TM* 297 (*WM* 302).

In hermeneutics, a temporal distance is transformed into an interpretative distance which then cannot be overcome. As Gadamer writes, "Time is no longer primarily a gulf to be bridged because it separates; it is actually the supportive ground of the course of events in which the present is rooted. Hence temporal distance is not something that must be overcome."[14] An interpretative distance is a situation experienced as "polarity of familiarity (*Vertrautheit*) and strangeness (*Fremdheit*)."[15] This means that the polarity exists between our belonging to a certain tradition, and between the otherness of the interpreted works.

Therefore, Gadamer says that the true home of hermeneutics is between familiarity and strangeness: "*The true locus of hermeneutics is this in-between.*"[16] Paul Ricoeur, with his concept of productive distanciation, disagrees with Gadamer, who (according to Ricoeur) wants to overcome the gap, but what he does is only to undermine Gadamer's position on dialogue. Ricoeur was not aware of both negative as well as positive meaning of distance and does not discern the difference between *Zeitabstand* and *Verfremdung*.

In 1960, Gadamer understood temporal distance (*Zeitabstand*) as the *only* criterion of truth. But in the in fifth edition of *Truth and Method* (1986) he changed the word "alone" (*nicht anderes*) with the word "often" (*oft*) and it now reads "often temporal distance can solve the question."[17] This shows that, in his later period, Gadamer realized that pointing to temporal distance as the sole condition does not solve the problem, and he gave up attempting to solve the legitimacy of prejudices. Many authors fail to see that Gadamer, by *Zeitabstand*, does not mean only filtering out unproductive prejudices.[18] Specifically, for Gadamer, temporal distance undergoes a constant movement and extension. Moreover, it is not closed, for it allows new meanings to appear. Therefore, temporal distance is not just the criterion for filtering out existing meanings, but also allows the emergence of *new* meanings.

As human beings always abide in a certain language and tradition and not in a hermeneutical void, it is not possible to access any text's subject matter objectively, but we must approach it. As he writes:

---

14. *TM* 297 (*WM* 302).
15. *TM* 295 (*WM* 300).
16. "*In diesem Zwischen ist der wahre Ort der Hermeneutik*" (*WM* 300; *TM* 297).
17. *TM* 376 n. 44 (*WM* 304 n. 228). Cf. *GW* 2:64.
18. One example is Thiselton, who says that Gadamer is too optimistic "about the temporal distance to filter out what is false and leave only what is true" (Thiselton, *Two Horizons*, 314).

throughout all the constant distractions that originate in the interpreter himself. A person who is trying to understand a text is always projecting. He projects a meaning for the text as a whole as soon as some initial meaning emerges in the text.[19]

These distractions cannot be avoided, because they are intrinsic to the hermeneutical process and their meaning is only possible when we read the text with expectations and questions. This is known as the theory of prejudices (*Vorurteil*), which is one of Gadamer's important contributions.[20] In most modern languages, the word *prejudice* has a negative connotation, as something unfounded, unreflective or subjective. But Gadamer draws this concept from a German legal terminology, where it means "provisional legal verdict."[21] Gadamer uses the term very positively, as the starting point and productive elements of our understanding and biases of our openness to the world. For Gadamer, the prejudice (pre-judgment) is any judgement that occurs and is brought "before the final examining of all moments that decide the subject matter."[22] Still, Gadamer does not return to uncritical understanding, he rather shows its positive meaning in order to criticize the unreflective role of reason as the universal method allowing people to transcend their historical context.[23]

This positive meaning of prejudices had to be rehabilitated, as Enlightenment and modernity excluded prejudices from the process of gaining knowledge.[24] Then again, the demand of the Enlightenment to overcome prejudice as an unfounded judgement, is shown to be a prejudice against prejudice itself.[25] This means that an anti-prejudicial approach still works

---

19. *TM* 269 (*WM* 271).

20. Gadamer knows also *Vorverständnis* and *Vormeinung* (*WM* 272–73; *TM* 270–71). Gadamer uses terms fore-conception, prejudice, fore-understanding, pre-understanding, prejudgment as synonyms. The idea of *prejudice* has a Heideggerian starting point as Gadamer finds the basis for it in early Heidegger (See *WM* 250–52), but it is only Gadamer who makes out of the notion of pre-understanding a hermeneutical doctrine and implies that the final meaning proceeds from the pre-understanding.

21. *TM* 273 (*WM* 275). Etymologically the word is built as pre-judice (German *vor-verständnis*) and it shows that the judgment is not possible before that what comes before it, pre-, vor-. In Gadamer's understanding the word "prejudice" is not a negative word. Etymologically the word is build as pre-judice (German *vor-verständnis*) and it shows clearly that any judgment one makes is influenced by any knowledge or experience that has preceded the judgement.

22. *TM* 273 (*WM* 275).

23. Objects Bernstein in Bernstein, *Beyond Objectivism and Relativism*, 36.

24. See "The Discrediting of Prejudice by the Enlightenment" (*TM* 274–78; *WM* 276–81).

25. "There is one prejudice of the Enlightenment that defines its essence: the

with their own pre-concepts, but fails to recognize them. As is evident, Gadamer turns this approach upside down, changing the presumed obstacles of understanding into operative factors in understanding.

Where do prejudices come from? Presuppositions come from the tradition in which we stand and "a person who does not admit that he is dominated by prejudices will fail to see what manifests itself by their light."[26] There is no pre-suppositionless interpretation and there is no a-historical situation from which the interpreter can approach the text.[27] For example, if one executes a specific experiment, the result of this experiment does not depend solely upon the elements of the experiment, but depends upon the *tradition of interpretation* in which both scientist and experiment stand.

That is to say, understanding is a dialectical process of the interaction between people and what is encountered. Self-understanding cannot be a free-floating consciousness, but is an understanding already placed in tradition and history. Gadamer underlines that "all such understanding is ultimately self-understanding," and, in this case, "that a person who understands, understands himself (*sich versteht*), projecting himself upon his possibilities."[28] Therefore, understanding does not simply mean the projection of our prejudices, but it requires an openness to otherness that is encountered when what comes is unexpected. This openness does not mean that we must forget our earlier meanings, or include neutrality or the extinction of one's self. Quite the contrary, it always includes positing other meanings in relation to the whole of our prejudices and of our world.

Gadamer further makes a distinction between prejudices that are fruitful and those that prevent us from understanding and thinking. Hence the fundamental question is: What is the ground of the legitimacy of prejudices? What distinguishes legitimate prejudices from the countless others that it is the undeniable task of critical reason to overcome? The first observation is that prejudices are subject to revision and correction by subject matter. In other words, prejudices are not productive elements if they are exposed to distraction from fore-meaning (comes from "fore-", meaning earlier or beforehand) that are not borne out by things themselves, or in the situation that the one who interprets and understands is subject to "the tyranny of the hidden prejudices that make us deaf to the language that speaks to us

---

fundamental prejudice of the Enlightenment is the prejudice against prejudice itself" (*TM* 272–73; *WM* 275).

26. *TM* 354 (*WM* 366).

27. Similarly also Rudolf Bultmann, see Bultmann, "Is Presuppositionless Exegesis Possible," 342–51.

28. *TM* 251 (*WM* 265).

in tradition."[29] The question of how to differentiate between them, or even stronger, how to control the good ones and minimize the bad, is connected with the enquiry of is there a critical impulse in Gadamer's hermeneutics. The question of correct interpretation is shown as both ideal and impossible, as there is no permanent and fixed meaning, but rather the meaning appearing in every hermeneutical situation in which the interpreter occurs. Gadamer, in this area, denies that there is an objective single correct interpretation that surpasses everything and he rather points to the requirement of personal involvement.[30]

Another concept that Gadamer rehabilitates is that of *authority*, which was considered arbitrary and institutionalized by the Enlightenment, treated with suspicion and assumed to displace understanding with blind obedience.[31] Gadamer considers this approach a distortion of the authentic concept of authority. Therefore, he argues that authority is *not* opposed to reason and freedom, nor is it based on subjection to reason, but is an act of acknowledgment.[32] He distinguishes between arbitrary and genuine authority and takes an example from education. If we take the example of a good teacher, his/her authority lies not in the power invested in him/her, but in the virtue and ability to draw listeners. Authority does not lie in punishment and sanction, but in the capability to bring to the fore the subject matters at stake.

Gadamer mentions an event, when he was as a youngster arguing with an experienced scientist about a certain issue and the scientist pointed him toward an issue he had never thought of or seen before. This scientist told him that Gadamer will also know that when he becomes as old as he is.[33] Therefore, authority in the hermeneutical sense is not an abdication of mind, but acknowledging the superiority of analysis and intelligence of the one who stands in front of us.[34] Authority further imposes that if the

---

29. *TM* 272 (*WM* 274).

30. "To understand it does not mean primarily to reason one's way back into the past, but to have a present involvement in what is said. It is not really a relationship between persons, between the reader and the author (who is perhaps quite unknown), but about sharing in what the text shares with us" (*TM* 391; *WM* 395). We deal here with an "epistemological paradox" (Grondin, *Philosophy of Gadamer,* 85): if prejudices are a condition of the understanding, how is it possible to know the things themselves?

31. See the chapter "The Rehabilitation of Authority and Tradition" (*TM* 278–91; *WM* 281–90).

32. "Authority in this sense, properly understood, has nothing to do with blind obedience to commands" (*TM* 281; *WM* 284).

33. See *GW* 2:40.

34. See *TM* 281 (*WM* 284).

interpreter stands in the tradition, in the history of understanding that is shared by several subjects, then this tradition has a normative importance.

Gadamer further claims that authority is not *regulated* by reason, but is handed down and carried over in tradition, which is another important element of the horizon of human understanding. Tradition (lat. *tradere*, to deliver) generally means the set of principles and beliefs carried through history from generation to generation. This concept has been discredited, as something that distorts knowledge due to its uncritical character and unreflective obedience. This rejection of tradition did not make much sense to Gadamer, as tradition is part of the human condition in the world, where people grow up with certain attitudes about themselves and the world even before they ask a question about it.[35] He writes:

> Rather, we are always situated within traditions, and this is no objectifying process—i.e., we do not conceive of what tradition says as something other, something alien. It is always part of us, a model or exemplar, a kind of cognizance that our later historical judgment would hardly regard as a kind of knowledge but as the most ingenuous affinity with tradition.[36]

Gadamer clearly does not post tradition and reason in opposition, however, he goes one step further than simply returning to a pre-modern period and states that the subject is *constituted* from prejudices. Prejudices are actually tradition and they are carried over by language—tradition is therefore linguistic. This comes out of the definition that *all* understanding is linguistic, and tradition must be also linguistic, as all understanding is linguistic.[37]

When compared with the Orthodox position on tradition, both approaches agree on the importance of tradition and share a fundamental prejudice about tradition as a framework constituted from presuppositions.[38] The difference is that Orthodoxy has in mind rather an unbroken continuity. Instead of having two horizons, Orthodox Christians talk instead about the single horizon that tradition provides. Critically, the Orthodox position should admit that having one horizon does not solve much, because

---

35. On tradition in Gadamer see the book Odenstedt, *Gadamer on Tradition*.

36. *TM* 283 (*WM* 286–87).

37. The definition in mind is: "All understanding is interpretation, and all interpretation takes place in the medium of a language that allows the object to come into words and yet is at the same time the interpreter's own language" (*TM* 390; *WM* 392).

38. "We are always situated within traditions . . . it is always part of us" (*TM* 283; *WM* 286–87).

tradition moves and is a living process, not a depository, but a "dynamic reality which interprets and is shaped by interpretation at the same time."[39]

In order to describe tradition more in detail, the concept of the hermeneutic circle must be introduced. It concludes that the tradition of the past *always* influences the subject during the process of understanding, and its prejudices always come to the fore before the act of understanding. Therefore, there is a circular movement within the tradition between prejudices and the current act of understanding. Gadamer recalls that the rule of a hermeneutical circle comes from ancient rhetoric and that "It is a circular relationship in both cases. The anticipation of meaning in which the whole is envisaged becomes actual understanding when the parts that are determined by the whole themselves also determine this"[40] A nice example is reading and understanding the sentence. In order to reach the meaning of the sentence, one must know the *meaning* of each word in the sentence. At the same time, in order to know the meaning of the word in the sentence, one must know its *context*, i.e., the meaning of the sentence. Hence the hermeneutic circle shows the ontological structure of understanding and always presupposes a certain pre-understanding—no one can claim to be free of a prior understanding of reality. The interpreter is not a *tabula rasa*, but there is always a horizon, filled with certain expectations, questions and preliminary explanations of facts. The hermeneutical circle means that if we want to access the interpreter, we must access him/her only through these pre-concepts. This is described as the fusion of two horizons (*Horizontverschmelzung*).[41] In the example of interpretation of the texts we talk about the horizon of a text and the horizon of a reader, but there are various forms of fusion.

Understanding Born Out of the Merging of Horizons

At this point, several models will be described for how this circular interaction can be approached. This is the central moment of Gadamer's hermeneutics and expands the *Zwischen* (in-between) moment. These models are explained in the following manner, as dialogue, application, mediality and play.

---

39. See George, "Oriental Orthodox Approach to Hermeneutics," 207. He makes a very interesting note about the two words: *tradere* (to transmit, tradition) and *traducere* (to carry over, translate), which relate. Tradition is not only transmission, but also a translation.

40. *TM* 291 (*WM* 296).

41. See *TM* 305 (*WM* 311). See also Rossen, "Horizontverschmelzung," 207–15.

Gadamer's distinguishing mark is his effort to present dialogue as a scientifically valid philosophical practice.[42] He goes even further, as his hermeneutics of dialogue is connected with language and linguisticality in the sense that words and meanings become what they are *only* in dialogue. He illustrates this with various statements throughout his work: "Language is not taking place in the statement, but in conversation,"[43] "Language is dialogue,"[44] or "Language exists in dialogue."[45] Not only are we in the dialogue and lead a conversation, but we *are* the dialogue ourselves. Gadamer illustrated his "hermeneutics of dialogue" by re-reading the early Socratic dialogues, where Plato is not depicted as one who possesses the truth, but is present at the birth of the truth. Something similar also occurs in genuine dialogue.

Gadamer distinguishes between three levels of conversations: (i) conversation where the other is just an object; (ii) a one-to-one relationship where the other is not approached in a responsive but in a calculative way, for example when listening to the other can help us to form a better counter argument for our response, and does not include true listening and hearing what the other has to say, as well as (iii), where finally there is a genuine conversation that is not concerned with what is behind the intention of the speaker, but is concerned with the subject matter of what is being spoken, as none of the participants presumes to own the full truth.[46]

Gadamer introduces genuine or authentic dialogue in the beginning of the third part of his *Truth and Method*:

> We say that we 'conduct' a conversation, but the more genuine a conversation is, the less its conduct lies within the will of either partner. Thus a genuine conversation is never the one that we wanted to conduct. Rather, it is generally more correct to say that we fall into conversation, or even that we become involved in it. The way one word follows another, with the conversation taking its own twists and reaching its own conclusion, may well be conducted in some way, but the partners conversing are far

---

42. "To become capable of conversation—that is—to listen to the Other—appears to me to be the true attainment of humanity" (*GW* 2:214).

43. *GW* 8:359. Similarly: "Dialogue is the manifestation of language, even if it is the dialogue of the soul with oneself, as Plato has called thinking" (*GW* 2:110. See also *GW* 5:27–48; *GW* 8:360).

44. "Sprache ist Gespräch" (*GW* 8:369–70, also *GW* 10:277). Also: "Language is always in conversation" (*GW* 2:144). See Wierciński, "Sprache ist Gespräch," 37–58.

45. "Sprache im Gespräch besteht" (*GW* 10:279).

46. See *TM* 351–55 (*WM* 363–68).

less the leaders of it than the led. No one knows in advance what will 'come out' of a conversation.[47]

This long citation identifies all the main elements of the dialogue. When the conversation begins, partners in dialogue do not know what will happen until the very end. They might have an intended direction, but a dialogue might have a will of its own and lead us in directions they cannot predict. This kind of a dialogue is characterized by openness. First, that means an openness and awareness that the preconceptions we bring into dialogue are part of the history and tradition. This awareness allows us, second, to be open to the position of the other, to what he/she has to say to us. Even the readiness for dialogue does not guarantee the success of the dialogue and conversation, because dialogue can never be perfect, closed or fully and successfully concluded. Its success is not measured by the level of what we learned *anew*, but by the level of *how* we encountered the other and were transformed by this encounter. Gadamer calls this the "transformative power"[48] of dialogue. This transformation is not one sided, but double-sided, where the other is changed through us, and we are transformed through the other. "Dialogue transforms both."[49]

Therefore, it is proper to talk about a hermeneutical conversation (*hermeneutisches Gespräch*),[50] where language corresponds with bringing the subject matter to the fore (*Sache zur Sprache bringen*). With this, on one side, the objectivist approach (i.e., text is reconstructed by the interpreter) is rejected, while on the other, relative subjectivism is also avoided as not everything depends upon the subject. For Gadamer, understanding happens when we participate, not in the *Sache* (subject matter) itself, but in a conversation *about* it. This hermeneutical dialogue does not aim to discover what was in the author's mind and to reconstruct the creative process, but rather aims for a genuine engagement with the *Sache*. It is a "fixed view of what is truly common, to which one belongs and we seek to comply."[51] One of the further characteristics of dialogue is the impossibility to repeat it. In

---

47. *TM* 385 (*WM* 387).
48. "The conversation has a transforming power" (*GW* 2:211).
49. "Das Gespräch verwandelt beide" (*GW* 2:188).
50. See *TM* 389 (*WM* 391).
51. In dialogue we are always at home, as Gadamer writes in one essay dedicated to Heidegger: "The conversation continues, because only in conversation can the language in which we are at home be formed—even in a more and more alienated world" (*GW* 9:338).

the moment when one suddenly requests a repetition of what the other said, the conversation is halted.[52]

In view of the above arguments, understanding of the other is a dialogical process that occurs in the fusion of horizons,[53] which is "actually the achievement of language."[54] Horizon is a metaphor that suggests a panoramic view from a certain viewpoint. As Gadamer says, "the concept of horizon suggests itself because it expresses the superior breadth of vision that the person who is trying to understood must have."[55] The possibility to have the perspective of the world is therefore conditioned by having a horizon, and this is acquired through language, as language provides limits and disclosure to the horizon. Horizon does not mean a physical sight, but a *mind's eye view*.

One might try to achieve an understanding of an object, but what always appears in the conversation is the "logos, neither mine nor yours and hence transcends the interlocutor's subjective opinions that even the person leading the conversation knows that he does not know."[56] Dialogue as a fusion means that the encounter of horizons is not the elimination of the other, but describes a mutual interaction and accommodation to the other. Fusion does not abolish or overshadow the other, let us say the past, but takes up the horizons and expands on them.

There are two controversial elements in Gadamer's account of the fusion of horizons, (i) that it is successful only if it ends in mutual agreement and (ii), that it opposes diversity as one is made out of two. One might object that, if even a conversation where the interlocutors enter seeking agreement and fail to achieve this, it should still count as successful if it results in the greater articulation of the position or in the greater sympathy for position of the other. One of the answers to these objections is that Gadamer does not mean "horizon" in its everyday meaning (the apparent intersection of the earth and sky as seen by an observer), but he uses it as a

---

52. *GW* 2:116.

53. Fusion of horizons is described three times in *Truth and Method*, and once in a postscript one decade later: *WM* 380; *WM* 401; *WM* 311, and *GW* 2:475 (Nachwort zur 3 Auflage, 1972).

54. "The guiding idea of the following discussion is that the fusion of horizons that takes place in understanding is actually the achievement of language" (*TM* 370; *WM* 383). See "To engage in a dialogue is to participate in the movement of play with the Other and become caught up in the game of the subject matter and its unfolding truth" (Vilhauer, *Gadamer's Ethics of Play*, 68).

55. *TM* 304 (*WM* 307–9).

56. *TM* 361 (*WM* 373–74).

HUMAN UNDERSTANDING AND TRANSCENDENCE IN GADAMER'S SCHOOL 69

technical term which had already been used by Husserl[57] and, as such, he de-emphasizes some meanings of its everyday use. Horizon as a technical term for Gadamer means that it expands, we can see beyond it by our own efforts, it always points toward something, has a limit and yet the limit can be overcome by our movement. It is filled with prejudgments and is always in the process of change.

The fusion of horizons illustrated in the model of dialogue relies on one very important condition—it considers *application* as an integral element of the whole process. Application, for Gadamer, means the involvement of a subject in the event of understanding. Application is usually assumed (for example moral application) as a step that follows when something has already been stated, but this notion is opposed by Gadamer. This is because, in hermeneutical theory, understanding, explanation, and application must be seen as a triunion in which they participate cooperatively.

In order to achieve this, Gadamer rehabilitates the pre-Romantic "forgotten"[58] tradition of hermeneutics named pietistic hermeneutics. He has in mind the eighteenth-century pietistic hermeneutics that recognized the function of application and points in more detail to the thinker Johann Jakob Rambach (1693–1735). Rambach in his *Institutiones hermeneuticae sacrae* (1723) brings the term "application" into hermeneutics. According to him, interpretation of the holy text always involves three moments: *subtīlitās intelligendi* (understanding), *subtīlitās explicandi* (explication, explanation), and *subtīlitās applicandi* (application).[59] First the interpreter (a preacher in this case) rationally investigates the meaning of the text in order to know what is written there (*investigandum*), then he formulates this meaning in his own words and explains it to others (*alii exponendum*) and at the end applies this meaning wisely to the particular life of the congregation (*sapienter applicandum*).

Gadamer's attitude toward Rambach is dual. He appreciates Rambach for bringing back the long-neglected factor of application, as there is a visible contrast with Romantic hermeneutics, which fused the first two moments (*intelligere* and *explicare*), and herewith obscured the task of application. Despite this appreciation for his return of application, Gadamer also criticizes Rambach because, for Rambach, these three moments are three separate components of one hermeneutics process, three different attitudes toward holy text, and as such, they express different levels of spiritual

---

57. Actually, Gadamer acknowledges his debt to Edmund Husserl the first time he mentions the word horizon. *TM* 301 (*WM* 307). For the connection with theology see Knotts, "Readers, Texts, and the Fusion," 233–46.

58. *TM* 307 (*WM* 313).

59. *TM* 306 (*WM* 312).

growth. For Gadamer they are not separate. Therefore, he radicalizes his model, where the application is not considered merely a *supplement* to the process of understanding, the third step, but it is the *core* of understanding and an inseparable part of the entire process.[60] He points out that the text cannot speak without applying to the one who speaks, "to understand a text always means to apply it to ourselves."[61] The situation is not set so that we first *know* something and only then apply it, but it is exactly the opposite, we *understand* through its application in a particular situation.

Gadamer elaborates this discussion on the models of theological and legal (or juridical) hermeneutics, which serve as his models for interpretation. The main credit of these two hermeneutics is that they show that understanding is completed *only* when applied. The law, for example, is to be made specifically valid through its interpretation and, similarly preaching should also not be seen as an explanation of historical fact, but "to be taken in a way in which it exercises its saving effect."[62]

Gadamer distinguishes preaching from all other hermeneutics because its content does not come from encounters with another expression/text, but from the pure persuasiveness of the truth of Gospel. Preaching is a special case. As such he contrasts it as an application with legal judgments. Neither of these hermeneutics sees the task of their interpretation as an effort to enter another world, but as an effort to *span the distance* between the text and the present situation. In legal hermeneutics, there are the lawyers (judges) who interpret the law in and, for their present situation in homiletics there are preachers, who read Scripture to preach it here and now.

The example of a preacher who applies biblical text to the present situation of the church shows that the sermon should comprehend much more than what the text means in its own world—the sermon must *explain* what it means in terms of our present moment. The focus on hermeneutical fulfilment in theology that happens and occurs only in preaching helps Gadamer to move away from a scientific and scholarly explanation of the meaning of the text and to focus more on the kerygmatic meaning. Gadamer talks about the *pro me* aspect of Scripture,[63] which certainly cannot be formulated beforehand as an objective concept, but at the same time cannot be

---

60. "Recognition of the application as an integrating moment of all understanding. . . . Understanding is always an application here" (*TM* 307; *WM* 314).

61. *TM* 399 (*WM* 401).

62. *TM* 307 (*WM* 314). In both cases, law and Gospel "if it is to be understood properly—i.e., according to the claim it makes—it must be understood at every moment, in every concrete situation, in a new and different way. Understanding here is always application" (*TM* 307–08; *WM* 314).

63. See for example *GW* 7:254.

formulated afterward. The objective and existential approaches occur at the same time and are distinguished, but not divided.

Theological hermeneutics additionally demonstrates that understanding is not a matter of getting to grips with a text, but it is a method of service. The explanation of the text in the homily remains subordinated to the biblical text. Here Gadamer finds proof that the explanation of the text is not controlling the text (*herrschen*), but it is serving the message (*Sache*) of the text. This is illustrated by the meaning of the Latin word *subtīlitās*, which is very similar to the English word subtlety, or fineness of detail. Its synonyms; delicacy, tenderness, gentleness, style, elegance, ingeniousness, wit, insight, and tact, indicate that knowledge as such cannot be acknowledged as a mechanical process.

Theological hermeneutics further provides a clear example of the limitations of knowing the author (*mens auctoris*) as a norm for the interpretation of the text. Especially in biblical hermeneutics, one cannot talk about authors because they are unknown and not even important, as biblical texts are already interpretations or mediations of the Christian message. When reading the Bible, we do not learn about historical events, but we learn how faithful communities in the past *interpreted* those events and how they understood them. Namely, the Bible is not a historical textbook, itinerary or scientific evidence, but it is a theological document, testimony and confession.

The conclusion is that neither pure historical research nor interpretative flights of fancy (style, tact) can independently lead to the truth of the text. Both dimensions of the truth, hermeneutic (existential application) and objective (methodological research) must be kept in active tension if one wants to hear the Bible's message.[64] Application is thus not a literally bringing of the past into the present, but it is the bringing of what is essential in the past into our personal present. Gadamer's concern is not archaeological, i.e., seeking to penetrate the past and explaining why conditions were as they were. He rather seeks the truth from tradition that will enlighten authentic existence in the immediate future. It is forward facing. The Scripture cannot be understood from an archaeological sense, for it presents a claim over the present actions of believers.

---

64. When Gadamer claims that application to a concrete situation is an integral element of interpretative understanding, he opens himself to the charge of relativism. It must be clear that this is not "truth-dissolving relativism" (*TM* 340; *WM* 350) in which all things are narrowed to the particularity and its prejudices. An interpreter caught in subjective relativism of this kind would never be able to turn toward the universal by which we are determined. Gadamer's example of Eskimo tribes and the reading in 300 years from now is famous (see *GW* 2:442).

Further on, when Gadamer insists that the subject participates in events of which he/she could never claim to be the source, and cannot take up a transcendental status as he/she is too much affected by it in order to be the condition of it, Gadamer gives an alternative to this discussion. It is the medial path, i.e., the mediality of human subjectivity.[65] There are many examples from his work that have a middle-voiced ring, for example Gadamer often used: *sich etwas sagen lassen* or *sich etwas gesagt sein lassen* (to let something be told to oneself).[66] These examples share that middle-voice and situate the subject within the event that affects the subject, without overpowering him/her.

With this, the character of understanding the event and the process of the verb are stressed, rather than the one who does it. The stress, as Gadamer says, is on the *relation* between the subject and the verb, as when he writes that the self that we are, *happens* to itself but does not *possess* itself.[67] The middle voice helps avoid a dichotomy between the subject and the object, while at the same time it preserves the subject and his actions. The middle voice should not be confused with passivity, as it holds together the event that happens and the subject that occurs within it. Gadamer calls this a miracle of understanding (*das Wunder des Verstehens*),[68] using miracle in the sense that, to be open to something that speaks to us (*sprechen*), is to cor-respond to it (*entsprechen*).[69]

Gadamer illustrates this mediality of understanding with the example of play (game), which is the hallmark event of understanding, "the primordial sense of playing being the medial one."[70] He mentions this concept for

---

65. Medium, the middle voice is a grammatical notion, a voice beside the passive and active. The subject is within the action, at the same time he is the one that performs the action. Example: I wash myself, I am washed, but I am also the one who washes, who does the action. One example is Greek word for "to get married" (*gameomai*), something happens to the bride and groom, who marry each other.

66. For more examples see Eberhard, *Middle Voice*, 62. When Gadamer talks about language, he says that "language speaks us, rather than that we speak it" (*TM* 459; *WM* 467). In his other essay, when planning for the future, Gadamer proposes steering, where the subject is always the one who determines the course, but he does it always within the given situation (*GW* 2:165). The mediality of hermeneutics is visible when focusing on the event that happens to the understanding subject, the topic is on the "in" of understanding. This is an explicit philosophical notion, as Gadamer writes in the preface to the second edition: "not what we do or ought to do, but what happens to us over and above our wanting" (*GW* 2:438). See also Eberhard, "Mediality of Our Condition," 411–34; Eberhard, "Gadamer and Theology," 283–300.

67. See *GW* 2:130.

68. See for example: *WM* 169, 297, 316, 347.

69. See *WM* 316.

70. *TM* 104 (*WM* 103). Here one must be aware of the development of the

the first time in the ontology of art as something that is not subjective and happens as an activity that reaches beyond the horizons of play and players. Gadamer's account of play always involves the "primacy of play over the consciousness of the player,"[71] "all playing is a being-played . . . the game masters the players"[72], play has the character of an event, and always needs the participants or the respondents and their reciprocal responsiveness. Players are not passive as it seems, on their side is the seriousness and full dedication to play, "someone who does not take the game seriously is a spoilsport."[73] Gadamer calls this a profound commitment, as when a child bounces a ball and counts how many times he/she succeeds.[74] All this must be applied when we conceive understanding: as an interactive event where the interlocutors become partners in a shared game that establishes the way they articulate the truth. The player must be engaged, but this *something*, subject matter, appears only in a to-and-from movement between the engaged spectator and the world.

What are the consequences of this understanding of the subject in the process of play? It seems that there are two answers. On one side, Gadamer wants to say that the role of the subject is to play according to the rules of the game. On the other, it cannot be ignored that he devotes a lot of space to the subject of understanding and states that the personal capacities of the participant in the game *are* important.

(i) Play happens by itself, as it is not performed either by the subject or by the object. It is not important *who* does, but *what* is done, i.e., the motion is relevant. Play is a motion; it generates its own rules. To play chess does not mean to control the game for any of the players, the stress is on *playing* and on the process. Gadamer compares this practice to two men sawing who are in harmony; it would seem that they understand each other and that their movement is conscious (*willenhaftes Verhalten*), but it is the movement *itself* to which both of them are subjected. This example shows

interpretation of Gadamer. Until this current era the concept of play has been mentioned only in the context of art and aesthetic consciousness (see for example the work of Richard Palmer who speaks about play only in this concept), but the work of Monika Vilhauer causes a turnover as she states that play explains the very structure of understanding and hermeneutic experience, and is much more helpful than the concept of fusion of horizons. See her book Vilhauer, *Gadamer's Ethics of Play*.

71. TM 105 (WM 110).
72. TM 106 (WM 112).
73. TM 103 (WM 108).
74. "We actually intend something with effort, ambition and profound commitment." The example with the child and few others (the one of tennis players or organist) are from his essay *Die Aktualität des Schönen* (GW 8:114), in English translation Gadamer, "Relevance of the Beautiful," 23.

that play does not depend on the subjects, but is also not independent of them. There is certainly some relation between activities and the passivity of the play, where Gadamer states that the play is being played, but at the same time the play plays and encompasses the players. Gadamer overcomes the question of activity and passivity of subjects by pointing to the relation between them and to the process that occurs.

(ii) It would be wrong to take Gadamer's talk about the "play of light and play of waves"[75] waves as proof that the game can go without human participation. The game indeed is self-sufficient, "the players are not the subjects of the play, instead their play merely reaches the representation through the players."[76] Still, the players are always there and are needed if the play is to happen. Gadamer states that to play means to forget and abandon oneself and personal experiences do not have importance for the game, moreover, they can harm the unfolding of the game. The conclusion about the role of a subject can be formulated in the following manner: even if the subject only participates in the game of truth and this game is set in motion by a work of art, the subject does not merely apply the rules of the game. Quite the contrary, the game depends on and expects the activity of the subject.

Transcendence Emerging amidst Our Being in Language

How is transcendence approached in the Gadamerian hermeneutical school? If the process of understanding is accepted as a fusion of horizons, it must begin with a discussion about language.[77] Such a discussion was not very common at that time,[78] moreover Gadamer even more urgently talks about the uncanny nearness of language (*unheimlich nahe*) that is, at most, an obscure and "most mysterious" (*Allerdunkelste*) question, calling it a "mystery of language" (*Dunkel der Sprache*).[79]

---

75. *TM* 104 (*WM* 109). See also *GW* 8:113.

76. *TM* 103 (*WM* 108).

77. "The guiding idea of the following discussion is that the fusion of horizons that takes place in understanding is actually the achievement of language" (*TM* 370; *WM* 383). For a thorough examination of Gadamer's see Arthos, *Inner Word*, 219–348.

78. This ontological turn based on language should not be mistaken with the so-called *linguistic turn* in Anglo-Saxon philosophy, about which Gadamer in the fifties knew very little (*TM* 487 n. 39; *WM* 421 n. 39).

79. *TM* 370 (*WM* 383).

Gadamer's aim is to describe and explain various ways in which people understand themselves and the world within and through language. He formulates this experience of relation between the interpretive understanding and language as:

> Language is the universal medium in which understanding occurs. Understanding occurs in interpreting . . . All understanding is interpretation, and all interpretation takes place in the medium of a language that allows the object to come into words and yet is at the same time the interpreter's own language.[80]

Here he claims that the entire process of understanding occurs as the event of language and that the experience of people with the world is always linguistic and,[81] moreover, that understanding itself shows a certain connection with language (*Sprachbezogenheit*).[82] Language in this sense is not considered to be a skill that people possess, but is rather identified with the horizon of the world and, even more, as a *Heimat* (home).[83]

Gadamer's position that the world of our experience has a linguistic nature is inspired by the work of Alexander von Humboldt (1767–1835), who claimed that human speech is a mirror of culture and is something at the disposal of humans. Gadamer agrees with Humboldt in this regard, but this is not enough for him. For him, language *is* the whole world, not merely a view of the world (not *Sprache als Weltansicht*, but *die Welt als Sprache*).[84] He mentions an example of what might happen if someone would lock a child in a room for years, so that it grew without any external influence, with the aim to discover the proto-language (*Ursprache*). This kind of *suspending the world from language* is obviously not possible, as it requires

---

80. *TM* 490 (*WM* 392).

81. See *GW* 2:184.

82. See *GW* 2:188. Language in the wide sense of the word includes whole communication forms, only in the narrow sense is it understood as speech (see *GW* 8:350).

83. See in lecture *Rückkehr aus dem Exil* from 1991, published in *GW* 8:366–72 as *Heimat und Sprache*. *Heimat* (home) is not only a place of residence that we can choose and change, because even those who live in exile can hardly forget their home (*Heimat*). What does it mean to return to home, if not to return to the mother-tongue, asks Gadamer. According to Gadamer, *Heimat* is first of all the *Sprachheimat* (home-language), our mother tongue contains in itself for each of us a piece of our homeland (*GW* 3:236). Language is our home, a place where we find a refuge, "where we are at home, which makes us so at home" (*GW* 10:369).

84. Humboldt limits the linguisticality of the world on *human spirit* (*WM* 443), and therefore Gadamer thinks that he did not get rid of individuality and view language as instrumental, and separates language from thinking. "Verbal form and traditionary content," says Gadamer, "cannot be separated in the hermeneutic experience" (*TM* 438; *WM* 445).

leaving the world.[85] This *Drinsein im Worte* (be inside the words) that fails to see words as objects is, for Gadamer, the fundamental condition of our linguistic behavior (*sprachliches Verhalten*). Therefore, he is very critical of artificial languages, because they are not part of any community (*Sprach-* or *Lebensgemeinschaft*).[86]

There is a long-standing belief (so called sign theory) that considers language a vehicle through which thoughts are transmitted. This theory takes words as representations of things and places emphasis on the capability to think, whereas the capability to work with linguistic symbols is secondary. Gadamer does not believe it is possible to end up in a situation where one is using language as a tool and therefore rejects the sign theory of the nature of language, pointing to the nature of a living language: "Language is not one of the means through which consciousness is conveyed in the world. . . . Language is not a tool, not an instrument."[87]

Gadamer finds support for his rejection with the Greeks, who had no separate word for language, as their term *logos* semantically meant thinking, meaning or reason, but never meant *onoma* (name).[88] Surprisingly, it is Greek thought that also bears the main guilt for the consequent forgetfulness of language (*Sprachvergessenheit*). Namely, it is Plato's *Cratylus*, where Plato in dialogue with sophists, developed an instrumentalist-nominalist relation between word and subject matter. This penetrates the entirety of Western thought as a form of latent nominalism, where words are just descriptions of thinking and thoughts.[89] This forgetfulness of language continued even into the twentieth century. For Gadamer, language is not a tool but somewhat a search for words that will express the situation. If one makes a statement "This chair is grey," it is not important that the human subject expressed a statement about the object, it is more important that the object is disclosed in a certain perspective:

---

85. See *GW* 2:147–49. This is not possible because we live in the world and in language. Gadamer calls language mysterious (*rätselhaft*), because we need to forget it. Very often he mentions a story about his daughter, who asked him how to spell "strawberry" (*Erdbeeren*). And when he told her, she replied: "Funny, when I hear it that way, I do not understand the word at all anymore. Only when I forget it again, am I at home in the word again" (*GW* 2:198).

86. *TM* 433 (*WM* 450). See also *GW* 8:342 or *GW* 8:420.

87. *GW* 2:148. See also Przylebski, "Gadamer's Critique," 231–42.

88. See *GW* 10:273.

89. Plato was usually an ally of Gadamer, for example dialogical Plato from the *Seventh Letter*. See Gadamer, *Dialektik und Sophistik*, but also *GW* 2:73; *GW* 8:435; *GW* 8:233.

> A word is not a sign that one selects, nor is it a sign that one gives to another; it is not an existent thing that one picks up and gives an ideality of meaning in order to make another being visible through it. This is mistaken on both counts. Rather, the ideality of the meaning lies in the word itself. It is meaningful already.[90]

Gadamer uses a word play here, where the language is not *Mittel* (tool), but *Mitte* (middle). His view is that language is the infinite universal medium and this implies that there is no point beyond language, because language is a medium *in* and *through* which human beings live. This implies that there is nothing comprehensible beyond the limits of language, as we always communicate from the center of language in which we are never able to take a stance outside its limits.

In regard to sign-theory Gadamer talks about the notion of utterance (*Aussage, Ausdruck*), which he sees as a product of the classical logic of judgment. His favorite examples to prove this are when someone quotes out of context and[91] another is the testimony of a witness in court. This means that in its written minutes testimony always receives a different meaning, because the original *circumstances* of the spoken testimony are ignored.[92] Minutes of meetings will always be reduced, because reports of what actually happened cannot capture the context of what was being said and *how* it was being said. Gadamer points to a basic critique of utterance or statement, that it never expresses all it should express. The limits of language experience are the essence of the hermeneutic concept of language: "Indeed, language often seems ill suited to express what we feel."[93] Here is a reference to the unspeakable, inexpressible, for which we lack words to express and even if we search for them, the unpronounceable is linked to language and therefore we need to talk about the universality of *Sagenwollens* (wants-to-say).[94]

90. TM 416–17 (WM 394).

91. See GW 8:359; GW 10:351; GW 8:248.

92. Gadamer often repeats the example of interrogation of the witness in the court, see GW 2:152; GW 2:195; GW 2:346; GW 4:14; GW 8:41. The true border of language is "in truth the limit that occurs in our temporality, in the discursiveness of our speech, of saying, thinking, communicating, speaking" (GW 8:359). The border of language is "essentially indigenous" (GW 8:361).

93. TM 402 (WM 405).

94. The key is the Greek understanding of language where the utterance is seen as carrying inner thoughts to outer speech, *hermeneia* and *dianoia*. Augustine perceived the word as the incarnation of the spiritual, which is present in the word, yet refers to something else. It is in this inner word, where universality lies. Gadamer points out that this should not be regarded metaphysically, as there is no pre-linguistic metaphysical world. GW 8:7.

We recognized that Gadamer's dimension of language is opposite to the theory that says language consists of fixed propositions and he claims that speaking is far more than to simply make an assertion. In this regard he writes about the *speculative* character of language.[95] He uses the original meaning of the word *speculative* (Latin word for mirror, *speculum*, -ī, *n*), where the basic structure of speech is expressed as an image that mirrors the castle in the pond. A reflection, which occurs with mirroring, has no existence in itself, but it is not *merely* a reflection as it is fundamentally linked with the mirrored castle. The mirroring underlines the fact that the image in the mirror does not have a being itself and is a duplication without the true duplicate.

This doubling is always the existence of one and expresses a dual unity between the endless unspoken (*Ungesagte*) and the final spoken (*Gesagte*). Everything expressed is dependent on the inner word, the unsaid and the metaphor of the mirror nicely catches this mirroring of the final and limited statement in the infinity of what seeks expression (*Sagenwollens*). The speculative nature of speech talks about finiteness. Speech remains definitive, but gives us an immensity of meanings. Not everything we want to say, we do say, but everything we say, opens the way to the unspoken.[96] It is this approaching-to-speech (*Zur-Sprache kommen*) that indicates how the infinite sense is interpreted in its final form—it does not receive any secondary being, on the contrary, revealing belongs to its own being. By this, Gadamer means that, when we are speaking, we are part of a process we do not control. The speculative nature of speech is the key to the mysterious unity of words and things (*Wort und Sache*), i.e., of the phonic element and meaning.

Human beings never manage to express what we want and words always stay behind: "The overriding principle of philosophical hermeneutics is, . . . that we can never say quite what we want to say. We are always left a bit behind and cannot not say quite what we wanted."[97] Whenever humans think, they do not direct their minds back to the original thought or back to the own thinking process, but direct those thoughts to the intended *Sache/Sachverhalt* (we can call it subject matter, truth content, kerygma, message, meaning, intention), to the matter that is *being* thought. What we search for in the words is not what is in the sign, but what that sign *signifies* (*das von Zeichnen Bezeichnete*). Gadamer condensed this idea into his famous

---

95. See *TM* 385 (*WM* 460–78).

96. See *TM* 469 (*WM* 478).

97. "Oberster Grundsatz der philosophischen Hermeneutik ist . . . daß wir nie das ganz sagen können, was wir sagen möchte. Immer sind wir etwas dahinter zurückgeblieben, haben das nicht ganz sagen können, was wir eigentlich wollten" (*GW* 10:274).

slogan: *"Being, that can be understood is language."*⁹⁸ Grammatically the emphasis here is placed on the relative sentence, so not any being is language, but exactly that being that can be understood and this is language.

This dual unity is one of the best ways Gadamer describes the fusion of horizons as the relation between human and divine and is illustrated in the hermeneutical model of incarnation.⁹⁹ As was shown earlier, Gadamer opposes the separation of word and thought present in the doctrine of the *logos* that dominated Western thought since Plato. The only exception to this forgetfulness is the Christian doctrine of incarnation, where the forgetfulness of language has never been completed.¹⁰⁰ Gadamer draws a parallel between the hermeneutical model and incarnation in order to show the proper understanding of relationships between word and thought. When God manifested himself to people in human form, this form was not a mere manifestation or appearance, nor the becoming, in which something changes into something else. It did not even consist of separating one thing from another. What comes to the fore is not an external form, which must be traced back to that which stands "behind" it. ¹⁰¹ Jesus became and remained God, which is the saving thought that saved language from spirituality: "The greater miracle of language lies not in the fact that the Word becomes flesh and emerges in external being, but that that which emerges and externalizes itself in utterance is already always a word."¹⁰²

But the problem remains. If truth is one and the same, like God the Father, how can truth then occur in time, like God the Son? In order to answer these questions, Gadamer returns to Saint Augustine of Hippo (354–430). He used the distinction between the inner mental word (*verbum intellectus*) and the external spoken word,¹⁰³ to return materiality to the Word without losing the spiritual perspective and the singularity of an incarnated God. Augustine utilized the stoic antithesis between external word and inner

---

98. *"Sein, daß verstanden werden kann, ist die Sprache"* (*TM* 470; *WM* 478).

99. *TM* 418–26 (*WM* 422–31). Gadamer deals with this in part III, 2, B of *Truth and Method* in several phases: The Christian doctrine of the word; Augustine's analogy of the inner word; extensive commentary on Aquinas divided in the Neoplatonist emanation theory and analysis of the analogy itself, the summary consists of opening new areas of thought relating to the inner word.

100. *TM* 418 (*WM* 422).

101. See *TM* 419 (*WM* 424).

102. *TM* 419 (*WM* 424).

103. It is very interesting, that in the chapter in TM Gadamer never directly cites Augustine, only makes allusions to *De Trinitate*, book XV, chapters 10–15. See *TM* 419–20 (*WM* 424).

word in order to grasp and explain the process of incarnation, and to approach the Trinity.

Stoics used this differentiation in order to make a clear ontological divergence between the world principle *logos* and its simple expression in words. Internal *logos* for them was the reflection that occurred before the utterance appeared, and they underlined the primacy of that reflection. External *logos* is therefore usually incomplete and secondary. Gadamer thinks that Christian theology, with its idea of incarnation, achieved far more than only explaining the relation between the Father and Son, it also succeeded in unlocking events from the spiritual ideal of thought. It showed how identity between spoken and unspoken, revealed and hidden, human and divine, is possible.

I began reason with Rilke's poem and the eternal playfellow that addresses and catches us, then followed various forms of fusion of horizons, such as dialogue, play and application that showed how something happens to us "*beyond our wanting and doing.*" Then I presented the model of incarnation that further explains how this mediality works.

Actually, the entire chapter is dedicated to the various forms of fusion of horizons. Gadamer even summarizes his hermeneutics as "not what we do or what we ought to do, but what happens to us over and above our wanting and doing."[104] This citation expresses what Gadamer meant by transcendence.

---

104. *GW* 2:438.

5

The Contributions of Gadamerian Hermeneutics

SINCE we have looked in detail at the development of Gadamer's project and its wider influence, in this chapter that concludes the virtual first part of the book, let us summarize the Gadamerian contribution to the understanding of the relationship between horizons of human understanding and transcendence. Simultaneously, we will point out where its weaknesses lie and where its complementary relationship with Orthodox hermeneutics may be beneficial.

Gadamerian hermeneutics is not theological hermeneutics but, as we claim, can still be considered hermeneutics of transcendence. Therefore, it has opened areas upon which theologians have continued to build: science and religion, interreligious dialogue, the Christian worldview and its restoration and religious aesthetics. A theological application of Gadamer's hermeneutical method can be based on various concepts. Right now, only those surveyed from the beginning are taken into account: historicity, language, tradition, prejudice and conversation.

Recovery of Hermeneutics in Theology

With this background, Roger Ebertz, professor at the University at Dubuque, encourages theologians to learn from Gadamer, because his hermeneutical method is an alternative to Christian scholarship.[1] The reason for this lies

---

1. See Ebertz, "Beyond Worldview Analysis," 13–28.

in the inconsistency of the Christian world-view, which does not see its position as perspectival, nor encourages learning from works by non-Christian authors. The hermeneutical method, on the contrary, is characterized by its dependence on history and on our being situated in it, since what is being studied is always conditioned by time and language.

The hermeneutical method further involves reflecting on one's own prejudices and underlines questioning as fundamental for understanding. The otherness of the past cannot be understood from a fixed ground, as the current horizon of the present does not consist of a permanent set of opinions. From this we can conclude that the theologian who tries to understand the voice of another always stands upon several traditions: as a person, an academic and a Christian. Therefore, the scholar always reads the Bible through these lenses and understands the subject matter as it speaks to his life, academic world and community of believers to which he belongs.[2]

The theologian is always embedded in multiple traditions that shape his prejudices and influence the way he understands a subject matter. Following Gadamer, prejudices cannot be ruled out and on the contrary, they enable the experience. The hermeneutical model therefore suggests that there is no final and definitive formulation of a Christian worldview, as any formulation is influenced by the context of the scholar, who always understands his object of study from his unique perspective. A hermeneutical method also implies the ongoing development of all understanding, where tradition is not a *fixed* entity, but a *living* reality.

Stating that there is no definite formulation of a Christian worldview without the prejudices of the theologian, cannot avoid the mimetic character of understanding that is closely connected to it. Since the time of Plato, *mimesis* has been understood as a copy, imitation or representation. So, for Gadamer, understanding as a mimetic performance "has nothing to do with the mere imitation of something that is already familiar to us. Rather, it implies that something is represented in such a way that it is actually present in sensuous abundance."[3]

According to this, understanding is not a repetition, but a recognition and involves the observer. Mimetic presentation involves three aspects: (i) self-presentation of the action, (ii) transformation-into-structure (*Verwandlung ins Gebilde*) and (iii), play or ritual when transcendence is presented to the audience. We can even talk about double-mimesis, since the subject matter of the play comes to the presentation in its performance (what is interpreted), as well as the audience (or spectators, since Gadamer talks about

2. See Ebertz, "Beyond Worldview Analysis," 25.
3. Gadamer, "Relevance of the Beautiful," 36.

theoros, a witness present at the sacred festival). The double-mimetic event is the basis of the participatory event in which what is understood and one who understands meet.[4]

Keeping all this in mind, William Schweiker takes the mimetic presentation of Christian tradition (text, rituals) as the entrance door to the study of religion, because it expresses how the religious community manifests itself. A double-mimesis includes religion being a mimetic figuration of experience, through which communities seek to express the relationship of the world to what is ultimate and beyond itself. But double-mimesis also includes the understanding of the community itself about the relation between them and the ultimate.

The fusion of horizons, as one of Gadamer's most important concepts, is a concept most helpful as an alternative to the traditional relationship between science and religion. It spells out differences between two disciplines, because it brings together the dimensions of unity and dynamism.[5] As shown in previous chapters, the horizon has many features: it is not an object, but the background; the horizon is the basis upon which objects are judged; the horizon is dynamic rather than static.

These attributes of the horizon challenge the idea of theologians and scientists as neutral observers who observe reality from somewhere outside. For the same reason, George Karuvelil indicates that the traditional concept of a privileged position, enabling one to look at the horizons of a group of people from a neutral perspective, is misleading. The alternative relation, described as the fusion of horizons, helps to overcome difficulties between science and religion, but still does not deny the existing conflict between the disciplines. Gadamer's concept of fusion of horizons requires a conscious effort. But at the same time, it allows for a complementary relation between science and religion, because the "focus of science is on the items within the horizons, whereas the focus of theology is on explicating a taken for a granted horizon."[6]

Another area of theological application of the fusion of horizons is in inter-religious dialogue. This is enabled by the fact that Gadamer's views do not deal only with understanding texts, but also with religious pluralism. David Tracy, for example, even claims that Gadamer's hermeneutical model

---

4. TM 116 (*WM* 122). Focus on double mimesis is strongly underlined in Schweiker, "Sacrifice, Interpretation," 795–96.

5. See Karuvelil, "Pragmatism, Existentialism, and Media Theory," 415–37, especially pp. 422–23.

6. Karuvelil, "Pragmatism, Existentialism, and Media Theory," 434.

of conversation is the most persuasive model showing how contemporary Western theology can clarify its aim of inter-religious dialogue.[7]

There are actually four main elements of Gadamer's hermeneutics that are important for inter-religious dialogue: (i) the acknowledgment of finitude and historicity; (ii) the focus of understanding on the other as alterity and (iii), the subject who does not control the process, as well as (iv), the other is allowed to become in the dialogue a genuine other, not a projected other. At the same time, the limits of this concept must be mentioned. Tracy emphasizes that genuine dialogue may still end up in *aporia* and that successful understanding is not guaranteed by Gadamer's model. Therefore, a fusion of horizons is not a necessity for dialogue, it is just an "*admirable ideological ideal.*"[8] Tracy's path, with his focus on Ricoeur (whose hermeneutics of suspicion presented in *Freud and Philosophy* is a radical correction of Gadamer's model), illustrates the limits of Gadamer's model, which does not reckon with the possibility of an interruption in dialogue, nor does it leave an opportunity to face a possible systematic distortion. The critique of Ricoeur helps Tracy to correct Gadamer's basic model of conversation that he accepts, as he said:

> I can see no good philosophical reason to reject Gadamer's basic model of hermeneutics as conversation driven by the to-and-from movement of the logic of questioning itself to the point where the interlocutors find themselves being played as they experience an event of new understanding. However, as we have just argued, there are times for the dialogue to stop for a time to face some possible systematic distortion.[9]

Tracy presents the Gadamerian model as a guide for interreligious dialogue, but does not claim that mutual understanding is a necessary achievement of a fusion of horizons. This opposes the interpretation of the Turkish theologian, Ismael Demırezen, who emphasizes a fusion of horizons as the goal of interreligious dialogue.[10] He tries to find a basis for dynamic pluralism in Gadamer's dialogical character of hermeneutics, which is a meeting point between plurality and monolithic unity. The reason is that Gadamer's notion of a fusion of horizons excludes the possibility of winning the argument over the other or coming to an absolute agreement.

---

7. See Tracy, "Western Hermeneutics," 1.
8. Tracy, "Western Hermeneutics," 9.
9. Tracy, "Western Hermeneutics," 18.
10. See his article Demırezen, "Gadamer's Hermeneutics as a Possibility," 113–30. Cf. Hedges, "Gadamer, Play, and Interreligious Dialogue," 5–27; Stenger, "Gadamer's Hermeneutics as a Model," 151–68.

Gadamer's dialogical hermeneutics is further helpful for interreligious dialogue with its relevance of historicity on reaching the truth and of fusion, especially as is visible in the conception of play, where the participants are rule-governed. His concept shows that interpretation is never neutral, but is an *"assimilation of one's own fore-meaning and prejudices."*[11] Since the truth that is reached is never an absolute truth, the common exclusivist approach to interreligious dialogue is excluded. All the same, it is implied that the members of confessions involved in dialogue must have their own identity and presuppositions, since such dialogue would not be possible without them.

This whole discussion concerning Gadamer's hermeneutics led to the recovery of theological hermeneutics, which is clearly visible in the work of one of its main protagonists, Jens Zimmermann. For him, Gadamer's ideas are the best possible starting point for the recovery of theological hermeneutics.[12] He sees Gadamer's work as very useful and sketches several things we can learn from him. First of all, the notion of reason which is, according to Gadamer, a way of participating in the structure of the *logos* of the world. This participation takes place in language, since everything that can be understood happens within the medium of language. Gadamer does not divide rationality into scientific fact and subjective contemplation and thus redefines human rationality as participating in transcendence. This participatory view of reason (*Vernunft*) is a retrieval of the Greek notion of *theōria*,[13] which is important for his dialogue with Orthodox theology.

The understanding that happens with the participation of a subject who partakes in the self-presentation of subject matter has been addressed as the mediality of understanding. Alexander Hampton claims this mediality also allows one to reflect their motivations of faith without requiring them to abandon their personal religious beliefs.[14] He sees that man's situation is hermeneutically characterized by the middle position between Adam and Christ. Theologically, man wants to *escape* the middle position and the commitment that is demanded by it.[15]

Gadamer examined this impatient human being and found the roots of his impatience in the Enlightenment and Cartesianism that attempted to

---

11. Demırezen, "Gadamer's Hermeneutics as a Possibility," 120. For Gadamer reception among Turkish theologians see Körner, "Gadamer Receptions Among Turkish Theologians," 205–24.

12. See Zimmermann, *Recovering Theological Hermeneutics*, 170. See also Zimmermann, "Confusion of Horizons," 87–98.

13. See Gadamer, *Reason in the Age of Science*, 18.

14. For this see his article: Hampton, "Conquest of Mythos," 57–70.

15. See Hampton, "Conquest of Mythos," 59–60.

overcome the middle position. Theology should follow Gadamer and rather *preserve* the middle position, which is the historicity of the understanding. As man's situation in the divine plan is historically situated, his limitation requires that transcendent realities are communicated in symbolic and imaginative language in order to be comprehended. For Gadamer it is a mistake to deny historicity and so to deny the finitude of the human position between the human and the divine.

The next issue that theologians must retain from Gadamer is the non-instrumentality of language, which reminds us that understanding is incarnational and it cannot be separated from its human dimension in time and history.[16] John Caputo therefore correctly states that Gadamer's hermeneutics is attractive to theologians because of his rehabilitation of tradition, which allows them to develop theories in which theology is neither limited by dogmatic formulations, nor totally free of them.[17]

When discussing the Christian revelation, it must be noted how Gadamer views the nature of the Bible, as a biblical inspiration and a biblical revelation. This is especially visible in his comments on Rudolf Bultmann, according to whom the Bible is to be interpreted like any other text. If we set the problem around the following question of if the preunderstanding that people have when they approach the Scripture is either a natural revelation that predisposes them, or is a gift given by faith, then Bultmann claims the first, Gadamer the latter. Gadamer's position is taken due to the unique hermeneutical situation of theology, where the partners in dialogue do not attempt to achieve agreement on the subject. The "theological task of the interpreter of the Scripture is not to translate God's speech into human language, but to be oneself translated into God's language, that is, to become one through whom God speaks."[18] Gadamer once said to Fred Lawrence that Bultmann forgot that New Testament books are not books in the ordinary sense of the term.[19] By this he meant that the relevance and meaning of the New Testament does not lie in the horizon of the Christian author, but in the fact that they proclaim something that surpasses their own horizon of understanding.[20]

---

16. See on this Zimmermann, *Recovering Theological Hermeneutics*, 185.

17. Caputo, "Gadamer's Closet Essentialism," 261.

18. McGrath, "Gadamer and the Hermeneutic Problem," 323. See also Ommen, "Bultmann and Gadamer," 348–59.

19. See Lawrence, "Gadamer, Hermeneutic Revolution, and Theology," 190; see also Ommen, "Bultman and Gadamer," 348–59.

20. Linge, *Hans-Georg Gadamer Philosophical Hermeneutics*, 210. See also *GW* 2:192, where Gadamer explains that by the *Wort*, he means a *singulare tantum*, the word that strikes that is in this sense used in the New Testament: "When I say 'word' [das

The New Testament, as an instance of a classic and *Urliteratur* has, according to Gadamer, three characteristics:[21] First, authors are faithful witnesses of the tradition that began with the first community, so they are not authors but rather immediate witnesses. Gadamer states that every religious message is an authentic witness, which must refer to the death on the cross. Second, New Testament texts have the status of eminent texts.[22] Christian Scripture is an eminent text and therefore establishes a norm, but also is constitutive for us and it has a *pro me* character. When we come in touch with the Gospel as an eminent text, we sense our immediate and binding affinity. As an eminent text, the Gospel has an autonomous meaning that is self-interpreting and self-authenticating. Especially in his French text "Herméneutique et théologie," Gadamer talks about the character of biblical texts as an eminent text.[23] Third and finally, the Gospel and the messianic promise do not have the status of a symbolic form common to all religious traditions, rather the Christian message of incarnation and Easter has the status of a sign. A sign is something given to one who is ready to accept it as such. Gadamer illustrates this with the story of two friends who were together in a Protestant service and one said "*Didn't the pastor prattle on?*" The other one responded, "*that may well be, but I didn't notice it.*" This means that the message existed for him as a sign—not as something that everyone can see, but when taken as a sign it existed as something certain. As Gadamer continues, the uniqueness of the Gospel message lies in the fact that it must *be* accepted because the claim of this message is that it alone can overcome death through proclamation of the death of Jesus.[24]

To criticize Gadamer, one can counter his principles with biblical revelation. Patrick McGrath SJ is one of those who show the incapability of

---

Wort], I do not mean the word whose plural are the words [die Wörter] as they stand in the dictionary. Nor do I mean the word whose plural are the words (die Worte) which with other words go to make up the context of a statement. Rather I mean the word that is a singular tantum. That means the word that strikes one, the word one allows to be said to oneself, the word that enters into a determinate and unique life-situation; and it is good to be reminded that behind this singular tantum stands ultimately the linguistic usage of the New Testament."

21. Description according to Lawrence, "Gadamer, Hermeneutic Revolution, and Theology," 190–92. See Italian original: Gadamer, "Temoignage et Affirmation," 161–65.

22. There are three categories of eminent texts: announcements or promulgations of the kind in common law, such as verdicts, then affirmations such as are found in poetry and philosophy and third, addresses such as religious texts, especially Scriptures Jewish and Christian, which are preached. See *GW* 2:475. See also English translation: Gadamer, "Text and Interpretation," 41–42.

23. Gadamer, "Herméneutique et Théologie," 388.

24. Bernasconi, *Relevance of the Beautiful*, 152.

Gadamer's hermeneutics to be applied to the Bible.[25] He says that Scripture as a divine revelation cannot be understood as an effect of history, but rather breaks all traditions and prevents any possible application of Gadamer's hermeneutics in four areas.[26] (i) Scripture violates Gadamer's principle that text is always a projection of the consequence of projecting a prejudice onto it. (ii) Scripture is not a conversation between *I* and *Thou* and it does not seek a common agreement. (iii) Scripture is never mastered by the interpreter and (iv), Scripture as divine speech cannot be separated from the divine speaker.

Reading of Scripture is namely a totally different type of reading, since it is a text of revelation and so an event of reciprocity, defined as when two agree on something, cannot be applied here. McGrath says that Gadamer lacks the category for revealed Scripture, because when God speaks he does not share an opinion, but reveals and speaks himself and this cannot be overcome by the reader.[27] Hence, it is concluded that Gadamer's hermeneutics of transcendence enables various theologians to critically develop a hermeneutical method in their own areas and simultaneously correct it.

Religious Experience as Aesthetic Experience

The last moment of transcendence is connected with its focus on the relation between the aesthetic and religious experience,[28] when religious experience is exemplified by the human experience in aesthetics.[29] Especially crucial is the difference between the re-presentation (*Vorstellung*) and the presentation (*Darstellung*). While *Vorstellung* implies a re-presenting of something independent of the work, the notion of *Darstellung* hints at what the work of art *presents* and how the subject matter comes forth to appear in the image. Its appearance therefore, is not secondary, but as *Darstellung* it is the essence itself: "A work of art belongs so closely to what it is related to that it enriches

---

25. But not the only one. See also Meek, "Hans-Georg Gadamer," 97–106; Obielosi and Ani, "Gadamer's Hermeneutics and Its relevance," 1–25.

26. McGrath, "Gadamer and the Hermeneutic Problem," 335.

27. Conclusion of McGrath, "Gadamer and the Hermeneutic Problem," 336–37.

28. Developed in *WM* 107–76. See also continuation of this topic in "Die Wahrheit des Kunstwerkes" (*GW* 3:240) or "Aktualität des Schönen" (*GW* 8:94). In his late work "Wort und Bild" Gadamer states that this interest has been present in his work from the very beginning. See *GW* 8:373.

29. This is called the "mytho-poetic reversal." See Davey, "Hermeneutics, Art and Transcendence," 375.

the being of that as if through a new event of being. To be fixed in a picture, addressed in a poem, . . . they are presentations of the essence itself."[30]

The aesthetic experience considered as epiphanic, where something reveals and presents itself within the boundaries of the artistic work, helps to the illuminate human understanding of transcendence. If we can understand something of the hermeneutical content of the aesthetic experience, we can understand an aspect of the transcendent as given with the religious experience. Nicholas Davey, professor at the University of Dundee, is one of these authors who emphasizes the epiphanic or revelatory character of aesthetic experience. Davey, in his recent articles, asks how it is possible that a painting reveals a new aspect each time we look at it and argues that this is not because an image describes transcendence which we can grasp, but because we are being addressed by an image, in other words, by the subject matter of the work of art revealed to us. The artwork therefore must have an autonomy and cannot be substituted by or reduced to a sign, since this reduction would silence its inner meaning. As has been seen, Gadamer's position is in favor of the autonomy of spiritual experience.[31]

When one looks at this epiphanic character of experience, as Davey demonstrates, there are three main consequences for theology: (i) transcendence is a part of our experience, (ii) hiddenness and disclosure are not exclusive and (iii), the experience always involves a transformative element. We suggest taking this interpretation and adapting it to theology and claim the following: (i) God is not something beyond our experience, (ii) God is revealed and hidden at the same time and (iii), understanding always involves transformation.

First, for Gadamer transcendence is not something beyond human experience, but is included in it. It does not contain even a reference to something extra-experiential or an entity beyond our present experience but, on the contrary, is a part of its very topography.[32] When we read a book for the third or fourth time or look at a painting again, we see what we did not see the first time and marvel over the things that are revealed to our eyes. But at the same time, we come to see the blindness of our previous judgments. This, says Davey, is the experience of transcendence that

---

30. *GW* 1, 152. What Gadamer means by *darstellen* (to present) is "a universal ontological structural element of the aesthetic, an event of being students—not an experiential event that occurs at the moment of artistic creation and is merely repeated each time in the mind of the viewer" (*TM* 152; *WM* 164).

31. See on this also Davey, "Doubled reflection," 161; Davey, "Truth, Method and Transcendence," 25–44.

32. Cf. Davey, "Hermeneutics, Aesthetics and Transcendence," 201; Davey, "Hermeneutics, Art and Transcendence," 378.

Gadamer has in mind, which "changes our senses of self by both expanding its possibilities, reveals the limits of its understanding and shows that our understanding and sense of self is utterly dependent upon that which transcends our individual being."[33]

Second, disclosure and hiddenness are not mutually exclusive for Gadamer. Davey shows that philosophy had forgotten how to defend the hidden and dark without moving into duality.[34] Consequently, theology also forgets how to see God as personal and active in the world, without making a friend of him and degrading him, or in an opposite way, how to leave God his majesty without making him unreachable. This is where Gadamer helps. When he says that art speaks to us and, as an event, brings something new into experience from unconcealness,[35] this does not mean the extinction of concealedness *per se*, but still continues to exist as hidden. For Gadamer, this is the tension that must remain. It would be wrong to talk about metaphysics in this case, for the reason that what is hidden is not another order of being, but although hidden and beyond our grasp, it is still present. When the truth reveals itself to us, it still continues to exist as hidden. As Davey says, "the withheld is not *not*,"[36] it is not *deus absconditus*. Actually, whatever is withheld upholds the understanding that *all* symbols are "upheld by the withheld."

Third, the aesthetic and spiritual experience share the strong transformative capacity of meaning. Art, when understood as a dialogical encounter with another who speaks through art, implies that the viewers are dialogically opened to its address, as well as also open to the risk of transforming its self-understanding. Both aesthetic and spiritual experiences share the assumption that the experience always leads to a new experience and reveals the tragedy of the life that aims at nothing outside itself. The call of experience is a call for transformation. Gadamer's approach to aesthetic and spiritual experience involves the strong transformative capacity of

---

33. Davey, "Hermeneutics, Art and Transcendence," 378.

34. Cf. Davey, "Hermeneutics, Aesthetics and Transcendence," 203–7, Davey, "Hermeneutics, Art and Transcendence," 379–82.

35. "No one can ignore the fact that in the work of art, in which a world arises, not only is something meaningful given to experience, but also something new comes into existence with the work of art itself. It is not simply laying bare of truth, it is itself an event" (Gadamer, "Truth of the Work of Art," 105).

36. Davey, "Hermeneutics, Aesthetics and Transcendence," 206. A quotation from Robert Sokolowski is proper: "Hiddenness is not just loss: it can be preservation and protection. Things need their right time to be seen . . . may be waiting for the right moment to be understood . . . Concealment is also preservation" (cited in Davey, "Hermeneutics, Aesthetics and Transcendence," 205).

meaning—meaning resides in experiences and does not depend on anything external to them.

This concept between the hidden and the disclosed is fully explored when Gadamer posits a difference between the time characterization of artwork and the pragmatic time experience of daily life that must be mentioned.[37] The pragmatic experience of time is a structure that needs to be filled with something, such as when we say "I have time for something."[38] A different experience of time is a fulfilled and autonomous time of festivals where every moment is fulfilled.[39] The repetition of the festival is not the repetition of the same, as a festival is never a commemorative event, but is an occurrence in its own "autonomous time." The festival does not become the past, because its celebration would be only its repetition, but more important is the recurring celebration, "a festival exists only in being celebrated."[40] The meaning of the festival lies in *what* is celebrated and this *what* is why the festival is repeated. The idea of a festival involves the mode of recovery or restoration of the original elements involved with the original festivals, such as Christmas and the Lord's Supper, thus autonomous time arises only through the recurrence of the festival itself. [41]

This experiencing of time creates a contemporaneity, a union of past and present.[42] Gadamer uses the concept of *theōria* in order to explain this participation, especially its original meaning of participation in a delegation sent to a festival for the sake of honoring the gods. Viewing the divine is not a neutral state of affairs, participation-less, but is the genuine sharing in an event, a real *being present*.[43] *theōria* is not a look at the world from a distance, but one of affinity and participation and "is a true participation, not something active but something passive (pathos), namely being totally involved in and carried away by what one sees."[44]

---

37. Developed especially in Gadamer's Salzburg lectures, published as "Die Aktualität des Schönen," now in *GW* 8:94–142 (English translation "The Relevance of the Beautiful," in Bernasconi, *Relevance of the Beautiful*, 3–53. But see also elsewhere for the festival, "Über leere und erfüllte Zeit" (*GW* 4:13753) or "Aesthetic and Religious Experience" (*GW* 8:143–55).

38. Gadamer, "Relevance of the Beautiful," 41. We are bored if time is not filled, and when there are too many tasks to do, time is overfilled.

39. Gadamer, "Relevance of the Beautiful," 42.

40. *TM* 121 (*WM* 129).

41. Gadamer, "Relevance of the Beautiful," 41.

42. Gadamer, "Relevance of the Beautiful," 46.

43. See Gadamer, *Reason in the Age of Science*, 17–18.

44. *TM* 122 (*WM* 130).

As a result, it has been shown which traits of Gadamer's hermeneutics are still helpful for theological hermeneutics and where an additional component from other sources would be beneficial. Since a hermeneutical method is characterized by dependence on history and involves reflecting on one's own prejudices, it can be concluded that the theologian who attempts to understand the voice of another always stands upon several traditions. The fusion of horizons is a thought most helpful in numerous areas, especially because it refutes the idea of a neutral observer as one who perceives reality from somewhere outside.

For Gadamer, the theological model of incarnation further showed that transcendence is not simply believing in God, but is a religiously experienced limit of human knowledge. The experience of aesthetics, with its idea of revealing the subject matter of an artistic work to viewers, provided further theological moments. It is not possible to say what the being *is*, as Gadamer repudiated classical otherworldly metaphysics, but on the models of icon and festival it can be shown how the *being* reveals and manifests itself as a word within historical understanding. Further, it can be said to be how the identity in difference is preserved.

The natural continuation of these thoughts involves a discussion of the second dialogue partner (the Other), which is modern Orthodox theological hermeneutics and, in particular, the works of its representative voices. Here, first of all I need to comment on the obvious unevenness, namely that I am bringing together both a person and a tradition. As was shown previously, Gadamer was understood not only as an individual thinker, but includes as well the effective history and continuation of his work in the West in the twentieth and twenty-first century. In a similar manner, modern and postmodern Orthodox hermeneutics are less concentrated around one person and yet show common distinct features, represented by figures, such as John Breck, Theodore Stylianopoulos, Andrew Louth, Vasile Mihoc, John Behr and Assaad Kattan.

The voices of non-Orthodox authors will also be mentioned who deal with the Orthodox tradition, such as Ivana Noble. A conversation between these two dialogue partners (Gadamerian and modern Orthodox hermeneutics) cannot only be based on the parallels and similarities between two concepts and their comparison. Therefore, the method involves a critical presentation of the strengths and weaknesses of each concept, presenting the boundaries of each contribution and identifying where they may need to be complemented.

6

The Emergence of Modern Orthodox Hermeneutics

HERE begins the second part of the book concerning modern and postmodern Orthodox hermeneutics. The purpose of this chapter is to provide the background of the development of hermeneutics in the twentieth century, including its main themes, figures and relations, without involving details to any significant extent. A more detailed description of the themes, as well as their critical reception, will be the content of the following chapters.

In order to understand the particular contributors to Orthodox hermeneutics, it is necessary to place the conception of specific Orthodox hermeneutics as it has developed. Hereafter, here we scrutinize the several ways in which hermeneutics entered and developed in its Orthodox context. I will offer a reference to the 1936 meeting in Athens, where the first paradigm shift occurred. An overview of the neo-patristic renewal in Greece in the sixties will follow, which offered a different pattern of how to overcome Western captivity. The events and conferences in the seventies will be briefly mentioned, when discussions over hermeneutics continued more explicitly in the context of biblical studies and finally, we will come to the current time, when a critical reception of neo-patristic movements occurred in the form of hermeneutical theology. Accordingly, during these periods modern hermeneutics within the Orthodox context settled in three directions: as patristic hermeneutics, biblical hermeneutics and hermeneutical theology.

In order to begin the discussion concerning modern Orthodox hermeneutics, its development, representatives, elements and problems, we must address a difficulty that appears with the term "Orthodox" hermeneutics. Although the main doctrines and canons of Eastern Orthodox churches were formulated centuries ago, a precise description of Orthodoxy seems to be missing. Absent a central institutional arbiter or body of defined doctrinal writings adds further uncertainty.[1] On what ground shall it be decided if a hermeneutical perspective is Orthodox? Moreover, what does "Orthodox interpretation" mean? Is it enough if the author of such an interpretation is Orthodox, or do certain elements need to be present in order to make the interpretation Orthodox?

For example, on the back cover of his commentary to Galatians, the Orthodox scholar Paul Tarazi says that his book may be considered Eastern Orthodox only in the sense it was written by an Orthodox scholar, not that it is written in order to support a predetermined Orthodox viewpoint. Thus the word "Orthodox" can be applied in various contexts where it implies a belonging to the tradition of the past. In the West, the word is used along with other nouns and adjectives (such as Lutheran Orthodoxy, Orthodox Judaism, etc.), so the Orthodox churches with their national prefixes (*Russian* Orthodox Church, *Greek* Orthodox Church, *Romanian* Orthodox Church) are only a few among other *orthodoxies*.

As a result, Orthodoxy is often devalued and considered as something exotic that can complement and enrich the mainstream. John Zizioulas urges that this devaluation of Orthodoxy should end,[2] as Orthodoxy has played this role far too often up to now. Honestly, this kind of image in the West has only been reinforced by immigrants from Russia, who immigrated to the West and, in order to preserve their Orthodox identity in an alien world, emphasized the mystical aspect of Orthodox theology (see the title of Lossky's book *Mystical Theology of the Eastern Church*, 1957). Therefore, there is a tendency to use the word "Orthodox" in a universal rather than the historical sense of the word, supported by the fact that Orthodox believers follow the one universal Christian faith and not a Western or Eastern version.[3]

---

1. For a general account of the doctrine, life and worship of Orthodox Christians, see for example Louth, *Introducing Eastern Orthodox Theology*; Ware, *Orthodox Way*; Bulgakov, *Orthodox Church*; Lossky, *Orthodox Theology*.

2. Zizioulas, *Being as Communion*, 26.

3. In this line see Stylianopoulos, who says that the title of his book can be easily misinterpreted (Stylianopoulos, *New Testament*, xviii), but he meant an Orthodox with low "o" for all Christians who hold to the historic faith of the church. See also: "Orthodoxy is no longer only 'eastern'. Today it is oecumenical, universal—not only in the geographical sense of the word, but also essentially and content-wise" (Bigović, *Orthodox Church in 21st Century*, 17).

Although Andrew Louth suggests talking about the *Eastern* Orthodox Church (as visible in the title of his book *Eastern Orthodox Theology*), John Meyendorff points out the disadvantage of using the phrase "Eastern Orthodox" in his lecture *Light from the East*, where he mentions his experience from one of his classes, when he was asked by a student if his denomination also has communities in California. The student thought, logically enough that Eastern Orthodox meant something geographically similar to Southern Baptists.[4] This is one of the reasons Meyendorff called for a move from *Eastern* to *Orthodox* theology, in order to challenge the secularized world and break down the barriers between East and West.[5]

The situation has become even more complex, with second and third generation émigrés no longer feeling like *Eastern* Orthodox Christians, but rather Orthodox Christians as such. In order to avoid labelling that does not clarify the situation and identity issue, Louth suggests three ways of approaching what Eastern Orthodox means: 1) we could list all Orthodox churches that exist, from Oriental to American, 2) list them as a result of their history or 3), devise a third way to name what is distinctive for Eastern Orthodoxy.[6] This is the context within which hermeneutics arose.

The First Shift of Paradigms

In the East, the hermeneutical problem never had such urgency as in the West, because for Orthodox theologians the hermeneutical problem does not lie in a theoretical basis but on the level of practice, life and *orthopraxis*. Moreover, Orthodox theologians share a common suspicion that, after the Reformation, the principle of the right of an individual to interpret the sacred texts led to a new ground for discussion. All this resulted, as Anthony McGuckin in his analysis states, in all of this intellectual ferment more or less passing under the radar of Orthodox churches during the first decades of the twentieth century.[7] Therefore, hermeneutics as a biblical interpretative method was limited to solving the problem of the distance between the biblical world and our world and to the explanation of biblical texts.

---

4. Meyendorff, "Light from the East," 339.

5. Meyendorff, "Orthodox Theology Today," 77–78. See also Meyendorff, *Living Tradition*, 168.

6. Louth, *Introducing Eastern Orthodox Theology*, xiii–xx. See also Cunningham and Theokritoff, "Who are the Orthodox Christians," 1–18.

7. As McGuckin writes: "The Professor's lecture room had become a higher seat of authority than the pulpit" (McGuckin, "Recent Biblical Hermeneutics," 303).

It was only the revolution in patristic studies at the beginning of the twentieth century that stimulated the hermeneutical question in Eastern Orthodoxy. In the Orthodox world, its chief impetus was the concept of the return to the Fathers, known as the neo-patristic synthesis, which has become the leading paradigm for Orthodox theology and its ecumenical activity. This return to the Fathers is connected with the name of Georges Vasilievich Florovsky (1893–1979), a historian of Russian thought, scholar in patristics, and ecumenist, as well as one of the most brilliant Orthodox theologians of the twentieth century.[8]

Florovsky expressed a need for liberation from the captivity of Western theology, in both its terminology and the way of thinking. Still, was not the first to call for this, as there were earlier patristic revivals. The most important of earlier revivals was *Philokalia*, an anthology of ascetic texts from the forth to fourteenth century (extensive selections from Maximus the Confessor and St Gregory Palamas), published in 1782 by St Macario of Corinth and St Nikodimos of Holy Mountain.

Moreover, patristic revival in the twentieth century was not even a strictly Orthodox phenomenon, as Roman Catholic scholars did tremendous work in this area. Florovsky's achievement is that he coined the phrase *neo-patristic synthesis*[9] and set a framework in which the discussion would continue with neo-patristic synthesis as a main hermeneutical principle in Orthodoxy. It asserted that "the teaching of Fathers is a permanent category of Christian existence, a constant and ultimate measure and criterion of right faith."[10] Florovsky collected his essays on church, Bible, and Tradition in the first volume of his *Collected Works*, he created the basis, but failed to further develop hermeneutical questions. He left it to others to develop the positive relationship between Scripture and Tradition.

---

8. Writes Kalaitzidis in Kalaitzidis, "Challenges of Renewal and Reformation," 153. Gallaher writes in a similar vein: "undoubtly the greatest Eastern Orthodox theologian of the 20th century" (Gallaher, "Waiting for the Barbarians," 559). Georges Florovsky was a major figure in the generation of Russians who preserved the heritage of their native land after emigration in exile. His true academic vocation and a major force in shaping of his theological thought was patristics, but as a founding member of the World Council of Churches he was also a pivotal figure in the involvement of Orthodoxy in the ecumenical movement. I recommend the bibliography on Florovsky by Matthew Baker and Nikolaos Asproulis.

9. This phrase was published for the first time in 1949 in his article "Legacy and Task of Orthodox Theology" (Florovsky, "Legacy and the Task," 69–70).

10. Florovsky, *Bible, Church, Tradition*, 107. For more on neo-patristic synthesis see Williams, "Neo-Patristic Synthesis of Georges Florovsky," 289–340; Gavrilyuk, "Florovsky's Neopatristic Synthesis," 102–24.

It was Florovsky who gave two papers at the *First International Conference of Orthodox Theological Schools* in Athens in 1936.[11] One is entitled "Western Influences in Russian Theology,"[12] where he talks about the pseudo-morphosis of Orthodox thought as Orthodoxy and was forced to use Western categories and foreign concepts in order to express himself. The other lecture was entitled "Patristics and Modern Theology,"[13] where he appealed to modern theologians to return to the tradition of the Fathers, as well as their practice and liturgy. This return to the Fathers was not meant as a return to letters and text *per se*, but to ignite the creative fire of the Fathers again and restore the patristic spirit. It must be stressed that a patristic revival for Florovsky did not mean a return to the past and its repetition or ignoring the present. Quite the opposite, for him the writings of the Fathers:

> should be more than just a collection of patristic sayings and statements: it must truly be a synthesis, a creative reassessment of those insights which were granted to the holy men of old. It must be patristic, faithful to the spirit and vision, ad mentem Patrum. Yet it also must be neo-patristic, since it is to be addressed to the new age, with its own problems and queries.[14]

Therefore, for Florovsky it was more typical to look *with* the Fathers than to look *to* the Fathers and he underscores the authority of Tradition as the hermeneutical principle that adds nothing new to Scripture, but *actualizes* it in the worshiping truth. The problems that come with Florovsky's concept will be analyzed in more detail in the next chapter, but let me at least mention Pantelis Kalaitzidis, who warns that patristic revival is not a unique Orthodox mark, as it is the starting point of each church renewal, the same as it was in the Protestant world with dialectical theology, or in the Catholic

---

11. Nov 29–Dec 6 1936. Wrongly called Pan-Orthodox congress of theology (due to the titles of Conference proceedings from the first two conferences). Descriptively this is correct, but the name of the conference was of Orthodox Theological Schools." There were eight conferences of this type organized over the years: 1936 in Athens, 1976 in Athens, Pendeli, 1987 in Brookline, 1996 in Bucharest, Romania, 2001 in Belgrade, Serbia, 2004 in Sophia, Bulgaria. The last, Eight International Conference of Orthodox Theology, organized by the Aristotle University of Thessaloniki, under the auspices of the Ecumenical Patriarch Bartholomew, was completed on Thursday, May 24, 2018, with a large number of speakers, delegates and students on the theme: "The Holy and Great Council of the Orthodox Church. Orthodox Theology in the 21st Century."

12. This lecture was presented in German and published in proceedings of the conference as Florovsky "Westliche Einflüsse in der russischen Theologie," 212–31; English translation "Western Influences in Russian Theology" is published in volume 4 of his *Collected Works*.

13. Florovsky, *Patristics and Modern Theology*, 3–7.

14. Florovsky quoted in Blane, *Georges Florovsky*, 154.

with the liturgical movement. The difference is that, in Orthodoxy, this return to the roots failed to appear as part of the interaction with modernity and its challenges, but as a "bulwark against modernity."[15]

This first paradigm shift, announced by Florovsky in 1936, was further brought into a Greek theology of the Fathers, especially in the so called "theology of the sixties."

Theology of the Sixties in Greece

The development of systematic theological studies in Greece began after its independence from Ottoman rule (1830), when the University of Athens was founded by Royal Decree (1837) as a theological faculty based on the German model within the state university and outside of Orthodox supervision.[16] One consequence was the appearance of academic theology pursued by lay professors, which undermined the experience of the Gospels and reducing salvation to an objective formula. The result was the westernization of university theology in Greece that missed the reflection of their own Orthodox identity.

Therefore, two main hermeneutical conditions have marked modern Greek theology since the foundation of the Greek state: creative theology of the Fathers of Florovsky's account and the influence of Western theology. These two factors worked in parallel. Extra-ecclesial organizations were of great importance for developing an awareness of Scripture, especially the establishment of the biblically oriented "Brotherhood of Life," community *Zoe* (founded 1907).

This movement had a huge influence on society, because it established study groups and published many materials on biblical books. With an aim to reform Church life, they put the Bible back in the hands of lay people and encouraged them to participate in church life. As Christos Yannaras (a critic of *Zoe*) saw it, there was a "dry Protestant pietism and an extremely Calvinist understanding of the church's Gospel. The Gospel is transformed into a totalitarian ideology merely regulating individual conduct."[17] *Zoe* used

---

15. Kalaitzidis, "From the Return," 12.

16. However, its importance should not be at all overemphasized, because in the nineteenth century the university hardly existed. Until as late as 1904 there was only one year in which there were more than three graduates in the theological school. See Yannaras, *Orthodoxy and the West*, 197. The second theological university was founded in Thessaloniki in 1925, but did not become operational until 1941–42.

17. Yannaras, *Orthodoxy and the West*, 227. Also: "Zoe represented the apologetic consolidation of Christian belief and the pietistic organization of the moral life of the faithful . . . however its influence on theology was insignificant" (Yannaras, "Theology in Present-day Greece," 198).

Scripture as a source of teachings and moral values that helped to enforce individual virtues. By 1936, this community had opened 300 catechetical schools with 35.000 students.

Zoe was considered an Orthodox reformation that did not lead to schism and represented a pietistic contrast to scientific theology before the sixties, but it ended in 1960, so it never became part of the revival. Therefore, the pietistic spirit and confusion of religious and national identity characterized itself during the first half of the twentieth century, but its indubitable contribution is that a whole generation of scholars trained in critical thinking appeared. These included Gregorios Papamichael, Nikolaos Louvaris, Hamilcar Alivizatos, Leonidas Philippides, Vasileos Vellas, Panayotis Bratsiotis and others.

This religious awakening and renewed interest in the Fathers and Orthodox tradition, as Athanasios Papathanasiou writes, was more precisely a "liberation from captivity to the scholastic models inherited from German universities after Greek independence from the Ottomans in 1821"[18] appeared during the sixties of the twentieth century and was paralleled by a renewed interest in the Fathers by Florovsky. Therefore, this movement was called *the theology of the sixties*, or neo-Orthodoxy and was characterized by an interest in apophatic theology, byzantine iconography, monasticism and Eucharistic community, as well as hesychasm and especially Gregory Palamas.

Official circles remained deaf toward this movement. For example, Savvas Agourides, professor at the University of Athens, proclaimed that the new perspectives only imitated the mystical trends of Russian diaspora theologians and conferred only marginal importance upon the new movement. Still, it is necessary to connect this revival and renaissance with the much wider social context of the events in the sixties, especially with the split in the *Zoe* movement, which conveyed an interest in the authentic Orthodox identity, and struggled to achieve distance from the individualism and legalism of the previous period. The most important theologians in this movement were Nikos Nissiotis (1925–1986), Christos Yannaras (*1935) and John Zizioulas (*1931).[19] Nissiotis's dissertation was the first where a Greek faced the problems raised by Kierkegaard, Sartre, Heidegger and Jaspers.[20]

18. Papathanasiou, "Some Key Themes and Figures," 233.

19. But also, John Romanides, Vasileos Gondikakis, Panayiotis Nellas, Georgios Mantzaridis, Nikos Matsoukas.

20. The next one in the first line was John Romanides, whose dissertation about sin and fall (*The Ancestral Sin*, 1957) challenged the Western juristic model. Professors from two faculties, Trembelas and Bratsiotis, reacted against it. See Yannaras, *Orthodoxy and the West*, 276.

The generation of theologians of the sixties was often criticized and, until the eighties of the twentieth century, were in a sort of exile or emigration.[21] First, because they were considered too progressive and conservatives were against them. Then, they were considered by others to be too conservative and were considered to be anti-Western as well as introverted. The most famous critic of the second type was the earlier mentioned Agourides. Although he took part in this renewal in its beginnings, he refused the idea of Hellenocentrism and enabled an antithesis between the East and West, which rejected the positive achievements of Western culture, such as human rights and scientific progress. The result of neo-Orthodoxy was much unexpected, as he writes:

> it is a sad fact that Neo-Orthodoxy coincided (chronologically only) with the worst type of depravity we have experienced in the Church for the past 150 years! . . . the Greek Church sank lower than it ever had before in its recent history.[22]

The neo-Orthodox movement was later overridden by the generation of the eighties, especially by the school of Thessaloniki; including Petros Vassiliadis, Ioannis Petrou and Miltiadis Konstantinou.[23]

Restoration in the Seventies

In the nineteen-seventies these local discussions were overtaken by more global discussions. One of the problems for global Orthodoxy prior to the seventies, as Alexander Schmemann reports, was that there were no regular meetings between Orthodox theologians and they could meet only at various ecumenical gatherings.[24] This was about to be changed at the beginning of the seventies with several meetings, symposiums and conferences that took a positive step toward cooperation between Orthodox theologians as one of the ways to avoid the "provincialism and self-centeredness that has

---

21. Kalaitzidis very thoroughly explains the destiny of each of the representatives in his article: Kalaitzidis, "Neue Strömungen," 189.

22. Agourides, "Orthodox Church," 151.

23. They founded the journal *Kath Odon* with the aim of contrasting the tendencies of the neo-orthodox movement. Universities are no longer places of new theological trends (Athens and Thessaloniki), but it is journals such as *Synaxis*, *Theologia* (from 2009), and the Institute *Artos Zoes*. This institute tries under the leadership of Agourides to renew biblical studies. They publish the Orthodox biblical journal *Deltion Biblikon Meliton*. They also publish translations of important Western theologians.

24. See Schmemann, "Inter-Orthodox Symposium," 151–52.

characterized Orthodoxy for far too long, in spite of the promising foundation laid in Athens in 1936."[25]

Actually, the period lasted exactly forty years until the next, *Second International Conference of Orthodox Theological Schools* was organized in 1976, with the theme "Orthodox Theology and its Application (Today)" at the Penteli monastery, Athens. Participants from the whole world and observers from the World Council of Churches, as well as other churches attended. Although the conferences of Orthodox theological schools had had a tradition since 1936, the greatest importance for Orthodox witness in the modern world and the restoration of reflection on hermeneutical issues have been two other series of conferences: the *First International Conference of Orthodox Theologians* in Brookline in 1970, which initiated the discussion about biblical interpretation in the Orthodox world, and the *Conference on Orthodox Hermeneutical Theology* in Athens in 1972, which set the ground for patristic exegetical study. This was the shift in hermeneutical discussion that I claim appeared in seventies.

Before we will talk about the restoration, let me emphasize that the references to hermeneutics in Orthodox theology can be found as early as the international theological conference held in Athens in 1936. Let me at least mention professor E. Antoniadis of Halki ("Die orthodoxen hermeneutischen Grundprinzipien und Methoden der Auslegung des Neuen Testaments und ihre theologischen Voraussetzungen") and professor Vellas of the University of Athens ("Bibelkritik und kirchliche Autorität"), as well as professor Bratsiotis of the University of Athens, and Ioannidis, Damalas, Zolotas, who worked mostly in the field of biblical studies and had been writing exclusively in Greek (only few translations in English and German are available).

The restoration I have in mind is expressed by Nissiotis's history, prolegomena, of modern Orthodox hermeneutics from 1965. Nissiotis explores the discussion concerning Scripture and Tradition and concludes that "hermeneutics should not be left exclusively to New Testament scholars and exegetes. Hermeneutics is the business of all theologians and of the church as whole, since all use the Bible, either as a basis for their theological work or for their devotional and liturgical life."[26]

The First International Conference of Orthodox Theologians in America (1970), was arranged thanks to the activity of the Orthodox Theological Society in America (whose president was Demetrios Constantelos) at the Holy Cross Seminary, Hellenic College, Brookline, Massachusetts. It hoped

---

25. Schmemann, "Inter-Orthodox Symposium," 152.
26. Nissiotis, "Unity of Scripture and Tradition," 204.

to become one of the most significant events that had recently taken place in Orthodox theology, as the last such meeting was held in Athens in 1936. It had no tendency to be pan-Orthodox, yet the speakers were from almost all the important Orthodox centers, such as Thessalonica, Athens, Paris, Leningrad, Bucharest, Halki, seminaries in Massachusetts and St Vladimir's.[27]

The two main questions discussed were the question of the autonomy of biblical studies and if the Bible can be studied directly or must be mediated through a study of the Fathers. Savvas Agourides from Athens gave a main paper, where he plead for acceptance of modern analytic methodology and fusion with the patristic exegesis. He called the Fathers guides *par excellance*—urging to return to them and do with synthesis the same as they did, to combine it with contemporary science.[28] But it was his respondents who raised the burning question regarding the role of biblical criticism. Both respondents pointed out the lack of biblical criticism in Orthodoxy and expressed a wish that future development in biblical studies would bring Orthodoxy closer to Scripture.[29]

The conference in 1970 was held in the form of a constructive dialogue and was considered successful, with a full awareness that it was only a beginning, a "joy of childhood" rather than the "stability of maturity."[30] Its importance is not only that it was the first international Orthodox meeting since 1936, but because the questions of criticism and hermeneutics in Orthodoxy were raised. The participants were mostly of a younger generation and it is this generation of theologians who had established the tone of Orthodox theology during the second half of the twentieth century. Several other international Orthodox conferences were organized in 1972,[31] but the most important was the first *Orthodox Conference of Hermeneutical*

---

27. Lectures were published in the *Greek Orthodox Theological Review* (1972) vol. 17, issue 1.

28. See Agourides, "Biblical Studies," 51–62. His paper was read in his absence.

29. Veselin Kesich, professor of the New Testament at St Vladimir's Theological Seminary, and Theodore Stylianopoulos, associate professor of the New Testament at Holy Cross Theological School. Stylianopoulos is strongly for historical exegesis of the texts, even of those that are connected to the dogmatic tradition of the church. For example, Paul Evdokimov says that an Orthodox biblical student has a freedom in his exegesis, apart from where the exegesis may contradict dogmatic truth. But asks Stylianopoulos, if there exists interpretation that is dogmatic, is then historical exegesis forbidden? Stylianopoulos, "Biblical Studies in Orthodox Theology," 80. See Evdokimov, *L'Orthodoxie*, 190–91.

30. Audi, "First Conference of Orthodox Theologians," 221.

31. Other Orthodox conferences in the same year were *Second International Theological Conference of Orthodox Theologians in America* held at St Vladimir's Theological Seminary, and the *Inter-Orthodox Theological Symposium* held in Thessalonica, Greece.

Theology held from May 17–21, 1972 and organized by the Inter-Orthodox Center of Athens at the historical Monastery of the Dormition of the Theotokos in Penteli.

This meeting responded to social and cultural changes by developing a hermeneutical theology. Hermeneutics in this case was understood as the patristic hermeneutical exegetical tradition, so the response to modern hermeneutical critique meant a return to the exegetical methods of the Fathers, as well as to critical thinking.

Presentations at the conference dealt with biblical topics (for example, Father Kniazeff studied prophetic mission in light of the Pentateuch, and professor Barois explored the proofs in Isaiah for the revelation of the New Testament), or with exegesis of the Fathers (Stylianopoulos studied the exegesis of Justin, and Andriopoulos of Origen). In their Statement, the participants agreed that "Orthodox hermeneutical theology" is called to express the Orthodox witness to the world, but the Statement further shows that they did not mean contemporary biblical research, but a patristic hermeneutical tradition considered as an "exquisite spiritual heritage and deposit" and "indispensable counsel and priceless guide to the correct interpretation of Holy Scripture."[32]

The main task of this Orthodox hermeneutical theology therefore was the detailed study and evaluation of the patristic exegetical tradition. The importance of this conference, in this historical overview, is that it brought into use the term hermeneutical theology and showed an awareness that critical thinking and hermeneutics were already present in the Fathers. An awareness of ideas and statements that were not present in the earlier period, for example in the Florovsky's account. Unfortunately, the questions of modern hermeneutical methods were not taken into account, rather the participants tried to find a balance between hermeneutical methods of the Fathers and the life of the church. This may well be considered a wasted chance, because from the critical thinking of the Fathers it is merely a step to take into account the methods of our own current world in the same way as the Fathers did in their time.

The Consolidation of Hermeneutical Theology

The period between the seventies and the eighties of the twentieth century is a period somewhat silent regarding hermeneutical discussion, although

---

32. This statement was published in *St Vladimir's Theological Quarterly* (1972) 16/3, 156–57.

there were some exceptions to this rule.[33] With the start of the third millennium, the number of conferences addressing the issue of the Orthodox Church facing the post-secularity and modernity of the twenty-first century increased, as well as conferences addressing other topics. A breakthrough was the *Sacred Text and Interpretation: Perspectives in Orthodox Biblical Studies* (2003) conference, with many important articles by contemporary hermeneutical theologians.[34]

Other hermeneutical works followed, by Michael Prokurat[35] and Vasile Mihoc.[36] This period features a redefinition of the relation between exegesis and hermeneutics, where hermeneutics is defined as a discipline that seeks to examine the premises that condition understanding beyond the question concerning the appropriate methods to employ. Therefore, hermeneutics is not simply a return to the Fathers or dealing with the words of Scripture, but is the process of a deeper understanding of God's plan of salvation;[37] so hermeneutics and exegesis are not synonyms and hermeneutics is not inevitably the reconstruction of the original meaning. This concept actually distinguishes between exegesis and eisegesis and takes into account the role of readers, the plurality of interpretations and, most of all, a focus on the subject matter and on the reader, rather than on original meaning. This is illustrated by the story of "The Sleeping Beauty" told by Merja Merras. If we attempt to see where the princess lived, why and what

33. Later we will discuss more thoroughly the work of John Breck and Theodore Stylianopoulos, also important is the article: Ugolnik, "Orthodox Hermeneutic in the West," 93–118. Ugolnik in his work shows a great knowledge of Western hermeneutics, from Luther to Tracy and Kierkegaard, but draws more attention to the continuity than to discontinuity and distance. He says that the whole idea of hermeneutics of restoration of the past and overcoming the gap sounds unfamiliar to Orthodox—because continuity and a living tradition lies between the modern and patristic exegesis (129). Other hermeneutical works with the eighties are from Paul Evdokimov, who deals with Bultmann's hermeneutics, and the work from the Indian Orthodox theologian George, who says that the question of how to understand the Bible is connected to the question of how to understand God and the church. He uses Gadamer when he talks about tradition as a hermeneutical category. See Evdokimov, "Principes de l'hemeneutique Orthodoxe," 127–35; George, "Oriental Orthodox Approach," 203–11.

34. It took place at the Hellenic College/Holy Cross Greek Orthodox School of Theology on October 28–November 1, 2003. Papers were published in volume 47 (2002) of *The Greek Orthodox Theological Review*.

35. See Prokurat, "Orthodox Interpretation of Scripture," 61–100. He puts an emphasis here on Orthodox elements and especially on liturgy.

36. See Mihoc, "Principles of Orthodox Hermeneutics," 293–320. He searches for the right criteria for assimilating what is right in Western exegetical methods. See Clark's article, which is an overview of the most important scholars working in this field of research. Clark, "Recent Eastern Orthodox Interpretation," 322–40.

37. See Nikolakopoulos, *Die unbekannten Hymnen*, 15.

happened to her, where the prince came from, why and what were his intentions, we miss the main point, that sometimes the odds can be overcome by a great effort.[38]

The main condition for the emergence of current hermeneutics (i.e., hermeneutical theology) within the Orthodox context is a new shift of paradigms, different than the one experienced in 1936. It was now based on the re-evaluation of traditional aspects and on a turn toward openness and dialogue with the West. There is a clear move to interaction and dialogue among the generation of current Orthodox theologians, in the West as well as in the East, which was a result of a deeper awareness about the world in which Orthodox believers live. So, for example, Andrew Louth writes that it is exactly this world, developed in a certain cultural history (Renaissance, Reformation, Enlightenment), with which Orthodoxy is now meeting and must communicate, as there is no other world.[39]

In many ways Orthodoxy is critical toward the way theology in the West developed as an academic discipline, separated from its spiritual aspect but, at the same time the fruits of Western scholarship can hardly be ignored. Archbishop Demetrios in his opening speech at the conference in 2002 accepted that no society can be a cultural island anymore and cannot be immune to influences from outside. Not even churches in Eastern Europe can afford the luxury of isolation. Therefore he suggested that the pluralistic world should not be seen as an obstacle, but rather an opportunity, where the Orthodox Church is "challenged to match her incarnational Christology with an equally incarnational ecclesiology."[40]

Daniel Munteanu adds that no one approaches the Bible as *tabula rasa*, because we are "products of cultural and ideological traditions." Each objectivity is constituted within a certain tradition, as we are rooted in prejudice and conditioned by the past or by effective history. Illustrative is a sentence from Alfred North Whitehead, "if we desire a record of uninterpreted experience, we should ask a stone to record its autobiography."[41] In order to avoid the fact that all these truths end in relativism and consequently lose the truth, the concept of truth must be inseparable from the principle of authority. Similar to the Early church, this leads to the interplay between Scripture, creeds and councils and the authority of tradition.

---

38. See Merras, "Do We Meet Modernity," 15.

39. In the introduction to John Behr's book *The Way to Nicaea*, ix.

40. Demetrios, "The Orthodox Churches," 3.

41. Munteanu, "Culture of Love," 201. Munteanu refers to Georgia Warnke's book (*Gadamer: Hermeneutics, Tradition, and Reason*, 3), but he does not seem to be aware of Gadamer's influence there.

In order to explain what is meant by hermeneutical theology, two current theologians who work with this kind of hermeneutics will now be introduced. The first representative is the metropolitan John Zizioulas (*1931), for whom the role of hermeneutics is described as *"the task of restating Scripture and Christian doctrine is termed hermeneutics. All theology is a matter of hermeneutics."*[42] Scripture says nothing and is silent until it is interpreted and therefore, according to Zizioulas, Christian theology is an interpretation and explanation of Scripture. He does not only conclude that it is important to explore the context in which the *kerygma* was initially formulated, but also that it includes the interpretation and exploration of our own situation. This second aspect also includes current intellectual movements and a correct relationship between them and theological interpretation.

This means that the theologian must be familiar with the intellectual climate of his own time, but even more, a theologian must have a "truly enquiring mind, a philosopher in the wider sense of being, sensitive to the deepest needs of human beings."[43] By referring to Gadamer he repeated similar thoughts at the symposium in Belgrade (2012), where he said that the task of a systematic theologian who tries to be faithful to patristic thought is to make *explicit* what is *implicit* in the expression of the Fathers. This requires not only faithfulness to the words, but also an openness to the questions the Fathers did not raise. There is an apparent difference with the work of the historian who limits himself only to what has been said. The work of a systematic theologian is not conceivable without hermeneutics, as the understanding of the past is not only reproductive but a productive activity as well.[44] Saying that theology is a productive activity, he refers to Gadamer's *Truth and Method*.[45]

Also similar to Zizioulas is the work of John Panteleimon Manoussakis, who talks about the "hermeneutic character of all theology (all theology as the logos of the Logos cannot but be hermeneutical)." This hermeneutic character of theology is based on two presumptions: first, that there is the primacy of the act of speaking—God *speaks* and reveals as the Word before it says what it *is* and second, the revelation in the Word is self-revelation. In Manoussakis's approach, a focus on communication and discourse is visible, that points to the need of a hermeneutical aspect in theology. Out of this

42. Zizioulas, "Doctrine," 3.

43. Zizioulas, "Doctrine," 4.

44. See Zizioulas, "Person and Nature," 108 n. 61.

45. A similar urge to interpret the past and engage it in dialogue with the present with a reference to Gadamer was repeated in 2015. Zizioulas, "Task of Orthodox Theology," 9–17, esp. 12.

need he stresses christological hermeneutics, based on the Incarnation as the overcoming of the distance between divine and human, and on what he calls the "*Eucharist's Endless hermeneutics*."[46]

This interpretative engagement with Scripture is clearly visible and applied in the work of the Orthodox theologian John Behr (*1966), and is based on an awareness of the operating matrix of Orthodox theology, which was one of the main topics of the 2007 international conference in Lebanon. There, Behr showed that as a fish cannot live without water, neither can theologians step out from the context in which they have grown up. It is a context shaped by the Enlightenment, confident in a neutral discourse of rationality and in the belief that the scientific method is the most secure way forward for the arts and humanities.[47] Behr is therefore not absorbed by historical uncertainties, he rather returns to Jesus' question to his disciples "Who do you say I am?" as the starting point of Christian theology. The particularity of Jesus' life led to many volumes describing the social and political circumstances of those early times, but this is wrong, writes Behr, as Jesus' question "calls for interpretation, to explain the meaning and significance of this person, his life and works."[48] The real Jesus in the New Testament is an already interpreted Jesus, says Behr. The preaching of the Christ becomes a hermeneutical lens, through which the content of Scripture is brought to us. Therefore, what comes to us in the medium of language is not Scripture, but Christ as the *content* of Scripture. The aim of reading cannot be to find the original meaning in the text, but to find the message of Christ, who "becomes the sole subject of the Scripture."[49] It can be concluded that Behr's theology is a hermeneutical theology.

One might argue and this will be correct, that Zizioulas understands his theological project as a kind of neo-patristic synthesis, whereas Behr is hardly interested in any genuine and fruitful debate with hermeneutics. It is therefore important not to mix hermeneutics with theological hermeneutics. Hermeneutics is theory of interpretation, about the implications, conditions and dimensions of interpretative activity. In principle, all forms of human communication could become the object of hermeneutical reflection. Hermeneutical theology, claims in addition, that theology is by its nature a hermeneutical exercise, since it deals with a tradition mediated by written texts and their interpretation. Hermeneutical theology investigates

---

46. Manoussakis, "Hermeneutics and Theology," 534.
47. See Behr, "Returning to First Principles," 21.
48. Behr, *Way to Nicaea*, 12.
49. Behr, *Way to Nicaea*, 28.

the interpretative nature of theology and its implications for the self-understanding of Christians.

It emerged in the sixties in response to systematic theology, emphasizing the particularities of time and place in theological formulation and calling for the rethinking of classical theological formulations. By taking many of its initial philosophical clues from Paul Ricoeur and Hans-Georg Gadamer, hermeneutical theology traces its roots to the methodology of Friedrich Schleiermacher and, later, the hermeneutical work of Rudolf Bultmann. Based on the assertion that God is a self-communicating God, hermeneutical theology is primarily concerned with questions of the reception and understanding of how this self-communicating God is both understood and responded to. It focuses on how we interpret the traditional texts (especially Scripture) through a kind of back-and-forth dialogue between the text and our lives. This position highlights the creative activity of all interpretation, the nature of knowledge as dialogue, as well as the openness within tradition to ongoing change and development.

So as to hermeneutically grasp the question of human understanding and transcendence, in this chapter we conduct an investigation of how hermeneutic theory has developed in the Orthodox context. We offer three different understandings of the concept of hermeneutics. The first is patristic hermeneutics, which relies mostly on the results of the efforts of the church Fathers and this look toward the Fathers is the main hermeneutical principle. However, patristic exegesis and the return to the critical thinking of the Fathers was missing. The second is biblical hermeneutics, which relies on methodology developed mostly in the West that enables the correct understanding of the words of Scripture. The third is hermeneutical theology, which overcomes the methodological approach that aims solely to bridge the gap between the biblical and our world. This is achieved because it embraces the exploration of our human situation and its interpretation, as well as the relation with the subject matter of the text, while focusing on the role of the reader, the plurality of interpretations and the importance of interpretation.

Since we focus in this book on the relationship between human understanding and transcendence, hermeneutical theology answers how what is transcendent (as active and enabling cooperation) can be witnessed within the horizons of human understanding without becoming created *by* the people as what reaches beyond them.

7

Sources of Orthodox Hermeneutics Revisited

THE previous chapter established the background and overview on which current Orthodox hermeneutics developed. This chapter will focus on the problem of negative identity formation and pay attention to the struggles and inspirational sources that have had a formative impact on Orthodox hermeneutics.

At the beginning of the chapter, I will continue my dialogue with Georges Florovsky and Christos Yannaras, who were briefly mentioned in the previous chapter and whose theories are demonstrative of two ways of dealing with Orthodox sources, both Russian emigrant and Greek. Their concepts are diverse and originate in different contexts, but they still reveal common features, as they explain why the patristic period developed into being normative for Orthodoxy.

I will not discuss the entire situation of Russian emigrants, nor will I deal with the whole theology of the sixties. This section about modern hermeneutics among Russian émigrés and Greeks will be followed by the section where I will point out the difficulties which come out of this debate and which are important for the whole discussion about the horizons of human understanding and transcendence.

These are two, which will be thematically addressed: patristic captivity and captivity in an anti-Western attitude. A detailed analysis of the Greek and Russian tendencies serves to find the origins of these captivities. Chapter 8 will later provide a more systematic and critical reception of sources of

Orthodox hermeneutics, a critique of the conclusions and alternative work with the sources.

Modern Hermeneutics among the Russian Émigrés

At the beginning we will deal with the first stance, which is the relationship to the source of Orthodox hermeneutics in the Russian area and among Russian emigrants. The first modern principles for Bible interpretation in the Russian area were formulated in 1776.[1] From the beginning of the nineteenth century a new generation emerged with an emphasis on a more careful reading and study of the Bible in Russian Orthodoxy, represented by Metropolitan of Moscow Philaret Drozdov (1782–1867), archbishop Alexander M. Bukharev (1822–1871) and archbishop Gerasim Pavskii (1787–1863), collectively called the "true founders of Russian Orthodox study of the Bible."[2]

These scholars understood hermeneutics as the formulation of methods for a correct understanding of the ancient text, but failed to include philosophical and psychological theories of understanding as was common in the West at the time. It is interesting to note that, while Philaret and Pavskii stressed the importance of the linguistic perspective in exegesis and the role of literary genres in interpretation, Bukharev was more interested in imaginative and mystical interpretation.

Development after 1917 is much more important for the theme of this study, when the Russian Orthodox Church became an enemy of the ruling ideology, many theological schools were closed and scholarly study of the Bible was restricted. Before the 1917 Russian October revolution, the church had a privileged position, with moral, theological and spiritual potential. But it proved to be powerless face to face with violence and militant atheism. The local council of 1917–18 re-established the patriarchate and instituted many decisions important for the life of the church. Its importance

---

1. By the Metropolitan of Moscow Platon (Levshin, 1737–1812) and have been obligatory for the Faculty of Moscow Theological Academy. The Metropolitan believed that Scripture should be understood in connection to time and place of the authors and therefore encouraged students to search for the literal and historical sense; at the same time, he urged orientation to the patristic heritage as a warrant of right interpretation. See Negrov, "Biblical Interpretation," 355. See also his book on the topic: Negrov, *Biblical Interpretation*, esp. chapter 6 on hermeneutical perspective.

2. Men, "K istorii Russkoi Pravoslavnoi Biblieistiki," *Bogoslovskie Trudy* 28 (1987) 272, cited in Negrov, "Three Hermeneutical Horizons," 86.

might have been as powerful as Vatican II, but it happened too late for these changes to be implemented.[3]

Theological scholarship ceased to exist and, in the meantime, Western theological scholarship continued to move forward. Much was accomplished elsewhere in the field of patristic studies, although these results were not accessible to Russians. Russian theological scholarship continued to flourish in exile from the West, especially in the Paris school, whose encounter with the West was fruitful for the re-interpretation of its own traditions and its presentation in an understandable way to the West.[4]

Unfortunately the results of the Paris school were not systematically studied in Russia and have never become a common heritage of Russian theological scholarship.[5] For this reason, we follow here modern hermeneutics among Russian émigrés and their main representatives, Georges Florovsky, Vladimir Lossky, Alexander Schmemann and John Meyendorff.[6] It is necessary to move with them to the neo-patristic school and the concept of the return to the Fathers because, as I will later explain, in a systematic way they solve the problem of the role of the Bible for the Fathers and the recovery of patristic thinking.

Florovsky was mentioned in the previous chapter in the historical overview in regard to his speech in Athens. He and Vladimir Nicholaevich Lossky (1903–1958) were considered founders of the neo-patristic movement and Lossky's *Mystical Theology of the Eastern Church* (1944) work became for many a handbook of neo-patristic synthesis. One of main differences with Florovsky is his emphasis on apophatic theology, which since then seems to have become universal for all Orthodox theology.[7] Their

---

3. Before the revolution there were 4 theological academies, 57 seminars and 185 "spiritual schools," but all were closed in 1918. If we do not count several illegal schools, "there was no spiritual education in the USSR until the Second World War" (Konstantinow, *Kirche in der Sowjetunion*, 182).

4. On Western Orthodoxy see: Noble and Noble, "Orthodox Theology."

5. Claims Alfeyev, "Orthodox Theology on the Threshold," 314. Let me mention at least one unpleasant event which happened in Ekaterinburg in 1998, when books written by Schmemann and Meyendorff were burned. See Kishkovsky, "Russian Theology after Totalitarianism," 268. The same author further points out that there is hope for the future, which is visible especially in the publishing of Schmemann's *Journals* in 2006, which are very popular in Russia. See also Alfeyev, "Orthodoxy in the Twentieth Century," 257–322.

6. In order to see similarities between Gadamer's hermeneutics, and Florovsky's and Lossky's, mostly concerning treatment os such notions as authority, tradition, freedom and reason, see Brüning, "Tradition and Traditions," 73–90.

7. For a deeper look into relation between Lossky and Florovsky, see Gavrilyuk, "Vladimir Lossky's Reception," 191–202.

ideas inspired many[8] and this challenge was also very quickly accepted by other theologians of the Russian diaspora. There was also a positive reaction in other traditionally Orthodox countries, such as Romania (Dumitru Stăniloae), Serbia (Justin Popović) and Greece (the generation of the sixties).

At the beginning of Florovsky's thought is an awareness that Orthodoxy was overrun by Western schemes and categories, which was a deviation from the traditional pattern formed in patristics. He called this a "pseudomorphosis of Eastern theology"[9] or the Babylonian captivity of Orthodoxy.[10] This was one of the reasons he performed a critique of Russian religious philosophy and marked a return to patristics as the main task for contemporary Orthodox theology. In one of his patristic seminars, one participant asked Florovsky if the authority of the Fathers meant that we must accept from them even the things in which they were conditioned by the situation and probably wrong. Florovsky answered with a resolute answer. No!, "only the *consensus patrum* is binding—and, as to myself, I do not like this phrase. The "authority" of the Fathers is not *dictatus papae*. They are guides and witnesses, no more. Their *vision* is "of authority," not necessarily their words."[11]

The content and methods of what should be recovered comes under the term of Christian Hellenism, as the last line in Florovsky's lecture "Patristics and Modern Theology" declares: "*Let us be more Greek to be truly catholic, to be truly Orthodox.*"[12] In his lecture, Florovsky uses this concept to point to the need for a process of spiritual Hellenization that is a "standing category of Christian existence."[13] Some could cast Florovsky's defense of Christian Hellenism as a "conservative rearguard" against Bulgakov's speculations,[14] and that Christian Hellenism was first developed in order to undercut the source of Russian religious philosophy.

This critique is not really justified, as Hellenism is connected with Florovsky's belief that the revelation of God is historical. Therefore, one of the consequences is its presumption that the Greek language is sacred, since the revelation was expressed in Greek categories and in Greek thought-concepts, so the translation cannot be inspired, only interpreted. In this sense it

---

8. Also among the Western scholars, let me mention at least Hans Urs von Balthasar, Henri de Lubac, Jean Daniélou, Werner Jaeger, Johannes Quasten, and Sebastian Brock.

9. Florovsky, *Ways of Russian Theology I*, 37, 72, 84, 121.

10. See Florovsky, *Ways of Russian Theology I*, 121.

11. From an unpublished letter to Debbie Bateman dated December 12, 1963, published in Gallaher, "Georges Florovsky on Reading the Life of St Seraphim," 62.

12. Florovsky, *Patristics and Modern Theology*, 7.

13. Florovsky, *Patristics and Modern Theology*, 6–7.

14. See for example Baker, "Theology Reasons," 87.

is understandable why Florovsky writes that we should believe that "Greek is the language of the New Testament and everything in early Christianity. We are all Greeks in our thinking as Christians."[15]

Therefore, for Florovsky, not only was undivided theology Greek in its essence, but Western theology up to Augustine was "basically Greek thought in Latin Dress."[16] These statements sound odd, as if Hellenism would deal with the language of ethnic Hellenism or contemporary Greece, but Florovsky had in mind a much more general concept, as he saw all culture of the church as Hellenic including its liturgy and theology.

The problem, according Florovsky, continued as the universal tradition was reduced during the Middle Ages, a "general eclipse and decay of civilization" during which time "the Greek language was almost completely forgotten, even by the scholars."[17] This is what he had in mind when he talked about the pseudomorphosis of Orthodox thought. On one side, his concept of Hellenism was developed to help engagement with the contemporary modern world, but on the other, Florovsky developed this engagement with the terminology and the idioms of the Fathers, not those of the modern world. But this still should not be understood as an identification of Orthodoxy and Greek thought, as Ivana and Tim Noble warn, for that would be a misunderstanding of Florovsky's intentions.[18]

The roots of Florovsky's patristic revival are various. First, they lie in nineteenth-century-Russia, where many translations of the Fathers had been prepared. Second, it is in the contemporary Roman Catholic theology (especially in France), which shared a renewed interest in the patristic period. Its most important figures are Henri de Lubac and Jean Daniélou from *nouvelle theologie*). But none of them created out of the patristic revival an absolute method, as Florovsky did.[19] One of the main marks of the theology

---

15. Quoted in Sauvé, "Florovsky's Tradition," 232.
16. Florovsky, "Legacy and the Task," 66–67.
17. Florovsky, "Legacy and the Task," 67.
18. See Noble and Noble, "Latin Appropriation of Christian Hellenism," 271.
19. Sauvé claims that the roots of creation of an absolute method of returning to history for the solution of the Western influence on Orthodoxy, lies in Hegel and claims Florovsky's philosophy of history to be Hegelian. Similarly, as Hegel attacked abstract idealism by using empirical historicism, there is a similarity with how Florovsky applies this in theology, such as: "that theology needs to be self-critical; that theology needs to be rooted in and explained by history; that reason alone is insufficient for theology; that each society is an organic whole and as such has a 'spirit' . . . that the theologian's task is to make each society aware of its values and belief, that tradition is used to make the past alive in the present, and to take what has been handed down from previous generations and transform it into one's own." At length, citation from Sauvé, "Florovsky's Tradition," 225–26.

of the Fathers is its existential character and its final reference in the life of the church and practice of virtue. As Florovsky writes, "Apart from the life of Christ theology carries no conviction, and, if separated from the life of faith, theology may easily degenerate into empty dialectics, a vain polylogia, without any spiritual consequence."[20]

Christian Hellenism in Florovsky's account did not lead to anti-Western polemics[21] and was more characterized by a sense of catholicity. Florovsky's ecumenical interest is visible in his lecture "Patristics and Modern Theology," which begins by citing John Pearson, Anglican bishop of Chester, who plead for a "return to reverend Fathers."[22] Later in the text, where Florovsky explains that this return is not a "blind or servile imitation and repetition, but rather a further homogenous and congenial development of this patristic teaching,"[23] he supports his argument with the thoughts of Cardinal John Newman.[24] Florovsky's characteristic understanding of ecumenism included that being ecumenical still did not mean to betray Orthodoxy. He was very critical towards attempts to find what is common among traditions and forget the rest, emphasizing that "the rest" is what "makes up the individuality of the traditions and denominations."[25] Noble and Gallaher share a similar understanding concerning Florovsky, as both focus on the ecumenical and Catholic (universal, *sobornost*) origins of his work and both stress the Western sources of Florovsky's thinking.

Florovsky's account did not even lead into a refusal of rationality. In this regard, Matthew Baker warns against making this mistake and replacing Florovsky's hermeneutics with Lossky's apophatism, which Florovsky himself criticized in the review of *Mystical Theology*. This mistake might

---

20. Florovsky, *Aspects of Church History*, 17.

21. An illustration is that in 1923 Florovsky contributed to the collection entitled *Russia and Latinity*, which reinforced the claim that an Orthodox believer was better off being killed by the Bolsheviks in Russia than converting to Roman Catholicism in France. One led to the temporal destruction of the body, but the other to eternal casting out of the soul. See Gallaher, "Waiting for the Barbarians," 663–64.

22. Florovsky, *Patristics and Modern Theology*, 3.

23. Florovsky, *Patristics and Modern Theology*, 5.

24. Noble sees as important also a note about Odo Kasel, Benedictine scholar of Abbaye Maria Laach. Mathew Baker, one of the most respected defenders of Florovsky sees as irony, that everybody criticizes Florovsky for supposed anti-Westernism and Eastern cultural chauvinism, whereas Florovsky is very ecumenical. See Noble and Noble, "Latin Appropriation of Christian Hellenism," 276; Baker, "Theology Reasons," 117.

25. Recorded interview transcribed by Florovsky's secretary, Masha Vorobiova, August 8, 1971, Andrew Blane archive. See Baker and Danckaert, "Georges Florovsky," 211–15.

lead to a wrong conclusion—that Florovsky's position opposes reason.[26] Baker admits that Florovsky's earliest philosophical essays register a strong critique of rationalism in European philosophy, in which he wants to achieve a clear distinction between philosophy and theology that is based on the radical difference between God and creation. According to Baker, Florovsky stressed the discontinuity between human reason and the divine, emphasized life over thought and stressed a strictly revealed basis for divine knowledge, while rejecting any notion of natural theology. Until 1950 Florovsky claimed the content of faith was a mystery and theology an apophatic theology.[27] But this was not Florovsky's last word, warns Baker, as he also talked about theological reason and this separates him from Lossky's way of neo-patristic synthesis. This is visible in the review of Lossky's *Mystical Theology*, where Florovsky asked why non-symbolic knowledge is not possible and claimed that knowledge is an integral part of this beatific life.[28] There is even evidence in the late twenties that Florovsky came to understand Christian theology as a true philosophy, founded on the historical self-revelation of God.

This rationale is further visible in Florovsky's *Ways of Russian Theology*, depicting St. Philaret Drozdov as the master of faith and using his aphorism *"theology reasons."*[29] Inspired by Philaret, the historical body of ecclesial responses for Florovsky are an integral part of the sacred tradition and theology reasons from within the patristic tradition as an uninterrupted connection with the past.[30]

Modern Hermeneutics Among the Greeks

The second tendency, distant in time and place but showing similar attributes in the renewal of patristics, is modern hermeneutics among Greeks, especially around the neo-Orthodoxy movement in the sixties, a movement presented in the previous chapter. The relationship between the West and Orthodoxy in Greece has been always ambivalent: on one side a rejection and a critique in the name of faithfulness to Orthodoxy, on the other, Greek theology was easily influenced by the West.[31] The reaction of neo-Orthodoxy

26. See Baker, "Theology Reasons," 102.
27. See Baker, "Theology Reasons," 83–84, see exact quotations.
28. Florovsky, "Mystical Theology," 207–8.
29. Florovsky, *Ways of Russian Theology I*, 208.
30. "To theologise in the Church means to theologise in the historical element" Florovsky, *Ways of Russian Theology II*, 296. See also Baker, "Theology Reasons," 100.
31. This influence was visible especially in academic theology after the foundation

in the sixties brought a rediscovery of Orthodox tradition and Byzantine monasticism, and a liberation from westernization, but also a strong feeling of anti-Westernism, which led to a negative identity formation.

This anti-Western attitude was especially present in the character of John Romanides (1921–2001), who had such an influence that one can in fact speak of pre and post-Romanidian theology.[32] In his book *Romiosyne* (1975), he came up with a new hermeneutical key, a distinction between Orthodox Greek and Latin Christianity on one side, and a heretical *Francosyne* on the other. In Romanides's eyes, there existed a Latin Christianity whose "Roman" character has been distorted by Franks and he accuses Franks of conniving against *Romiosyne* (the Greek form of Romanism) and Orthodoxy. Even so, his work never gained an audience beyond its own microcosm,[33] which is why our main attention is given here to Christos Yannaras, whose work has been accepted throughout the Orthodox world.

Christos Yannaras (*1935) is one of the most important contemporary Greek theologians[34] and his primary accomplishment is best described as a theory of the unbroken continuity of Christian Hellenism from the classic period until today. Since he was a representative of the generation of the sixties, as such he aimed to overcome the dry intellectualism of earlier theology and the pietistic tendencies in Greek theology, in order to achieve liberation from Western captivity and to connect Orthodox thinking with its patristic roots.

Yannaras points to the period after the foundation of the Greek state as the domination of the West with its pietism and rationalism.[35] Movements like *Zoe* were popular among the bourgeoisie, who loved everything European and created a Protestant type of service of the Word. Eastern Christianity since late Byzantium had been contaminated by Western rationality and so it lost its own roots and was experiencing a long-term identity crisis. In order to achieve this emancipation and to explain the mode of being of

---

of the Greek state (1864), which was characterized by dry scholasticism. Kalaitzidis summarizes the long trajectory following: "From the wars between the pro-unionists and the anti-unionists, or between the Thomists and the anti-Thomists in the last centuries of Byzantium, it would enter a phase of almost total Westernization during the Turkish occupation, followed by a period of dry academic Scholasticism throughout the first hundred years of its liberation (after the 1830s), including a strong pietistic and moralistic trend imported from Europe and exemplified in Christian fellowships such as Zoe" (Kalaitzidis, "Image of the West," 142).

32. George Metallinos calls it so. Quoted in Kalaitzidis, "Image of the West," 145.

33. Kalaitzidis, "Image of the West," 150.

34. Andrew Louth writes so about Yannaras in: Louth, "Introduction," 1. See also Louth, *Modern Orthodox Thinkers*, 250–52.

35. See Yannaras, "Orthodoxy and the West," 123–24.

the Orthodox Greek identity, he brought a new hermeneutical key, which was the Greek culture.

The main condition for this structure of Greek identity *sine qua non* was a structural anti-Westernism and a radical contrast between Orthodoxy and the West. Yannaras's hermeneutics was formulated in 1970 in his conference presentation titled "*Orthodoxy and the West*," which was followed by the publication of a book with the same title.[36]

Yannaras found inspiration in the work of Heidegger, from whom he took his thorough critique of the development of Western philosophy dating from the time of Plato.[37] In his book *On the Absence and Unknowability of God: Heidegger and Areopagite*, Yannaras made use of Heidegger's interpretation of Nietzsche's proclamation of the death of God and argued that God in the West had been reduced to the best solution, *first cause, highest value*, in order to justify Western social structures (papacy, hierarchy, monarchy). The characteristics of Western thinking according to Yannaras, are: (i) transformation of religious faith into an ideology of a determined worldview and obligatory methodology that he calls a technology of faith, (ii) a method controlling everything, the totalitarianism of method, (iii) polarization of life and culture between intellectual individualism and authoritarian objectivism and (iv), the Roman church's lost sense of the ecclesial life and the sense of the church as the body in which people share life. With the help of Heidegger, he undermined the roots of Western civilization in the Medieval Ages and took him as an ally in the critique of Western metaphysics.

Yannaras's opposition to the West took several directions. First, there was opposition against the immorality and impersonality of Western consumerist society, which he considered to be an in-authentic style of life. Further, there was opposition to the development of Orthodox theology from the Reformation until today and against the manner in which the authentic culture of the Greek East was silenced.[38] Yannaras warned that modernity meant an uprising of one-sided, absolute and all-pervasive rationality, which originated in Augustine and culminated in scholasticism. This rationality is different from the one of the Byzantine East, which was considered to be more holistic. His main argument stated that in the beginning there was a

---

36. This book is based on his previous articles, it was published in 1992 in Greek and translated in 2006 in English.

37. Although Andrew Louth warns that Yannaras's relation to Plato and Aristotle is much more positive than Heidegger's. Louth, "Introduction," 5–6.

38. Still, Yannaras acknowledges that this silencing was not absolute, and one of the resistances was publishing *Philokalia* (see chapter 12 of Yannaras, *Orthodoxy and the West*). It is exactly the spirituality of *Philokalia* that is crucial for Yannaras's theology.

form of Christianity, embodied in the Greek culture and this was the true Orthodoxy.[39]

The new form of Christianity arrived from the Western part of the Roman Empire and although culturally less developed, overwhelmed the Greek form of Christianity. Therefore Yannaras talks about the "Western deviations" and "spiritual problems that have been created by Western religionizing of the Church."[40] For Yannaras the new form of Christianity is an individual religion, ruled by "private convictions, the acquisition of individual merit, and the institutional control of faith and morals,"[41] and he considers it to be a heresy far more dangerous than the ones from the early church period, because it offers a new way of life and thinking.

The first of those who rejected the Greek heritage and enforced the creation of a new form of Christianity was St Augustine of Hippo (354–430), but Augustine would remain a lonely thinker if the Franks would not have settled a new Roman empire. Yannaras claims that the Franks linked Augustine's understanding of Christianity to *religio*, as something that supports the morality of the individual and offers him security and certainty. He considers this shift from Christianity to *religio* to be the greatest debasement of Christianity.[42]

He indicates the importance of the role of the Medieval Ages and of scholasticism (even calling current Western theology a Scholasticism) that changed the understanding of God. Scholastic thinking is based on an ontic understanding of *being* (God as *prima causa*, supreme divine being), where *being* is that which causes the existence of other things. This resulted in the "banishment of God . . . this Being, which is God, is separated from the sphere of the human experience."[43] This led to the emergence of boundaries between the transcendence of God and human capacities and further led to the rejection of unity and possibility of participation in the divine truth,

---

39. From Heraclitus until the Neo-Platonists the truth has been verified as the event of common experience, therefore Yannaras cites a famous fragment of Heraclitus: "Everything that we share, we know to be true, what we have that is peculiar to us, we know to be false." Yannaras puts this communal verification of the truth in contrast with the individual perception of the truth, which appeared in the fifth and sixth century in the new form of Christianity (Yannaras, *Elements of Faith*, 153).

40. Yannaras, *Orthodoxy and the West*, viii.

41. Yannaras, *Orthodoxy and the West*, 24.

42. See Yannaras, *Elements of Faith*, 156. In a similar manner scholasticism and Reformation continued, which though rejecting scholasticism, still made a mistake and remained faithful to Augustine.

43. Yannaras, "Orthodoxy and the West," 117.

"the analytical scholastic methodology represents, then, a deeper posture which is essentially anthropocentric."[44]

Therefore, Yannaras talks about spiritual schizophrenia in the Western posture as a deep wedge between religion and life, when religious life is divided from daily life and experience. This separation lead to the spiritualization of symbols, as for example in the Eucharist, where the bread and wine ceased to be bread and wine, but are spiritualized into body and blood. Yannaras shows here a very broad understanding of the symbol and is not aware of the work of the Western thinkers on this, such as Paul Ricoeur or Paul Tillich. He also seems to totally ignore the Protestant understanding of the Eucharist and its relation between sacral and profane, which is not the same as the Roman Catholic understanding.

Besides that, this sharp separation between a rationalistic West and more spiritual East is not really correct, as the West had (and has) its mystical traditions as well. On the other side, the East was not always itself freed in history from the systematic approach to dogmatic formulations, in as much as a modern Orthodox scholasticism is not only characteristic for Greek theology, but also for other theological schools, since it is clear and easy to teach. To conclude, since there were always more lines and trends of thinking in Orthodoxy, not only the mystical and apophatic, it would be wrong to absolutize only one trend.

Orthodox Captivity in Patristics

The political map in the twentieth century (I have in mind especially the events of 1917) influenced the religious map and increased the presence of Eastern Orthodoxy in the West. Certainly, Orthodoxy was present in the West much earlier. Let me mention the Russian missionaries arriving in Alaska in 1794, or even earlier, as well as the Orthodox parish founded in London in 1677.[45] Orthodox theology responded to this situation by developing the concepts of a Western and Babylonian captivity of Orthodoxy. These theories aimed to find unique Orthodox elements, but resulted in another extreme, which will be addressed in the following sections: in an Orthodox captivity in patristics and in an Orthodox captivity in anti-Westernism.

So far, we have paid attention to the struggles and inspirational sources having a formative impact on Orthodox hermeneutics but, while focusing on the movement of the return to the Fathers, a problem of negative identity

---

44. Yannaras, "Orthodoxy and the West," 116.
45. See on this the article Noble, "Rights of the Indigenous People," 164–73.

formation as a key to what Orthodox hermeneutics took place. By patristic captivity, we mean the identification of *"closer to the Fathers"* with *"further from the Bible."*[46]

On one side, the return to the Fathers as the warrants of correct interpretation makes perfect sense. Unfortunately, the connection between the Fathers and the Bible has been broken for a long period. The problem actually does not lie in the church Fathers themselves, but in the long traditionalist period (from sixth to nineteenth century.) when actual exegetical work shifted from direct engagement with the Scriptures to dependence on the church Fathers.

Rare exceptions are Maximus the Confessor, who said that Scripture is the lamp on the lamp-stand of the church, Simeon the New theologian, who based his works on direct engagement with the Bible and Photius the Great, who showed linguistic and philological skills when dealing with the questions of the Bible. For example, the patriarch Cyril Lucaris (1572–1638), has been condemned because of his "Calvinistic" tendency to advocate the authority of the Bible over the Fathers. When one looks closely at the Fathers, there are several things that cannot be questioned. The Fathers were devoted students of the Bible and most of their works were expositions and sermons on biblical texts.

There is much that one can learn from those in the patristic era: primacy of Scripture, Christ as the center of interpretation, interdependence between Tradition, church and Scripture, coherence of theology, spirituality and daily life, importance of theological tradition in interpretation, emphasis on the Spirit rather than on the letter, contextual intent (*skopos, akolouthia*), use of Scripture for pastoral ministry and focus on an ongoing living tradition. The criterion is not only their doctrinal importance, but that they were *pneumatophoroi* (Spirit-bearers) and guides to the will of God and to the authentic Orthodox tradition.[47]

Tsirpanlis similarly warns that the intellectual exercise of their writings is not of the highest importance, but it is *experience* that highlights the

---

46. Some of the sources that critically deal with patristic legacy are: Hovorun, "Patristics after Neo-Patristics"; Noble et al., *Wrestling with the Mind of the Fathers*.

47. In Western Christian terminology, the age of the Fathers marks the time from the age of apostles and apologists up to 451 (the date of the Council of Chalcedon), or to the Second Council of Nicaea (787). For Orthodoxy, as McGuckin sees, there is no strict historical line, as it counts among the Fathers also Simeon the New theologian (949–1022) or Gregory Palamas (1296–1359) in the same way as John Chrysostom (347–407) or Maximus the Confessor (580–662). The time criterion is for Orthodoxy very loose, as the Fathers in Orthodoxy are "those definitive and highly authoritative theologians of the church in its classical ages who represent purity of doctrine allied with the great holiness of life" (McGuckin, *Concise Encyclopedia*, 358).

passion for divine things and unity of heart and mind in their work. This patristic experience is why their work is considered "*a work of holiness*,"[48] and why their exegesis is unavoidable for Orthodox scholars. Without this patristic legacy it is not possible to even think or talk about the revival of the Orthodox Church. This opposes the theory that the Fathers are theologians of the past and that the patristic era ended in a certain historical period. From this perspective it becomes clear that any clash between returning to the Bible and returning to the Fathers is artificial. The most common patristic principle is the obligation to study the Bible, which proves that permanent contact with Scripture was very important for early Christians and only this contact allowed them to develop their piety.

On the other hand, the return to the Fathers turned into a patristic captivity in the moment when "*closer to Fathers*" was identified with "*further from the Bible*." While in Western Christianity the authority of the Fathers has been subjected to a return to the Bible, in Orthodoxy the affirmation of authority in effect downplayed the authority of the Bible. We saw this hermeneutical approach among the Russian émigrés. An illustrative example is used by Savvas Agourides, who quotes an anecdote from Mount Athos when one of the abbots said: "Why should we resort to tough food when the holy Fathers gave us this food chewed and ready for our delicate stomach?"[49] Here the problem is spelled out clearly. Why should we struggle with reading the Bible when all the explanations are already given in the works of the church Fathers?

When studying the return to the Fathers in modern Orthodox theology and hermeneutics, we must take on board several other problems, including to what degree this return involves exegetical critical principles that the Fathers used in the interpretation of the Bible. Here a problem appears if the patristic commentaries are to be considered as the standards for current biblical exegesis and if modern Orthodox hermeneutics presupposes that there is a universal and unproblematic agreement between the actual reading of the Fathers and the Bible. The Fathers in their works not only underlined the Scripture's importance for reasons of piety, but also urged one to examine and observe the text.[50] This is clearly seen in the fact that the majority of their corpus remained in the form of commentaries on the

---

48. Tsirpanlis, *Introduction to Eastern Patristic Thought*, 19.

49. Story quoted by Agourides, "Biblical Studies," 51. Another anecdote proving that in the views of many Orthodoxy simply *is* patristic Christianity, are the words of the guide saying to visitors at Mount Athos: "Here it is still the fourth century" (mentioned by Casiday, "Church Fathers," 167).

50. Mihoc points out that the Fathers very often used verbs such as: look for, examine, think, observe, consider. See Mihoc, "Actuality of Church Fathers," 8.

biblical texts. Even their sermons were actually interpretations of biblical passages, i.e., they were more homilies than sermons.

Therefore, I suggest talking about "patristic homiletic hermeneutics." Homiletics as the study of the composition and delivery of a sermon is already tightly connected with hermeneutics and exegesis. After all, what else is a sermon, if not the interpretation of biblical texts and Christian doctrines and their following application in the community of the believers? Therefore, homiletic hermeneutics is actually a tautological expression. If we still understand patristic hermeneutics as an interpretation of Scripture and its study as a search for the exegetical principles of how to understand the message of the Scripture, then homiletic hermeneutics focuses on the tight connection between theological truths found in Scripture, and theological truths preached and lived by the church. It would be wrong to consider that there are two different exegeses, where one would be for educated people and the other for simple believers, just as it is wrong to claim that there is a sharp distinction between biblical exegesis and systematic theology.

This lack of distinction is why a common misunderstanding appeared regarding the relationship between Scripture and the Fathers, according to which the Father's interpretation of Scripture was dismissed because it had been believed that their interpretation did not aim at exegesis of the text but was only for the purpose of preaching. Not only that, but critical scholarship refuses patristic exegesis as not sufficiently critical, and Orthodoxy itself follows this approach by saying that it is enough only to venerate God's word without any critical thinking. They say *while the blood of martyrs may be the seed of the church, the sweat of the exegete can only be the seed of heresy.* This attitude, although well accepted as an identity mark by a number of Orthodox academics themselves and by Western academics criticizing the Orthodox, stands in opposition to the relation between the Fathers and critical exegesis of the Bible.

The Fathers felt free to use the critical tools of their time and use them for exegesis. They used critical thinking, even questioning the authenticity of some biblical books, such as Origen of Alexandria, who undertook a critical study of Hebrews and concluded that it did not belong to the Apostle Paul. Our view is that patristic criteria is not so anti-scientific as it seems and that scientific linguistic methods and ideas are not so different from patristic ones. That is, the acceptance of methodology can also be very easily argued from the perspective of the Fathers, since they managed to combine the theological and biblical dimensions of biblical texts. Certainly, they did not know the strong academic character of science, but there are still not so many differences between the Father's methods and current methodology.

For example, Bultmann's call for demythologization was already known to the Fathers, as they were also analyzing and reconstructing the meanings of mythical expressions, such as the anthropomorphic expressions of God. Nikolakopoulos extensively compares Clement of Alexandria's and Bultmann's commentary of "*Jesus sits at the right of God*" and concludes that their deductions and conclusions are exactly identical. At the same time a certain level of caution is in place. Nikolakopoulos further thinks that the Fathers should enjoy prominence as signposts, but they should not be repeated or "slavishly copied in Orthodox interpretation, but rather operate as guiding patterns."[51]

Finally, let me simply clarify that, although we distinguish between patristic exegesis as the theory of exegesis and patristic hermeneutics as a systematic reflection of Christian doctrine, I do not believe that it is possible to draw a thick line between the ways the Fathers interpreted biblical texts, the way they reflected the Christian doctrine and hermeneutics as a theory of exegesis. I believe that applying these categories onto the patristic mind would not be correct, as these three different understandings were not separated at that time and there was no sharp distinction between biblical exegesis and systematic theology.

Anti-Western Faith Identification

The previous section focused on the patristic sources that had a formative impact on Orthodox hermeneutics, more precisely on how the patristic period became normative for Orthodoxy and the limits of the period. The identification of "*closer to the Fathers*" with "*further from the Bible*" was labelled as a patristic captivity. Now attention will be given to the struggle around the role of the West and critical thinking, which is labelled as a captivity in anti-Westernism that further contributed to the expressions of Orthodox identity. This captivity occurred when "*closer to Orthodox identity*" was identified with "*further from the West.*"[52] We saw this hermeneutical approach among the Greek generation of the sixties.

First it is necessary to note a divergence between the theological part of Orthodoxy that is accustomed to discussions with Western thinkers and churches and the part of the Orthodox world that sees such discussions as

---

51. Nikolakopoulos, "Orthodox Critique," 342. See also Nikolakopoulos, "Orthodoxe Hermeneutik," 473–86.

52. An important volume on this topic is a volume published by Fordham University Press, see Demacopoulos and Papanikolaou, *Orthodox Constructions of the West*.

hostile. In most cases it is easier to choose anti-Westernism, as John Zizioulas claims:

> Today there is a tendency among the Orthodox to stress the responsibility of the Western Christians for the evil of division and for the wrongs done to the Orthodox Church by our Western brothers.... Deep however in the tragic reality of Christian division lies also an inability of the Orthodox to overcome and rise above the psychology of polemic in a true spirit of forgiveness and love. Confessional zeal has often proved stronger than forgiveness and love.[53]

One of the reasons for this hostility are the different trajectories of East and West. Around the end of the eighteenth century, the West experienced the French revolution and the rise of Kant's rationalism, while the East at the same time experienced an ascetic-mystical revival centered on Orthodox spirituality and related literature (such as *Philokalia*), which strongly influenced Slavic Orthodoxy and was at odds with Western rationalism of the time.

The most common type of anti-Westernism is a one-sided Orthodox critique of Western modernity, which focuses on its negative consequences such as secularization, de-Christianization or loss of Christian roots, while at the same time it tries to solve these impasses with the Orthodox heritage and praises the Eastern Church for its purity and correctness. The reasons for this refusal and hostility lie in the differences between the Western and the Eastern ways of thinking.

Orthodoxy is a *way of life* beyond formulations and statements,[54] placing more emphasis on passive values rather than on active human virtues, is considered less individualistic and has a strong communitarian spirit, does not support the logic of an autonomous individual who can make decisions freely and who can question established authorities. This is similar to another objection that, since the church did not canonize the inspired author, but only the inspired writings, the historical work with the author of the writing is not even necessary.[55] The next difference between Orthodox biblical interpretation and independent academic criticism lies in the question of the role of the interpreter. In critical hermeneutics, the interpreter is given the highest authority and his/her judgment becomes the

---

53. Zizioulas's lecture held on December 4, 1999 at Balamand Monastery. Zizioulas, "Orthodox Church," lines 79–84.

54. Florovsky said that the church is first of all the worshiping community, doctrine comes afterwards. Florovsky, "Elements of Liturgy," 172.

55. Mentions: Oikonomos, *Bibel und Bibelwissenschaft*, 54.

"*last and highest court.*" Orthodoxy focuses more on apostolic authority that liberates rather than enslaves.[56] Certainly, such a short list of differences between East and West is not exhaustive and surely superficial, yet it does illustrate different paradigms and positions. My aim is to relativize these differences and expose such a black/white clash as artificial.

One of the forms of anti-Westernism was oriented against the academic study of the Bible. The critical objection was that this form of academic study wrongly presumed that it had a system of standards or principles for such study. This sort of critical thinking was opposed because it was the product of the modern world, closely related to the rise of the modern world in Western Civilization. Orthodoxy did not follow this development for various reasons, as the political situation in Southern and Eastern Europe in the twentieth century with its existential problems also prevented the development of *academia*.[57] At the same time it must also be mentioned that Orthodox judgments over Western methods were very often one-sided and simplified, resulting from not really having sufficient knowledge about what they called "*Western methods.*"[58] Two exceptions to this are the scholars Theodore Stylianopoulos and John McGuckin.

According to Theodore Stylianopoulos, Protestantism ends up in a dead-end because it loses the balance between the principle of Scripture and church.[59] He accepts the possible role and importance of the new voices, such as of Ricoeur, Gadamer and Tracy, but he sees that they emphasize the *cultural* distance between the Bible and modern thinking and neglect the revelatory authority of Scripture in its relationship to the church. They grant an excessive weight to the distance and presuppose it as a primary hermeneutical problem.

The American Orthodox theologian and priest, John Anthony McGuckin, in his critique of the Western approach shares doubts about the possibility of objective historical research, which he calls "philosophical acumen,

---

56. There is a nice music parable, which I leave here unshorten: "Dominical and apostolic utterance become, as it were, the set key signatures, within which the present music of the re-expression of the evangelical kerygma can be extrapolated: that music which is the essential expression of the Church from age to age. It is an 'oppression' only in the sense that the fugal form necessarily guides the composer in the creation of a fugue, or in the way a sonnet is required to rhyme" (McGuckin, "Recent Biblical Hermeneutics," 317).

57. Western Orthodoxy is certainly an exception, especially the Paris School around the St Sergius Orthodox Theological Institute. For different directions of Western Orthodoxy see the latest book on the topic: Noble et al., *Ways of Orthodox Theology*.

58. Notices also Nikolakopoulos, *Die unbekannten Hymnen*, 43.

59. See Stylianopoulos, *New Testament*, 157.

both arrogant and uninformed."[60] He has especially in mind the accumulation of knowledge, one of the attributes of objective research, which puts itself in the role of "finally objectively explained now." McGuckin rejects the possibility that research occurs in an isolated and impersonal space, where objectivity is "scrutinised by an infallible academic voice." Quite the contrary, the text, context and interpretation do not appear in an abstract space, but in a specific and particular time and space, here and now. So McGuckin calls attention to the fact that a hermeneutical process always includes an interpretative community. What McGuckin says follows the same trajectory as in Gadamer's and Heidegger's objection against historicism, that also claimed to objectively understand, but somehow forgot its own context and historicity. The interpreter's context in the Orthodox Church is the community of fellow believers; where its Western counterpart presumes distance and estrangement and searches for restoration, the Orthodoxy presumes continuity.

Let me summarize in one paragraph the main ideas from this chapter. I presented the inspirational sources that have a formative impact on Orthodox hermeneutics and the problem of negative identity formation as a basis for what Orthodox hermeneutics should be, was explored. I presented the representatives of two dominant movements and tendencies in the twentieth century in order to present how modern Orthodox hermeneutics developed in these two contexts. First was modern hermeneutics among Russian émigrés, exemplified by Georges Florovsky and Vladimir Lossky, who were the founders of the neo-patristic movement. Florovsky's concept of Christian Hellenism was shown to be a hermeneutical principle. Then, in order to achieve and explain the mode of being of Orthodox Greek identity, Christos Yannaras was presented, as he brought a new hermeneutical key, which is Greek culture. The main condition for this structure of Greek hermeneutics is a structural anti-Westernism and a radical contrast between Orthodoxy and the West. These presentations of representatives were followed by naming the problems that arose out of them, which are called captivities. I concentrated on two captivities: patristic captivity and captivity in an anti-Western attitude. In our opinion these captivities are the most dominant hermeneutical criteria that rule contemporary Orthodox theology. The return to the Fathers revolved into a patristic captivity in the moment when *"closer to Fathers"* was recognized as *"further from the Bible."* The captivity in anti-Westernism followed when *"closer to Orthodox identity"* was identified with *"further from the West."* This discussion is very important for the theme of this book, because these positions showed the

---

60. McGuckin, "Recent Biblical Hermeneutics," 308.

weakness of the Orthodox approach, identified that a vertically understood transcendence divinizes too much and leaves no space for the human element, for suspicion and otherness. This is the position that will be overcome by the post-patristic position (chapter 8) and complemented by the liturgical hermeneutics lying in Gadamer's concepts (chapter 9).

8

The Move beyond the Neo-patristic Synthesis

In the previous chapter we addressed the problems of modern Orthodox hermeneutics. This chapter first contains an analysis of the so-called negative work with the sources of Orthodox faith. Second, it encompasses alternative and more positive and constructive work with the sources. Both critical and alternative work will help to overcome negative identity formations.

Several voices of the younger generation of Orthodox theologians will be included, such as Pantelis Kalaitzidis, who sees the category of development turning into mythology, Aristotle Papanikolaou, who criticizes negative self-identification, Brandon Gallaher, who compares the present situation in Orthodoxy with the situation of the people of a Greek town waiting for the barbarians to come and conquer them, Ivana Noble, who notes the lack of the moment of innovation, and Assaad Kattan, who suggests how hermeneutics as a Protestant discipline can be used in the Orthodox context.

These voices are further complemented with alternative work with the sources that represent a move beyond, especially because they also show the influence of non-Orthodox authors, as is seen in the work of John Breck and Theodore Stylianopoulos.

Critical Reception

In a similar way to the way the patristic revival has been considered a shift of paradigm, contemporary Orthodox theology is confronting a new shift of paradigms and new challenges in the twenty-first century.[1] The church is moving toward post-modernism where, as John Behr says, there is no more *terra ferma* for truth.[2] Whereas in Eastern Europe and Russia the church experienced secularization from the Communist ideology and governments, the situation in the seventies in Western Europe was characterized by the post-modern movement and with a return to religion.[3]

If one takes into account that each text has its context, which for patristics was Greek philosophy and culture, it is very obvious that current theology faces a totally different context. Pantelis Kalaitzidis in his lecture in Prague in 2012 emphasized that modernity and post-modernity (or late modernity, as he likes to say) and the framework they define constitute the broader historical, social and cultural environment within which the Orthodox Church is called to live and carry out its mission. He denied the existence of any ahistorical, monolithic and super-temporal tradition and underlined that theology always appears within a particular cultural and historical context.[4] His words add a great deal of material to our theme of human understanding and transcendence.

Therefore, in the following section I will follow several critical voices that aim to overcome the captivities mentioned in the previous chapter. Currently there are many critics of Florovsky's synthesis, but Pantelis Kalaitzidis is currently one of the most outspoken critics of a theological return to the Fathers. Therefore, I will begin with him and then continue with others.

Pantelis Kalaitzidis, director of the Volos Academy for Theological Studies, accepts that the return to the Fathers was connected with the attempt to protect Orthodoxy but, at the same time, warns that there were two directions of its development: on one side toward openness (the twentieth

---

1. Some of the new challenges are: (i) mission as a service and not as a dominion; (ii) accepting the principles of democracy and human rights; (iii) engagement in the ecumenical movement and encouraging plurality and variety in the church. For a more detailed description see in: Kalaitzidis, "Challenges of Renewal and Reformation," 158–60.

2. See Behr, "Returning to First Principles," 22.

3. Which was mistakenly understood by some Orthodox theologians as the end of modernity So Kalaitzidis in Kalaitzidis, "Orthodox Theology and the Challenges," 5–13. Kalaitzidis calls this a pseudo-argument and for him post-modernity is the late modern era, not the end of modernity. See Kattan's article; he founds Kalaitzidis claiming this in his book *Orthodoxia kai Neóterikotéta*, published in Greek, 2007. Kattan, "Revisiting the Question," 128–29.

4. His lecture "Orthodox Church and (Post)Modernity: The Conditions, the Context, and the Problems of an Encounter" was presented at the International Scientific Doctoral and Post-Doctoral Conference *Presence and Absence of the Orthodox Theological Reflection of Modern Ideologies and its Ecumenical Impact* organized by the PTF UK, IBTS and Jabok, delivered on February 3, 2012.

century after all is the time of the renewal of Orthodox theology), but on the other side it was a time of introversion, conservatism, and a fundamentalist understanding of Tradition, which was substituted for traditionalism.[5] Kalaitzidis compares this direction toward introversion with the fundamentalism that is more common for Protestant churches and talks about the fundamentalism of tradition and the fundamentalism of the Fathers, as those prevented Orthodoxy from remaining an integrated part of the modern world and entering into a critical dialogue with the Christian West.[6] The consequence of such a development is a theological interpretation that has its refuge in the past and considers the teaching of the Fathers to be an archive of faith. Kalaitzidis further argues that the church neglects other even more important aspects of Orthodox teaching, such as theological holism or spiritual heritage.[7] The effort to de-westernize Orthodox theology lead to the fact that all other topics were overshadowed.

The clash between Kalaitzidis and Hilarion Alfeyev is interesting, as both assess the critique of neo-patristic synthesis. Alfeyev (*1966) objects that the time of neo-patristic theory was ahead of its time in the period when it appeared. Therefore, he proposes what he calls a "*contextual method*," a method based on Florovsky's synthesis, but much more fitting to the challenges of the twenty-first century. Florovsky's understanding was based on an assumption of the patristic heritage as a sum of *Patrologia Latina* and *Graeca*, and based on this, he understood Christianity as Byzantinism. In his time he could not anticipate the discovery of Syriac and other writings (for example, as published in *Corpus Scriptorum Christianorum Orientalium*), which challenge his belief that Christianity can be reduced to Byzantinism.[8] Kalaitzidis accepts most of Alfeyev's conclusions, but he does not like an idealistic view about patristic thought as something that did not lose its relevancy, while still maintaining its value for the current time and its challenges.

According to Kalaitzidis, the consequences of the patristic revival are numerous. First is the neglect and devaluation of biblical studies, which were considered to be a distinctive Protestant matter, contrary to patristic studies that are considered to be a uniquely Orthodox field of research. However, this procedure is not unique at all, as *sola scriptura* was simply replaced with *consensus patrum*, and soon it was forgotten that the church

---

5. See Kalaitzidis, "From the Return," 8.
6. See Kalaitzidis, "Theological, Historical and Cultural Reasons," 148.
7. For this see Kalaitzidis, "From the Return," 33–35.
8. For usage and application of contextual method see Alfeyev, "Patristic Heritage and Modernity," 158–65.

Fathers were known as *interpreters* of the Bible. Further, there appeared a shift in patristic theology, which suddenly began appreciating patristic texts more highly than biblical texts and so patristic theology showed the marks of a-historicity. All these approaches and negative consequences of the neo-patristic movement lead to the introversion of Orthodox theology, as well as its absence from theological discussions in the twentieth century.

Kalaitzidis sees the more important negative impact of the patristic revival to lie in the polarization between the West and East as "Orthodoxy's total rejection of the West, and to the cultivation and consolidation of an anti-western and anti-ecumenical spirit."[9] Interestingly, Kalaitzidis does not blame Florovsky for this, but the way in which this *"return to the Fathers"* was perceived by some of the heirs of Florovsky's legacy. He calls this a "major paradox,"[10] because Florovsky himself did not rely merely on the patristic literature, but was also influenced by works coming from the West. Moreover, Florovsky, according to Kalaitzidis, never adopted the idea of an opposition between East and West, but emphasized that Catholicity needed both parts of Christendom, both East and West.[11] What prevailed in Orthodoxy was not Florovsky's spirit, but the spirit of anti-Westernism and anti-ecumenism of Vladimir Lossky, Justin Popović and Dumitru Stăniloae.

The Fathers were taken as the exclusive property of the Eastern Church and the entire study of patristics and of the Latin fathers in the West was ignored. This polarization assumed that the East had all the wealth of the Fathers with mystical and liturgical experience, whereas the West had only dry scholasticism and rationalism. In their essay, Tim and Ivana Noble add to this the claim that the conviction concerning superiority over Western theology was already present in the neo-patristic movement, not only in its effective history. Even if earlier Orthodox theology was inspired by the return to the Fathers today in post-modern society, there is "a clear and imperative need for a breath of fresh air, for the overcoming of a certain provincialism and complacent introversion within Orthodox theology, for an openness to the ecumenicity of Christianity, to the challenge of religious otherness, and the catholicity of human thought."[12]

Kalaitzidis is also very critical of Yannaras's account of the West and feels that this view of Western civilization is simply a mocking caricature of the West. He feels that it is wrong to generalize and speak of the West as if

9. Kalaitzidis, "From the Return," 19.

10. Kalaitzidis, "Theological, Historical and Cultural Reasons," 148.

11. "As Siamese twins" (Kalaitzidis, "Theological, Historical and Cultural Reasons," 149).

12. See their article on Western Orthodoxy: Noble and Noble, "Orthodox Theology in Western Europe in the 20th Century."

it would be one philosophical, cultural and theological unit, a "monolithic cultural space, down to its tiniest and most contingent details."[13] In Yannaras's view, the whole of Western theology is reduced to Thomas Aquinas and scholasticism. But Kalaitzidis asks why he constantly mentions neo-scholasticism and neo-Thomism, which actually never had any influence in history, rather than Karl Barth or Dietrich Bonhoeffer? Yannaras seems to know Martin Heidegger, Karl Marx, Jean-Paul Sartre and Immanuel Kant, but he puts them all together in one bag. Further on, Kalaitzidis asks why Yannaras ignores the Reformation and Martin Luther, who might be his allies in the anti-rationalistic battle and fails to show the complexity of the Western world? All this indicates that Yannaras's critique of Western Christianity is one-sided, as he sees only mistakes and errors there.[14]

Brandon Gallaher from the University of Exeter is the next critical and representative voice of post-patristic theology. He asks a very controversial question. How patristic is Florovsky's account of a neo-patristic synthesis?[15] Gallaher sees Florovsky's paradigm as unsatisfactory, as he determines what Orthodoxy *is not* and so, by this negation continues affirming what Orthodoxy *is*. This negative affirmation leads to the conclusion that the identity of Orthodoxy is not isolated or autonomous from the Other, but is *dependent* on it.[16] Moreover, Florovsky misses the fact that early Christians followed Jewish liturgical practices in their liturgy. If early Christianity transfigured the idioms of philosophy during their particular time, asks Gallaher, and if Christianity is still developing, why cannot Christianity today transfigure the idioms of current philosophy in this *current* time and culture?[17] Gallaher searches for different origins of the vision in Florovsky's thought and finds them in Romantic idealism, Johann Adam Möhler and Friedrich Schelling.

Gallaher compares the situation in Orthodoxy with the that described in the poem by Constantine Cavafy (1863–1933) "*Waiting for the Barbarians*,"[18] where the people of a Greek town are assembled in the agora

---

13. Kalaitzidis, "Image of the West," 155.

14. Kalaitzidis also sees a change in Yannaras's late works, when he mitigated his views in 2006 in his *Contra religionen*. See Kalaitzidis, "Image of the West," 157.

15. See Gallaher, "Waiting for the Barbarians," 672.

16. See Gallaher, "Waiting for the Barbarians," 660.

17. An ally of Gallaher, Paul Valliere, criticizes the neo-patristic movement for several reasons: establishing an equation of Orthodoxy with the apophatic approach, closed philosophical engagement with modern culture attempted by the Russian religious school, and rejection of any alliance with modern philosophy. See in Valliere, *Modern Russian Theology*, 299–300.

18. Cavafy, "Waiting for the Barbarians," 15–17.

and wait for the barbarians, who will come any moment and conquer them. When the message comes that there *are* no barbarians anymore, a confusion arises. Orthodox theology is also in a similar situation of waiting for someone against whom it will define its identity and who will embody the negative. The West has played this role so far, but paradoxically, by identifying against the West, Orthodoxy has become even more dependent upon the West.

Florovsky, as Gallaher interprets him, is a good example of this. Florovsky rejects post-schism theology because it lost the universal consciousness of Christian Hellenism, but the sources of his polemic are exactly those that he criticizes (German Idealism and Russian philosophy). Gallaher therefore adds a hermeneutical perspective as crucial for contemporary Orthodox theology as "the acknowledgement that when reading the Fathers it always reads them within the hermeneutical horizon of time."[19] Gallaher accepts that the present world picture is dominated by Western culture, but it is no shame to admit it, as the Western worldview serves as a "spectacle through which the theologian interprets the Fathers and creatively rearticulates the mystery of their pre-modern faith for our postmodern era."[20] If there is a need to revise the neo-patristic synthesis, which Gallaher sees as a necessity due to the hermeneutical horizon of time, it is necessary to return with humility to the Western sources that influenced and built the background of the Eastern Orthodox heritage.

In this regard, Gallaher asks if the West and East are truly opposites. He uses the christological doctrine of the synthesis of opposites, where humanity and divinity are united, but not unchanged.[21] He uses this synthesis of opposites as a hermeneutic principle to mediate between the Christian East and Christian West. By this he means two things: first, that Orthodox theology should not focus on purely Eastern thinking and second, Gallaher thinks that his hermeneutical principle allows for Orthodox theology to discover its identity through a positive encounter with all that is Western, also including modern philosophy.

Gallaher turns Florovsky's well known paradigm upside down, that "one should be Greek in order to be Orthodox," into "one can be Orthodox only in the encounter with what is other and different than itself." Therefore, what Orthodox theology needs is not the demonization of the West, but what he calls political *perichoresis*, "conscious proactive theological

---

19. Gallaher, "Waiting for the Barbarians," 680.
20. Gallaher, "Waiting for the Barbarians," 680.
21. See Gallaher, "Waiting for the Barbarians," 681–93.

engagement with the Other from the basis of one's tradition."[22] The Other does not always have to be the *alien* Other, but can also be a *friendly* Other. One of the achievements of this critique of anti-Westernism is that the anti-Western attitude is not something Eastern, but it is also present among thinkers in the West. Recent decades have also shown other modes of rationality besides the "Western" one (Claude Lévi-Strauss, Robin Horton, and others) which are not necessarily either irrational or arbitrary.

Westernization, even in the way it is understood in the East, is therefore not a one sided, linear and fixed phenomenon, but is rather a dialectical process. Gallaher's proposed hermeneutical approach especially allows not *deleting*, but *bracketing* of the distinction between the East and West and allows a more sober view on the benefits from each side. Certain benefits from the West cannot be ignored, such as the sources and texts that Western academic scholarship has provided. But it is not only about handbooks. Orthodoxy can learn how to be attentive to clear and rational argument, learn about fairness and freedom of thoughts and expressions and learn about creative debate, discussions and compromises, as well as not merely to assert Orthodox positions.

Aristotle Papanikolaou from Fordham University, as a further voice in critical reception, talks about the common meta-narrative. According to this, contemporary Orthodox theology is divided between the Russian religious thought of Vladimir Solovyov, Pavel Florensky and Sergei Bulgakov and the neo-patristic synthesis of Florovsky, Lossky, and others. This meta-narrative involves a strict division between Orthodox theology from a neo-patristic perspective and Western theology and has been taught throughout the Orthodox world until the present time. Papanikolaou claims it is false.[23] He attempts to refute the East-West division by pointing to the neo-patristic character of Bulgakov and by pointing out Bulgakov's ideas as a part of Lossky's thinking. He calls this division a "post-colonial attempt by Orthodoxy to re-establish an intellectual tradition that is uniquely Orthodox." [24] Although sophiology was the most influential philosophy before Florovsky, it failed to survive in any influential form past Bulgakov. Actually, contrary

22. Gallaher, "Waiting for the Barbarians," 683.

23. Agrees with him also Kattan, who in his recent study supplements the common narrative with the meta-narrative, which included debate about the freedom: the freedom of theological thinking to discover new ways and to adopt philosophical considerations; the freedom of hermeneutics of the Fathers, accepting that the Orthodox theology of modern times is also a piece of tradition; and the freedom of theology to redraw the line between mutable and immutable. See Kattan, "Die Freiheit des theologischen Denkens," 181–90.

24. Papanikolaou, "Eastern Orthodox Theology," 538. See also Papanikolaou, "Contemporary Orthodox Theology," 114–17.

to the usual interpretations of polemics between Florovsky and Bulgakov, Florovsky's critique of Bulgakov was not against his use of philosophy *per se*, but against the influence of German idealism that led to an unsatisfactory distinction between the *created* and the *uncreated*.

According to Papanikolaou, a new sign of a theological basis for a mutually exclusive opposition between East and West appeared in the radical apophatism of Vladimir Lossky, who was paradoxically ecumenical and did his dissertation on Meister Eckhart.[25] One of the reasons for this anti-Westernism is his direct attack against the influence of rationalism in theology, as is visible in Bulgakov's work. Lossky's attack has remained the basis for further constructions of anti-Westernism until today, demonstrated in the self-identification of the East as against the West, as well as against Western liberal democracy, human rights, and individualism. Papanikolaou sees only two exceptions to this negative role of the West in contemporary Orthodox theology, both Sergey Bulgakov and Dumitru Stăniloae. Otherwise, current Orthodox theology is a "post-colonial attempt to find its intellectual way after years of oppression."[26]

A further problem with neo-patristics is that its notion of history is divided from the notion of development and progress. Theologians of neo-patristic synthesis encountered the question of normativity, where the living tradition could no longer be equated with history, so it had to be constructed eschatologically.[27] The problem, underlined by Ivana Noble, a Czech Hussite theologian from Charles University, in her presentation in Leuven in 2011, is that the living tradition was made normative as a permanent reference point. Noble, by so arguing joins the critique of Kalaitzidis and Papanikolaou and claims that this normativity of the living tradition disabled the delivery of this tradition as living to other generations. She follows the trajectories of Florovsky, Schmemann and Meyendorff, who all defended the concept of a living tradition. Still, at the same time, Florovsky's notion of authentic development, not as continuation but rather a pseudomorphosis of Tradition, remains at odds with mainstream Orthodoxy. Noble, in her article asks how can we speak about the living tradition as normative for history and compares various approaches. She argues that Florovsky's way to keep tradition alive inevitably needs to include the moment of innovation. But innovation may have two consequences: either the tradition would be ignored and

---

25. This is according to Papanikolaou, "Tradition or Identity Politics," 19. Vladimir Lossky had followers, such as John Romanides and John Zizioulas, who further extended this opposition to trinitarian theology.

26. Papanikolaou, "Tradition or Identity Politics," 20.

27. "Whose achievements were postulated as coming not from the history, but from the end times" (Noble, "History Tied Down," 284).

replaced, or this very requirement of innovation would be ignored. Still, she sees the concept of catholic transfiguration as more problematic than that of re-Hellenization for one simple reason: re-Hellenization did not lead to negative identity. The catholic transfiguration about which Florovsky speaks "would remain problematic, as it would involve a kind of departicularization of the particular, and hence the danger of turning the tradition into mythology, criticized by Kalaitzidis, would remain."[28] This lack of innovation leads Ivana Noble to ask if this does not cause neo-patristics to fail to pass along the "living tradition as truly living and liberating, in the way they experienced it themselves."[29]

Further, the German Orthodox theologian Assaad Elias Kattan, professor of Orthodox theology in the Centre of Theological Studies at the university in Münster, gives important insights into the hermeneutical character of theology in contemporary Orthodox theology. He asks if hermeneutics as a Protestant discipline can be used in the Orthodox context. This seemingly provocative question attempts to resolve common misunderstandings. Kattan considers as crucial the necessity of distinguishing between exegesis and hermeneutics: exegesis is a discipline that attempts to understand the text adequately, whereas hermeneutics focuses on how that understanding happens and emerges. This follows the current understanding of hermeneutics pointed out in the previous chapter. Hermeneutics is not an interpretative method or a survey of various methods of how to apprehend the text, rather it seeks to "examine the premises and frameworks that condition understanding beyond the question concerning the appropriate method to employ."[30] This is exactly the key point that opens the door for hermeneutics into Orthodox theology and proves that a refusal of Western thinking and Western methods has nothing to do with hermeneutics, as hermeneutics is *not a method*. According to Kattan's understanding, Orthodoxy needs hermeneutics as a discipline for understanding, including its premises and the framework provided.

Kattan finds inspiration in theologians who are less known in the West. First among them, the Byzantine-Orthodox Metropolitan of Mount-Lebanon, Georges Khodr (*1923), whose main thesis is that even inspired human words are mere endeavors.[31] Although Khodr has not developed these

---

28. Noble, "History Tied Down," 287–88. See also Kalaitzidis, "From the Return," 7–8.

29. Noble, "History Tied Down," 284. See also Noble and Noble, "Latin Appropriation of Christian Hellenism," 277 n. 24, where authors criticize Baker's defense of Florovsky's synthetic approach and propose the possibility of non-synthetic dialectics.

30. Kattan, "Hermeneutics," 48.

31. He has been interested in the issues of language and the vocabulary that is used

ideas, Kattan concludes that human words for him are only interpretations of the experience behind the words. This effort to express God's inexpressible truths places a huge responsibility on the relativity of human reception, which is incompatible with the Orthodox approach that defends verbal inspiration. Khodr in his autobiography (1979) talks about one Gospel becoming *many* Gospels, still without losing their wholeness. Here he follows the thoughts of the church Fathers, but the important shift is that Khodr concentrates more on the reader's position. In this sense, he talks about the encounter between the divine word and various readers. This means that there might be many meanings of a biblical text and it is occasioned by the fact that the biblical text can be apprehended by many different readers in many different contexts and situations.

This is exactly the new step in Orthodox hermeneutics that Khodr represents, a focus on the plurality of the reader's dimension. Here, Kattan finds a comparison with Gadamer, who said that understanding is an act of encounter between the horizon of the text and the one of the reader. For an illustration, something different can be seen in the work of Paul Tarazi, who concentrates primarily on the historical and literal understanding of biblical texts. He introduced his hermeneutical project in the introduction to his commentary on first Thessalonians as based on two pillars: (i) that the meaning intended by the author can be reconstructed and (ii), that there are not two valid meanings. He believes that understanding is a passive reception of meaning, but it is after all an active encounter of the interpreter and the text. After all, understanding can never be exhaustive nor completely grasped, as Kattan and Khodr believe. The reason for Tarazi's misconceptions is that he did not reflect sufficiently on his hermeneutical theory.[32]

Assaad Kattan takes the rejection of the idea that Western culture has already achieved a change from modernity into post-modernity (with the consequence that there is then no need to solve the problem of modernity) and combines this idea with Kalaitzidis's call for a constructive debate between Orthodoxy and modernity, as well as with the issue of hermeneutics and absolute theological criterion.[33] Truly, hermeneutics has had as its goal

---

in order to express the religious message. See the description in Kattan, "Hermeneutics," 49–53. See also Kattan, "Les lignes directrices," 379–91. For more see Khodr's book *The Ways of Childhood*, translated and published in 2016.

32. In order to be fair, in 1991 Tarazi wrote an introduction to the Old Testament, and it seems he slightly modified his hermeneutical position, and became more aware of the need for dialogue and encounter in the act of understanding. Tarazi, *Old Testament Introduction*, 1.

33. See Kattan, "Revisiting the Question," 128–43; and Kattan, "La théologie orthodoxe," 180–96.

to create a comprehensive theory of understanding and, as such, was part of modernity's effort for universally valid projects. But this optimism and certainty was questioned in the twentieth century and the interest in the primacy of questions and the focus on any encounter with the text came to the fore. Hermeneutics abandoned its modernistic elements and is no longer a phenomenon of modernity.

Alternative Work with the Sources

The above-mentioned critical reception that addressed negative identity formation, the rise of traditionalism, lack of innovation and plurality of mediations of the transcendent, is further complemented with the alternative work of theologians who moved beyond critique, relied on the works of non-Orthodox authors and worked more constructively with their sources. It is important to note that in this case there was a type of negative identity formation "against" others, as was criticized earlier.

The work of John Breck and Theodore Stylianopoulos is most important in this regard, as they represent the *move beyond* neo-patristic synthesis. One could argue that they can be as well understood from the perspective of a neo-patristic synthesis, taking the Bible as a starting point. In fact, both scholars spill much ink to marry a number of patristic interpretative tools such as Breck's typology with historical criticism. In addition, Stylianopoulos, following in Florovsky's footsteps, even coins the term *biblical synthesis*. It is true that both scholars are indebted to Florovsky's pattern, because denying this would mean to deny the hermeneutical concept of *Wirkungsgeschichte* (history of effects). Still, this only shows that they continue to work in a certain context of which they are aware, on which they react and which they develop.

A systematic rehabilitation of patristic methodology and hermeneutics is first visible in the work of Fr. John Breck (*1939), an American Orthodox theologian whose field of research is the interpretation of Scripture. His work flows out of two sources: first out of his engagement in the ecumenical dialogue in the eighties and then out of his discontent with the current Orthodox praxis. Breck's main contribution lies (i) in the re-establishing of *theōria* in hermeneutics and (ii), in the emphasis on liturgical life and the Holy Spirit in the Orthodox Church. These moments complement negative identity formation and offer a positive way to preserve respect for both patristics and critical thinking at the same time.

The starting point of Breck's work is a presentation of Protestant, Catholic and Orthodox views on the hermeneutical problem, namely how to translate the liturgical and cultural context of Scripture to a modern reader and his life situation. Breck achieves this by stating a difference between hermeneutics and biblical exegesis: while exegesis attempts to grasp the text in the original context, hermeneutics attempts to find the meaning of a text for the recipient/reader.[34] He talks about a hermeneutical bridge, and defines a hermeneutical problem as actualization; the main hermeneutical question for him is how to translate the original context to the current reader, how to combine the life situation of Christians and the Bible in one's own context.

Breck calls this the *anamnesis* (remembering), which is not the remembering of past events, but it is their renewal and actualization. The Protestant approach overcomes this problem with the preached word, but Breck considers this too individualistic in the sense that this approach relies on spiritual illumination of an individual in his/her personal reading of Scripture. This individual illumination of a single person eliminates the sacramental and ecclesial context as, at the same time, it isolates pneumatology from ecclesiology and separates them. The Catholic approach has continued differently and overcome the division with the emphasis of magisterium, but this does not fully solve the main hermeneutical question either.

For this reason, Breck offers his Orthodox answer, which is based on the return to patristics, yet at the same time is also based on an indispensable scholarly exegesis of Scripture.[35] What Breck did is that he distanced his thinking from historical-critical and literal analysis and used a method focused on typology.[36] He did this under the inspiration of non-Orthodox authors, namely Frances Young and Bertrand de Margerie.

His book *Scripture in Tradition* (2001),[37] in which he returns to the problem of hermeneutics and explains the role of Scripture in the Orthodox Church, is characterized by the reaction to modern approaches that focused on a literal meaning of Scripture, and so ignored the lives of readers. Methods do not suffice, says Breck, since "they are fragmentary, do not speak to the spiritual needs of people."[38] Methods remove Scripture from its original ecclesial and liturgical context and *interrogate* the text rather than

---

34. Breck, *Power of the Word*, 26–30.

35. This is the approach presented in Breck, *Power of the Word*, 26.

36. Noble claims that Breck prefers typology, but still does not refuse allegory. Noble, "Your Word is a Lamp," 56. But this is not completely correct, as Breck clearly claims that allegory does not suffice as it creates a difference between history and the text. See Breck, *Scripture in Tradition*, 23.

37. This book is highly regarded, Weiss calls it the "cornerstone of Orthodox Scholarship." See Weiss, Review of *Scripture in Tradition*, 143.

38. Breck, *Scripture in Tradition*, 17.

allow themselves to be addressed and challenged by it. This is in contrast to his book *Power of the Word in the Worshiping Church* (1986), where he defends historical critics. There he formulates the hermeneutical problem, and finds an Orthodox answer to this problem that will be faithful not only to tradition and inspiration, but also to the necessary scholarly exegesis of the Bible.[39]

Breck offered a middle position between these two books (1986 and 2001) regarding the relation to methods in his speech from 1989, where he talked about the relation of Orthodox biblical studies to Western biblical approaches.[40] They are mostly negative, but critically and positively can complement Orthodox biblical studies. Breck still does not totally reject critical thinking, but tries to find the right role for it and wants to complement critical thinking with *theōria* and typology.

Breck strives to rehabilitate the texts as they were identified by the early Christians and therefore he deals with the issue of the Alexandrian and Antiochene Schools.[41] Both schools claim that Scripture is inspired by the Spirit, and both are primarily based on the literary-historical sense and only in their second phase did they approach the text allegorically or typologically, as both schools wanted to decipher the deeper sense. Whereas in the thinking of the Alexandrian school there are two levels of sense, Antiochenes knew only one that connected both of them. Although the difference between the schools remains, as Alexandrians wanted to uncover allegorical symbolism and Antiochenes wanted to preserve historical reality, according to Breck typology was still normative for both schools from the very beginning.[42] Breck distanced himself from historical-critical and literary analysis, adopting the typological aspect of a patristic interpretation.[43]

39. See Breck, *Power of the Word*, 25–26.

40. Speech on the occasion of the fiftieth anniversary of St Vladimir's Theological Seminary, published as Breck, "Orthodoxy and the Bible Today," 141–57.

41. See Breck, *Scripture in Tradition*, 21–31. Also see Breck, *Power of the Word*, 49–92, chapter titled "The Patristic Setting for 'Theoretic' Hermeneutics."

42. Breck, *Power of the Word*, 56.

43. He did this, as Clark notices, in order to popularize the work of Frances Young. See Clark, "Recent Eastern Orthodox Interpretation," 331. The book mentioned is *Biblical Exegesis and the Formation of Christian Culture*. There is no anachronism in the statement that John Breck was influenced by Frances Young. Namely, Breck's *Power of the Word* from 1986 shows the influence of Bertrand de Margerie and his book *An Introduction to the History of Exegesis* (first French edition from 1980), especially in the concept of the *theōria* as the fulfilment in the community. The influence of Frances Young (book 1997), especially typological aspects of biblical and patristic typological interpretation, is articulated in Breck's book *Scripture in Tradition* from 2001 (see 21–31). For clarification, typology appears also in the *Power of the Word* (38–41), and while Breck speaks there about the double movement of the type and how Jesus was present

This rehabilitation of typology involves the Holy Spirit in the hermeneutical process and illustrates that interpretation is not merely a method, but a synergy visible in the Eucharistic liturgy that becomes a new dimension in the hermeneutical process.[44] It is the Holy Spirit who constructs historical events, makes them present and actualized in the liturgical life of the church.[45] Breck was inspired by the account of the Jesuit writer Bertrand de Margerie (1923–2003) on the aspect of prophetic fulfilment in the typological relationship.[46] Therefore, he created a hermeneutical model that makes use of the historical element of the typological relationship, which is converted into the liturgical life of the interpretative community while, at the same time, is also fulfilled in this community. Breck in his work puts together Holy Spirit, Tradition and Church, and says that the biblical event can be only re-actualized in a community of believers through the Eucharistic celebration because Scripture cannot interpret itself. Breck felt urged to emphasize the idea that *theōria* is a vision that can only be fulfilled in the church and liturgy because this is where the words of scripture are fulfilled and where they end. Thus, for him the liturgy is not just a possibility or alternative, it is vital.

Breck developed a system of eight principles, which he calls "*presuppositions and principles of patristic exegesis.*"[47] They must all be amplified to understand the entire system that Breck projected. (i) The Word of God relates to three different realities: eternal *Logos*, scriptural testimony and the proclamation of Him. (ii) The Word of God must be perceived from the trinitarian perspective: The Spirit leads to the knowledge of the Son, and the Son renews the relationship with the Father. (iii) The Word of God must be understood from the perspective of theandricity (human-divine nature, as Scripture is God's word to people, and not a human word about God), which accepts the cooperation between divine and human elements

---

among Israelites in pre-incarnate form, the influence of Georges Barois (*The Face of God in the Old Testament*, 1974) is visible. Kattan sees the influence of Veselin Kesich, see Kattan, "Orthodoxe Theologie und moderne Hermeneutik," 70. But, in *Scripture and Tradition* is visible a new development of the aspect of typology (esp. 25–31, "The Type as Both Event and Interpretation"), which has as a starting point Frances Young's book (see Breck, *Scripture in Tradition*, 25, esp. footnote 9).

44. Similarly as Breck writes also Andreas Andreopoulos. See his text: Andreopoulos, "The Gospel as an Image," 7–22.

45. See Breck, *Scripture in Tradition*, 35–41, 104.

46. See Margerie, *Introduction*, 180.

47. Breck, *Scripture in Tradition*, 38–44. First there were five principles (1990, Breck, "Orthodoxy and the Bible Today,"), then there were seven (1996, Breck, "Orthodox Principles of Biblical Interpretation"), expansion to the current eight is from 2001 (Breck, *Scripture in Tradition*).

in the process of creation of the canon, as well as for its interpretation. (iv) The proper place, *locus*, for interpretation is the Church. (v) The emphasis is on the relation between Scripture and Tradition; Orthodoxy fully accepts the priority of Scripture in questions of life and faith, but still understands it as a product of Tradition. (vi) The Old and New Testament together build salvation history, with its relationship of promise and fulfilment, type and antitype. (vii) This principle Breck calls an exegetical reciprocity, which means that everything points to Christ and every text can reveal the messianic message. (viii) To interpret Scripture means to interpret it *from within*, and presupposes living according to it, as no one can interpret the Scripture if one does not live according to it.

Theodore G. Stylianopoulos (*1937) is an American Orthodox biblical scholar who teaches at the Holy Cross Greek Orthodox School of Theology. He continues in a similar direction as Breck, by preserving the positive evaluation of patristics and overcoming anti-Westernism with a positive evaluation of scholarly methodology.[48] Stylianopoulos even more strongly enforces the importance of the methodology of interpretation for the integrity of biblical truth and the unity of the church. He sees the problem of contemporary Orthodox hermeneutics in a balance between biblical scholarship, which receives appraisal even in Orthodox circles and the *"theological emptiness"* and *"spiritual dryness"* that is an inevitable part of biblical exegesis.[49]

The task of hermeneutics, as he sees is it, is therefore to balance theories of knowledge and interpretation with a spiritual reading of the Bible.[50] Particular methodology as such is not a chief concern in the Orthodox Church, rather it is how to be faithful to the harmony of the church with the witness of Scripture. It is important to note that this anti-methodological accent is a sign of the later Stylianopoulos view, where he very clearly argues for a contemplative anti-methodological interpretation, focused on faith and liturgy. A distinction is made between exegesis, interpretation and hermeneutics. *Exegesis* deals with the original meaning of the text, while *interpretation* is an evaluative task about values that the readers see in the text. *Hermeneutics* is a reflection on the methods and presuppositions and embraces the entire process, including reflection about the presupposition, principles and methods.[51]

---

48. Worth mentioning is a recently published Festschrift in his honor, see: Pentiuc et al., *Studies in Orthodox Hermeneutics*.

49. Stylianopoulos, "Holy Scripture, Interpretation," 25.

50. Stylianopoulos, "Scripture and Tradition," 30.

51. See Stylianopoulos, *New Testament*, 81–87.

He names this approach a *"dynamic conservatism"*[52] and anchors it in the high regard of Scripture, as well as the importance of prayer in the study of the Bible, its primary meaning as historical and the purpose of exegesis, which is to illuminate theological truths and ethical values in Scripture. These elements are his main contribution that complements the broader argument about the patristic captivity of Orthodox theology. This is, in his case, addressed by an alternative and positive concept, where both sides are preserved and is similar to Breck's project.

One side of Stylianopoulos's theology is profoundly biblical and he states that the way to renew the church and fulfil its mission in the twenty-first century is to "tap the deep waters of the biblical and patristic tradition."[53] He admits that the growth of biblical studies in Orthodoxy was inspired by modern biblical criticism in the West, although this is intertwined with what he calls some "problematic presuppositions"[54] of the Enlightenment. The other side indicates his main inspirations are the works of St Symeon and John Chrysostom. St Symeon is considered an example of a monastic who devoted his life to the study of Scripture and for whom Scripture was the decisive criterion of truth, the "bedrock theological grounding of his theology and spirituality."[55]

Chrysostom presents a similar situation. It is he from whom one should acquire such ideas as (i), love for the Scriptures and personal devotions, as scholarly work with Scripture without love for the Scriptures is fruitless, (ii) the Bible as a combination of God's divine word and the human character, because the revelation does not happen in a vacuum but among and through people and (iii), the Bible belongs to the church, the living community of believers, in which Scripture is "written, preserved, transmitted, collected into a sacred library, used and interpreted."[56]

While Breck sees a hermeneutical problem in the actualization of the text, Stylianopoulos sees a hermeneutical challenge in the relation between faith and reason. He says that hermeneutical models fail to have the spiritual power to understand Scripture and that without faith their effort is useless and vain. Reason has its role, for sure, but it is limited and cannot rationally analyze or prove the existence and acts of God. What is needed,

---

52. Stylianopoulos, *New Testament*, 81.

53. Stylianopoulos, *Good News of Christ*, xi. If we browse through his other books, for example *The Way of Christ* (2002) Bible passages are mentioned on every page. In these books, as McGuckin writes in his review, it is visible that the Bible is a part of the church for Orthodoxy, and that the Orthodox Church is truly biblical.

54. Stylianopoulos, "Holy Scripture, Interpretation," 11.

55. Stylianopoulos, "Holy Scripture, Interpretation," 6.

56. Stylianopoulos, "Comments on Chrysostom," 197.

according to Stylianopoulos, is a balance between the hermeneutics of faith and the hermeneutics of reason, otherwise it will become either rationalism or fanaticism.[57] Similar to the manner in which Florovsky called for neo-patristic synthesis, Stylianopoulos calls for a *"neo-biblical synthesis."*[58] By this, he means the close study of biblical authors, their message and their work. But at the same time this also means to draw from their experience of faith and both elements must be balanced.[59]

In order to keep those elements in balance, Stylianopoulos's hermeneutical position has three aspects.[60] First is a historical aspect (exegetical, descriptive). This task is accomplished by a contextual and grammatical interpretation that pays attention to an author's intent, language, and genre. This approach is not only historical because, as Stylianopoulos says, it is also a matter of "religious conviction, theological truths and spiritual insights of the authors."[61] Second is an evaluative aspect (interpretative, doctrinal) where the emphasis is moved from a biblical author to the reader. Stylianopoulos is aware that much of the content of Scripture depends on the reader's own faith, willingness, worldview and presuppositions. Third is the applicatory aspect (transformative, contemplative) that includes the application of biblical texts to personal lives, as well as to the church and the world. This hermeneutical position presupposes and requires the balance of the exegetical, doctrinal and contemplative aspects. As he writes, an ideal interpreter is one who is a scholar, theologian and saint at the same time.[62]

This balance of exegetical, doctrinal and contemplative elements is fully described in his theory about the four fidelities, which Stylianopoulos elucidates when he describes how to interpret the Bible according to its

57. See Stylianopoulos, *New Testament*, 96–98.

58. Stylianopoulos, "Comments on Chrysostom," 192. Mark Sheridan's response correctly notes that historical-critical and other current methodologies are insufficiently described in his book. Sheridan, Review of *The New Testament: An Orthodox Perspective*, 606.

59. One must raise objections against Stylianopoulos that his overview of the hermeneutical crisis in the West is very general (much more general than his overview of Orthodox hermeneutical attempts). Supplementary, when he mentions Western hermeneutical thinkers (such as Schleiermacher, Dilthey and Gadamer), he does not use primary sources, but fully relies on secondary sources, primary works do not even appear in the bibliography. His poor knowledge of Western theology is also visible when he talks about *sola scriptura*, where he obviously does not know that there are three *sola* in Reformation theology, which must be understood together. See also Kattan's observations in Kattan, "Orthodoxe Theologie und moderne Hermeneutik," 78–79.

60. See Stylianopoulos, "Holy Scripture, Interpretation," 26–29, already largely expressed in the chapter 7 of his book from 1997.

61. Stylianopoulos, "Holy Scripture, Interpretation," 27.

62. See Stylianopoulos, "Holy Scripture, Interpretation," 29.

own nature. Only the integration and practice of all four principles builds a perspective from which the Orthodox believer can approach the Bible.[63] (i) The first is fidelity to the witness of the Bible as the Word of God and as the primary source of revelation, (ii) then there is fidelity to the common tradition of the ancient church as the tradition of the apostolic truth, (iii) fidelity to a sincere critical work as the third principle and (iv), fidelity to the Holy Spirit who accomplishes the goal of understanding the Bible as the last piece in the puzzle. A critical study cannot be the sole source, because salvation comes from an encounter with God and not by scholarly erudition. Yes, reason has its place but salvation by grace, first of all, engages faith, repentance and love.

Stylianopoulos talks about levels of interpretation that must be discerned, but still correlate with each other, each having its own elements: *historical*, which requires training, seeks original meaning and tries to reconstruct the biblical world; *theological*, which requires technical training, but "concentrates on the theological claims as themes of the Bible"[64] and *mystical*, which is related to the above, but does not require any technical training, as its training is in the community of faith, where we read and hear the stories. The point here is not to be precise in historical understanding or precise in theological concepts, but in the spiritual receptiveness of the believer embracing symbols, narratives and biblical images.

The purpose of this chapter was to achieve a re-reading of Orthodox hermeneutics and prepare the ground for the next chapter, where the presentation of the forms of modern and postmodern Orthodox liturgical hermeneutics, based on Gadamerian concepts, will follow. Therefore, we included the critical reception of post-patristic theology concerning the way the neo-patristic school in its Russian and Greek forms worked with its sources, more precisely the patristic and anti-Westernism captivities.

The connection with the theme of this book is important to mention at this point. As expressed in the introduction, the main question is how can what is transcendent, as active and enabling cooperation, be testified to within horizons of human understanding without becoming created by people? How can the balance between historical mediation and the silence that dismisses the mediation be preserved? How can the participatory relationship between the immanent and the transcendent as we find it in Orthodox theology be preserved without divinizing the world? Orthodox hermeneutics with the attributes of negative self-identification, antithesis

---

63. See Stylianopoulos, "Perspectives in Orthodox Biblical Interpretation," 330–37. See also Stylianopoulos, "Orthodox Biblical Interpretation," 554–58.

64. Stylianopoulos, "Perspectives in Orthodox Biblical Interpretation," 336.

between East and West and traditionalizing of the church fails to achieve this balance, as it refuses plurality.

It is post-patristic theology, both its critical reception and alternative work with the sources that achieves the result of seeing the strengths and weaknesses of its positions. We need post-patristic theology in order to see the strength of Orthodox hermeneutics, identified in terms of belonging to community, as well as to see transcendence as something that comes from outside, as does the Holy Spirit and not as the result of collaboration between people and history. We need post-patristic theology in order to see the weakness of the Orthodox approach, namely the problem that the vertically understood transcendence does not provide enough space for the human element, for suspicion and otherness.

9

Human Understanding and Transcendence in Current Orthodox Hermeneutics

THIS chapter discusses Orthodox hermeneutics from the perspectives achieved in the previous chapter and I will begin with the reception of Gadamer's thoughts in the Orthodox world. Although the work of Gadamer became well known in the West by the end of the twentieth century, it took a while longer until it found its way into Orthodox theology. First, the reception of Gadamer by Andrew Louth will be presented, who provides one of the best interpretations of Gadamer's work Then that is followed by two theologians of a younger generation: Assaad Kattan, who frequently referred to Gadamer during recent years and Nicolae Turcan, who sees a critique of traditionalism in Gadamer's hermeneutics.

The ideas from this section will build the foundation for the following two sections. Namely, from Gadamer there are several helpful ideas, such as the importance of the life of the interpreter, understanding as the continuity of an experience, genuine conversation, temporal distance and the interpreter's involvement in the interpretative act. These thoughts form the basis for the balance of the chapter on Scripture and Tradition and the relation between contemplation and science.

The Reception of Gadamer in Orthodox Hermeneutics

The structure of this book, where the first part deals with Gadamerian hermeneutics and the second with modern and postmodern Orthodox theological hermeneutics, requires an additional section where we more closely approach the reception of Gadamer's work in Orthodoxy to identify the most important areas thematized, as well as to address them from the perspective of modern and postmodern Orthodox theological hermeneutics.

Even though Gadamer's work was influential during the last third of the twentieth century, it did not immediately find its way into Orthodox theology. One of the reasons is that his concept of hermeneutics had a philosophical background that was not automatically recognized even by Protestant and Catholic theologians as helpful in complementing theological concepts.[1] For theologians working in the East, it was even more difficult to appreciate Gadamer. Thus, it is small wonder that Orthodox theologians working in the West were the first to begin implementing his thoughts. I will present three of them.

Andrew Louth (*1944), the professor of Patristic and Byzantine studies at the University of Durham, in his *Discerning the Mystery* (1983) grasps Gadamer's thinking as "one of the most interesting attempts to reflect on the distinctive approach of the humanities" and contains "a profound and far-reaching attempt to reorient the humanities."[2] Louth endorses several of Gadamer's issues. First of all, it is his critique of the scientific method as a way of reaching the truth that ignores the one who approaches this truth and attempts to discover a meaning as existing independently of both the process and subject of understanding.[3]

He explains his idea that the Enlightenment's paradigm of method raised a resistance to this claim and it was only Gadamer who provided the most radical way of resisting its totalitarian claim. The idea that the attempts of Vico, Dilthey and Romanticism failed succeed was obvious to Louth, because for them the meaning was not the sense of the literary text itself, but the sense *behind* the text in the mind of an author and his/her world. Louth emphasizes that this reconstruction of the original historical context meant that the personality of the one who understands is ignored. Gadamer calls this a false objectivity—the reconstruction of the original meaning is not possible, as the interpreter has a historical context of his own.[4]

---

1. David Tracy, Kevin Vanhoozer, Anthony Thiselton, Werner Jeanrond, Heinz-Günther Stobbe, Bernd Jochen Hilberath, Peter Stuhlmacher, Francis Schüssler Fiorenza, Wolfhart Pannenberg, and Bernard Lonergan, are only some of the names important for application of Gadamer's hermeneutics into theology.

2. Louth, *Discerning the Mystery*, 29. It needs to be noted that when he wrote the book, Andrew Louth was not Orthodox.

3. See Louth, *Discerning the Mystery*, 30.

4. "Both the writer and I who seek to understand him belong in history: I cannot reconstruct his historical situation and think myself into it, as if I had no historical context myself" (Louth, *Discerning the Mystery*, 30).

Louth finds it very helpful that Gadamer construes understanding as an agreement between two people about something, where the reader does not engage with the writer himself, but with the subject matter of the text.[5] The implications are clear to Louth—the individualistic approach that attempts to abstract the individual from the historical context and supposes a presupposition-less understanding, is rejected in favor of understanding as an *engagement* with the tradition, rather than an attempt to escape from it.[6]

Therefore, the second area positively evaluated by Andrew Louth involves the recovery of tradition, which he sees to be similar to the pattern of the Fathers of the church since, for the Fathers, the knowledge of God can only be found within the tradition of the church.[7] He writes that in the movement from the Enlightenment and Romanticism, there is a tendency to break the thread of the tradition as something that confuses and falsifies. For Louth, tradition is the continuity of a human communication of an experience, rather than something that limits our freedom, but it is the context within which one can and is allowed to be free.

He explains that there is no antithesis between tradition and reason, but quite the opposite. Tradition is an act of reason, therefore there is no need to forget our prejudices. This is similar to Gadamer's effective history (*Wirkungsgeschichte*), which does not include only awareness of the historical context, but moreover includes awareness of history in the effect it has on the present historical situation of the interpreter.[8] Thus, Louth felt a kinship with Gadamer on this point. Tradition as *Wirkungsgeschichte* is a process of self-discovery that can never be complete, a process of revising our preconceptions and not seeking to escape them. The effect of all this is that the act of understanding is seen in a wider context than the historical method allows us. Thus, we are in a better position to appreciate the traditional way

---

5. "It is enough to say that we understand in a *different way, if we understand at all*" (*TM* 307).

6. See Louth, *Discerning the Mystery*, 37. This is quite opposite to Romanticism which had a concept of a hermeneutical circle as just a provisional state, which ends with perfect understanding. For Gadamer the circle is the description of the interplay between text and our subjectivity.

7. Louth quotes Cyprian's words from *De Ecclesiae Catholicae Unitate*: "Habere iam not potest Deum patrem qui ecclesiam non habet matrem: he who no longer has the Church for his mother cannot have God as his Father" (see Louth, *Discerning the Mystery*, 64).

8. "In fact, the important thing is to recognize temporal distance as a positive and productive condition enabling understanding. It is not a yawning abyss but is filled with the continuity of custom and tradition, in the light of which everything handed down presents itself to us" (*TM* 308).

of understanding the Scriptures "as it is found par excellence in the Fathers, a way of understanding that sees not one but many senses of Scripture."⁹

Louth makes use of Gadamer's note about a process of *un*deception, we have been deceived but we are now freed from deception and are oriented toward new experiences.¹⁰ This growing in experience is not primarily an increase in knowledge, but it is rather an escape from what deceived us, it is learning by suffering, *pathei mathos*, a concept that Gadamer uses for the process of undeception and exploration of human finitude.¹¹

Louth sees that behind Gadamer's reflection about the nature of understanding lies an analogy between understanding and genuine conversation, where the reader (interpreter) not only recognizes the otherness of the other (as in therapeutic conversation), but also recognizes the truth-claim of partners in the conversation and listens to what they have to say. In other words, when I listen, I do not try to understand the other and so to gain dominance over him, but I try to listen to what he has to say and to learn from him. This is analogous to reading the past that Louth recommends—we must accept the validity of tradition not simply in the sense of acknowledging it, but to listen to what it says to us.¹² Louth sees this in parallel with Gadamer, who says that the interpreting of the work is not an attempt to reconstruct the original historical context, but rather a matter of listening across a historical gulf that is not empty, but filled with the traditions that bring this work to us.

Assaad Elias Kattan (*1967), German Orthodox theologian of Lebanese background, is a theologian who has in recent years very often referred to Gadamer's thinking. In his lecture from 2010, called "*Essentialism Reconsidered*"¹³ Kattan sees three existing patterns of relationship between hermeneutics and Orthodox theology: (i) one pattern that stresses the insufficiency of hermeneutics, (ii) another that depicts the Holy Spirit as the link between the past and present and (iii) one that is challenged by Gadamer. He chooses the third possibility and underlines very directly that

---

9. Louth, *Discerning the Mystery*, 106.

10. See Louth, *Discerning the Mystery*, 37.

11. "Thus experience is experience of human finitude. The truly experienced person is one who has taken this to heart, who knows that he is master neither of time nor the future. The experienced man knows that all foresight is limited and all plans uncertain" (*TM* 365).

12. See Louth, *Discerning the Mystery*, 41.

13. His lecture "Essentialism Reconsidered: The Myth of a Non Hermeneutical Approach to Orthodox Tradition," was presented the International Conference of the Volos Academy for Theological Studies: *Neo-Patristic Synthesis of Post-Patristic Theology: Can Orthodox Theology be Contextual?* in Volos, June 3–6, 2010. Published in a slightly modified version as Kattan, "Gadamer Ad Portas," 63–71.

some aspects of the Orthodox way could be challenged and revolutionized by Gadamer's insights since, as he is aware, this has not yet been done in Orthodoxy.

He has especially in mind the challenge of Gadamer's analysis of the impact of temporal distance, and the involvement of an interpreter's individuality in the act of understanding—neither element has been satisfactorily analyzed in the Orthodox hermeneutics of tradition. Especially inspiring and of importance according to Kattan is Gadamer's concept of temporal distance,[14] which presupposes that the act of understanding is impossible without fore-structure and that the interpreter belongs to the act of interpretation. Gadamer frees prejudices from the captivity caused by the Enlightenment and makes them a starting point for the rehabilitation of tradition.

The popular notion of tradition among the Orthodox sees tradition as a closed and unchangeable entity and this must be challenged, according to Kattan and to be seen as a dynamic and open testimony of the Holy Spirit in the church. Tradition in Gadamer's view seems, on one side to be conservative, as he returns to the Greek-Roman paradigms, yet on the other he rehabilitates it in a way that shows a reading of the text in the wide horizon of tradition. There is a critical potential in the form of temporal distance as a *sine qua non* of every understanding. If this is true, then the need emerges to reconfigure how the writings of the Fathers are used, as they can no longer be ready recipes for current problems. It is also not possible to ignore the achievements of psychoanalysis and uncritically endorse anthropologic paradigms.

Gadamer's insights and Kattan's interpretation invite us to see tradition with new eyes. Gadamer uses a metaphor, the fusion of horizons in order to call attention to an interpreter's involvement in the interpretative act. This fusion happens as an application, which is an integral part of the understanding that the interpreter's presuppositions are not static entities, but must be verified and adjusted. If we take as the main consequence that subjectivity is elevated to the rank of a hermeneutical principle as true, how legitimate is it then to regard tradition as highly objective, infallible and absolute? Kattan thinks that this sensitivity to the role of the interpreter might contribute to a healthy and fruitful discussion among the Orthodox over the limits of tradition.

In 2010, Nicolae Turcan (*1971), an Orthodox theologian from Cluj-Napoca, published a study titled "*Church Tradition: Reflection on*

---

14. See Kattan, "Gadamer Ad Portas," 65–69.

Hermeneutics and Holiness"[15] that contributes to the issue of the challenges of Gadamer's philosophical hermeneutics. This study concerns the Orthodox concept of Tradition and Gadamer is used to help him to better understand *how can I, as an Orthodox thinker, understand church Tradition related to Gadamer's thought?* Can we use Gadamer to better understand our church Tradition?

For Gadamer there is a dialogue with the texts of tradition, as well as a dialogue with the *Thou* of the text. For theology, this dialogue goes further, because the *Thou* of the sacred text is the *Thou* of prayers, God. The author agrees with Gadamer regarding this, but also emphasizes the difference and sees that religious experience is more than a hermeneutical experience. Turcan marks the difference between traditionalism and church tradition and offers an analysis of these two from the perspective of contemporary Orthodox theology. Gadamer's understanding of tradition as a *living* dialogue with the texts remains between traditionalism ("the dead belief of the living people"), and the Tradition of the Holy Spirit who remains in the church ("the living belief of the dead people"). Traditionalism is seen as a disease, as a form of dead hermeneutics. Church tradition, quite differently, is revealed as a tradition of the Holy Spirit, which hermeneutical discourse moves in an inevitable way to prayer and ecclesiastical life. The consequence of such an understanding is that it diminishes the differences between those who follow the tradition and those who create it, underlining the idea that both are created by Tradition.

In his conclusion, Turcan sees Gadamer as an important moment in our theological thinking concerning church tradition and thinks that his hermeneutics can be a good critique of traditionalism, but should be complemented with the theological moment. The dialogue with the texts must become a dialogue with the divine, who is the inspirer of these texts.

This concludes our discussion of the way Gadamer has been received in the Orthodox context. The following sections will be based on the themes addressed by the reception of Gadamer in Orthodox hermeneutics that are identified as important for Orthodoxy. On the basis of these themes, the horizon of human understanding and transcendence will be approached. These areas are, the role of Tradition and Scripture as classics and as bearers of meaning and the discussion concerning contemplation and science.

These and the following themes will be approached thematically, but the representative voices of current hermeneutical theologians will be noted, such as those of John Breck, Anthony McGuckin, Kallistos Ware, Aristotle Papanikolaou, Vasile Mihoc, Michael Prokurat, and others.

---

15. Turcan, "Tradiția bisericii sau despre hermeneutică și sfințenie" 227–37.

Scripture and Tradition as Classics

The theme is now to show how Tradition is connected with Scripture. Tradition has assuredly an important relationship with Scripture in that it provides a hermeneutical key for the interpretation of Scripture. Before I begin, a few general comments must be noted, as discussing the term tradition (*paradosis*) leads to several problems. First, one deals with how to write this word, and second, with how to define it, especially in contrast to the Western discussion on the topic.

The dispute about tradition has existed since the Reformation, but the simple opposition developed in the controversy between Protestants and Roman Catholics shows that both sides misunderstood its nature. The mistake concerning the controversy about tradition is that Scripture and tradition are objectified as something that we seek to understand. The Post-Reformation era simplified the term as something dealing with the past, rather than referring to the whole of the Christian faith and created a difference between the *tradition*, which is used for apostolic teaching, and the *traditions*, which are used for the process of delivery of this primary event. The term *traditions* therefore designates different forms in which the primary Gospel is expressed and received. Protestants still maintain this distinction. In other words, the Reformation controversy separated what had been an organic whole and contrasted the normative value of Scripture and tradition by placing the Bible higher. For the Orthodox position, the act of tradition and the process of delivering this tradition through history is one and the same *Tradition* and Orthodoxy uses the capital "T" for that.[16] The advantage of this formulation of Tradition is that it sees the Bible as a normative writing, but at the same time leaves room to speculate about the intentions of the writers.

The best official document on this topic according to Kallistos Ware is the "*Moscow Agreed Statement*," issued by the delegates of the Anglican-Orthodox Joint Doctrinal commission meeting in Moscow from July 26 to August 2, 1976. Although it is not confirmed as the representative expression, Ware considers it the best expression of Orthodox doctrine on the relationship between Tradition and Scripture, especially because there were not any objections to its conclusions. This document is undervalued, but still expresses the Orthodox view: the Bible should be affirmed as a coherent whole, as a unity. Furthermore, Scripture is the main criterion whereby the

---

16. See Lossky, "Tradition and Traditions," 10–22.

church tests Tradition, and Holy Tradition completes Holy Scripture in the sense that it safeguards it.[17]

Although the Holy Scripture was canonized on the basis of the Holy Tradition, the part of the Tradition that is not written and included in Holy Scripture is also Holy Tradition. "*Scripture in Tradition*" is the project of John Breck, who alleged that "rather than see Scripture as the original and primary medium of revelation and tradition as mere human reflection upon its witness, we need to give full weight to the fact that Scripture as written text is born of tradition."[18] Scripture and Tradition should not either exclude or complement each other, but should be seen from the perspective of their historical development. Scripture was "born and shaped within the community of faith."[19] In this regard, Vasile Mihoc notes that for the Early church, Scripture is not the only authority, as Jesus himself remains the supreme authority and Scripture has value only so far it witnesses Jesus.[20] From this one must conclude that *sola scriptura* cannot be sustained, because not everything that Jesus said is written in Scripture and not all divine revelation is contained in the Bible.

The most comprehensive way to explain the problem of the relationship between Scripture and Tradition is to use the concept of the hermeneutical circle, which points to circularity in the relation between Scripture and Tradition. Scripture is the measure according to which Tradition is judged, but the Bible was also created within the church and Tradition.[21] This circularity remains the main principle of Orthodox hermeneutics and cannot be overturned. Church, Tradition and Bible are interconnected, which means that each is contained within the others. Therefore, the church is the place where the Bible lives in the continuity of Tradition, while the church confirms the authority of biblical books based on Tradition and through this Tradition the church interprets the Bible. At the same time, Orthodoxy proves its own authority from the Bible itself.

McGuckin, in this regard very interestingly talks about the self-renewal of tradition. By this he means that it is normal that some texts from an earlier era, for example the sermons of the Fathers that were important in

17. According to Ware, "Unity of Scripture and Tradition," 231–46.

18. Breck, *Scripture in Tradition*, 10.

19. Breck, *Scripture in Tradition*, 3. Also: "Scripture exists within tradition" (Vassiliadis, "Canon and Authority," 26).

20. Mihoc, "Principles of Orthodox Hermeneutics," 295–96. There is a similar problem with Luther, according to whom biblical books are useful only as long they show the Gospel.

21. On the hermeneutical circle within Orthodoxy see Mihoc, "Principles of Orthodox Hermeneutics," 308, and Breck, *Scripture in Tradition*, 9.

their time have now been forgotten or ignored and he sees in it a process of self-renewing tradition. It would be false authenticity, "*archaization*" he calls it, if one should attempt to revive texts that have nothing in common with the current community and church and, moreover, texts that may even be obstacles to receiving and hearing the message of salvation.[22] This is the area where Gadamer's concepts of the history of effect and temporal distance very much relate.

John Breck has another helpful concept when he denotes the two degrees of inspiration: revelatory inspiration in the case of the Bible and anamnetic inspiration for Holy Tradition.[23] This helps to preserve the inspiration of the Bible and yet to understand the Bible as theandric, theanthropic and synergetic cooperation between God and human authors. God and humans are authors on the same level. Therefore, Scripture is fully divine and fully human. It is this divine-human character of the Bible that introduces the need for critical thinking.[24] Namely, the human side of the divine-human character of the Bible gives one the right to find a legitimate place for it, since the "reasoning brain is a gift from God."[25] Nevertheless, we cannot accept the reasoning brain in its entirety, because the Bible is not only a collection of historical documents, but a testimony, a book of the church that encompasses God's word.

For exploration of the human side of the Bible, one needs critical inquiry and for the divine part of the Bible one needs faith and meditation. This means that reading Scripture is not so much a matter of reading something back into Scripture (*eisegesis*), but recognizing the fundamental message that is there. After all, inspiration from the Orthodox perspective cannot be limited to the Bible, but is expanded to the whole life of the church. Not only is the writing inspired, but the reading, talking and practice as well. Biblical inspiration would not be enough.[26]

Still, if exegesis is a divine-human enterprise based upon synergy or cooperation between the divine spirit and a human interpreter and is expressed in the form of a hermeneutical circle, what is the role of the exegete, hermeneutician and reader? This role is decisive. Even the church Fathers repeated many times that the life of the interpreter is the main condition for

---

22. See McGuckin, "Recent Biblical Hermeneutics," 311.

23. See Breck, *Power of the Word*, 106.

24. See Karavidopoulos who stresses the advantages of historical critical methods, but rejects them if they lead to conclusions that are different than the dogmas of the Church. Karavidopoulos, "Offenbarung und Inspiration," 157.

25. Ware, *Orthodox Way*, 110.

26. See Galitis and Mantzaridis, *Glauben aus dem Herzen*, 79.

reliable interpretation and that methods of interpretation come into very close connection with the spiritual life of the interpreter.

Especially monastic hermeneutics, such as John Cassian, show that interpretation is possible as a synthesis of the Holy Spirit, who inhabits the scholar, as well as human creative efforts, where a scholar must submit himself to the Spirit's guidance. However, the individuality or self-sufficiency of the exegete is not possible as an option, for the theory of synergy involves an interrelation of the corporate dimensions, such as church and Tradition, including a mystical self-evolving experience. In other words, the Bible must be read within the same Spirit who inspired it, but at the same time humans must work, read and repeat the reading in order to discover the meaning. The scholar or believer must therefore always begin from within the community, which includes liturgy, preaching, prayer and sacraments, for this will prevent readers from a too individualistic mysticism and from heretical misunderstanding.

Hilarion Alfeyev, in this context, talks about the Eucharistic body of Christ and the Eucharist that unites the community with God and each other, when the personal experience of each individual believer should be incorporated in the collective memory of the church. Alfeyev quotes St Germanus that the church is an earthly heaven, where the heavenly God lives and moves, which is a very important aspect of Orthodox ecclesiology and is based upon the biblical teaching that Christ did not abandon the disciples after his Ascension, but remained among them to the very end of the age (Matt 28:20).[27]

Furthermore, in order to preserve the hermeneutical circle between Scripture and Tradition, we must use the collocation first used by David Tracy, who told Aristotle Papanikolaou that the Orthodox have an advantage over Roman Catholics and Protestants, because they know how to think like a tradition.[28] Papanikolaou rejects this exclusive relationship between Orthodoxy and tradition and claims that although Orthodoxy has never lived the Western story, the Orthodox are still caught up by it. Furthermore, the most explicit treatment of tradition appears only as a reaction to the "Protestant rejection of tradition, and the Roman Catholic juxtaposition of tradition and scripture."[29]

---

27. Alfeyev, *Mystery of Faith*, 97–98.

28. His lecture in Prague "Tradition and Identity Formation," presented at the International Conference *Tradition and Innovation: Reflections on Different Streams of Orthodox Theological Thinking in Exile and its Impact on Ecumenical Dialogue*, delivered on May 19, 2013. In the modified version published as Papanikolaou, "Tradition as Reason and Practice," 91–104.

29. Papanikolaou, "Tradition as Reason and Practice," 91–92.

Paradoxically, Papanikolaou urges the Orthodox to be more traditionalist, not less. However, he accepts Tracy's statement and redefines it. In order to achieve this, he uses a simple but expressive example—he parallels tradition to dance-classes. Because, one cannot begin with an advanced class, but must begin with the beginners and follow the principles and the techniques tested by time in order to advance. The point is that advancement in dancing also includes understanding of the things surrounding (let us say, the theory of dance) and includes an awareness of how these practices were developed. Exactly this development of the dancer points to the fact that they become a part of a certain institutionalization that transcends the mere learning of dance—steps. Papanikolaou uses this example in order to show that there is no tradition without institutionalization, but it says much more.

He claims that tradition develops not only within time, but also within the community and that advancing in dance is not a static process, but is an interaction between history and the individual. This interaction between the rules and the practice is not a matter of the past, but is a matter of presence, the matter of a specific and particular act (the dancing figure), of a Christian becoming a part of this tradition. With advances in his spiritual life, learning more and more steps, procedures, history, the dancer (Christian) comes to the moment when he forgets the steps and begins to feel the music/Tradition and *becomes* it. Papanikolaou writes that "being a Christian is a traditioned existence that is more than what we proclaim in creeds or even Scripture; being a Christian is an embodied realization of the greatest commandment, which for the Orthodox is a living communion with the life of God."[30] This is easier to grasp if we remember the oral origin of Tradition, which is easy to forget because post-Guttenberg modern culture is almost entirely based on writing.

So far it has been shown that Scripture is not only the work of God but, at the same time, the work of men and women and sacred authors from different times and places. The question that arises out of this situation is how *human* words can carry such *holy* meanings. In order to answer this question, Orthodox theologians often explain that this lies in the person of Christ, who is the best example of how the human and divine can be united and permeated together. The Incarnation of Christ into a human body, as the paradigm for a divine and human character, is parallel with the Bible as an incarnation of God's saving will embodied in human categories and language. This parallel shows that the human and the divine can coexist

---

30. Papanikolaou, "Tradition as Reason and Practice," 100.

and neither of them will be changed.[31] This Orthodox formulation of the character of the Bible as a human-divine reality is a mystery in the same way as Christ. Many questions arise, such as were holy authors aware of the meanings of their words? Can we know what was in their minds and hearts? Can we know how God revealed himself to them?

Mihoc answers differently and writes that the words of the Bible are not divine and cannot capture divinity, but have a certain ability to give us some knowledge of God. He uses Gregory of Nyssa's term *anakrasis* that expresses the way *Logos* is "mixing" with the biblical words, but the mixture is imperfect, because human words are limited.[32] This means that the divine God adapts to the abilities of our language and this is the role of anthropomorphisms in the Bible (God speaks, sees, etc.), to accommodate to our capacity of apprehension. Therefore, it can be said that the exact words are not inspired, only their *meaning* is inspired. This is actually why the church is required for the interpretation of the Bible, since by itself it is not autonomous.

Thus, if the exegete wants to grasp the meaning of Christ (1Cor 2:16), one must be a member and part of the community. The Bible cannot be separated from the church since there is a hermeneutic circle between the church and the Bible. The church refers to the Bible as its basis but, at the same time, the Bible is produced by the church, the New Testament as well as the Old Testament.

Relationship between Contemplation and Science

When discussing the relationship between contemplation and science, particularly the question of whether they are mutually exclusive, we must address the issues of knowledge, the divine-human nature of Scripture, critical thinking, and the concept of typology and *theōria*.

At this point a distinction between two types of knowledge must be mentioned, the first coming out of human communion with God and experienced through the spiritual intellect residing in one's heart, the second arriving through the senses and intellectual powers. Each of these types has its own method and field of inquiry, but what is even more important, they are not necessarily in opposition.

---

31. See on this Hopko, "Bible in the Orthodox Church," 68–73; or Stylianopoulos, "Scripture and Tradition," 23.

32. See Mihoc, "Principles of Orthodox Hermeneutics," 298–99.

Alkiviadis Calivas, professor emeritus at Holy Cross School of Theology, calls it a *"unitary approach to knowledge,"* of heart and mind.[33] This unitary knowledge is hidden from human eyes, because people are weak and their abilities are limited to only the material aspect of things. Moreover, it is hidden from them due to the separation of faith and science, which, when separated, are false barriers. Namely, science and faith are two ways of dealing with reality and opening the mysteries of the created world, but cannot be separated from one another. Therefore, it is very important that modern Orthodox hermeneutics studies the methodologies and trends in human and natural sciences and assesses exclusivist positions, reason-dominated worldviews and faith-dominated worldviews, as barriers to the more holistic understanding of knowledge. The critical resources of Western hermeneutics for the study of the Bible are vast, but it would still be a mistake to think that these resources can manage to grasp the fullness of the Bible, especially its spiritual dimension. The mystical and monastic approach, when isolated, will similarly fail to grasp the fullness.

The main concept that helps lies in the nature of Scripture, where discernment between the divine-human enterprise is preserved. We spoke about it briefly in the previous section as divine-human communion is the "first principle upon which all theological thinking is grounded."[34] That goes back to the patristic period, does not rely on opposition to the West and is in the heart of theologians such as Lossky, Florovsky, Yannaras and Zizioulas.[35] The cause for biblical criticism lies in the fact that the Bible is a result of the human spirit, but its content is the word of God inspired by the Holy Spirit. This means that the exegesis should also deal with both natures of Scripture, the human as well as the divine.

There are two theologians who deal with hermeneutics related to the divine-human character in Orthodox theology of Scripture and Tradition. The first is Vasile Mihoc, professor of the New Testament at the University of Sibiu, Romania, who orients his work around the problem of *what out of the Western exegetical methods has value for Orthodoxy?* On one hand, he admits that the apostolic and post-apostolic tradition remain essential

---

33. See Calivas, "Science, Technology and Faith," 35.

34. Says Papanikolaou, "Tradition or Identity Politics," 21.

35. Even in spite of the differences between Lossky and Zizioulas, their theology of personhood is remarkably similar, and for both it is the most adequate form of expressing divine-human communion. There are accusations that the theology of personhood is a Western influence on Orthodox theological discourse and therefore is not Orthodox. Papanikolaou radically rejects this, and states that the Orthodox theology of personhood is the clear manifestation of thinking as tradition and a logical development of divine-human communion. See Papanikolaou, "Tradition or Identity Politics," 21.

for Eastern Christians, but on the other this does not exclude relying on modern research and methods. Hermeneutics in the Orthodox understanding is not simply dealing with the words of Scripture, but is the process of a correct and deeper understanding of God's plan of salvation. Therefore, historical methods are not to be refused, as they are essential tools.

Another example of an Orthodox theologian who uses critical thinking as a part of the divine-human relation, is Konstantin Nikolakopoulos, professor in the New Testament Department of the Orthodox Theology Institute in Munich. In his *Die 'unbekannten Hymnen' des Neuen Testaments* (2000) habilitation he offers an overview of hermeneutical methods in Western and Eastern churches, and notes a different understanding of science between the emphasis on the historicity of Christianity in the West and the aspect of holy mystery in the East. Nikolakopoulos calls these two approaches *analytic* and *synthetic* and calls for a convergence between them as absolutely required.[36]

The analytic approach requires a direct analysis of the text of the Bible without giving mystery the possibility of presenting itself, while a synthetic approach must have the entire picture, i.e., the expressed mystery of God, yet the return to the text is missing and there is nothing that guarantees protection against errors. Each of these two very different approaches has its advantages and its weak points, although neither of them possesses the absolute meaning, which is both supernatural and historical. In his latest book *Das Neue Testament in der Orthodoxen Kirche* (2012) Nikolakopoulos is especially attentive to the theandric character of the Bible, which in his case means that he recognizes the need for the methods of interpretations of Scripture and does not exclude them.[37]

Although Nikolakopoulos does not say it, what we have here is the basic definition of the hermeneutical circle as a move from the individual to know the whole and from the whole to grasp the individual, where each needs the other. Reading the Bible in a closed hermeneutical circle means that there is an interaction between the reader, who comes to the text with his own context and way of thinking and the biblical context itself.[38]

36. Nikolakopoulos, *Neue Testament*, 304.

37. See Nikolakopoulos, *Neue Testament*, 20–21. The part on the relationship between Orthodox interpretation and historical-critical method is very important here. (see pages 303–17).

38. "We seek understanding and faith through the reading of God's word, yet we can only truly understand that word through eyes of faith. Faith depends on the word, yet proper interpretation of the word requires faith" (D-Vasilescu, "Orthodox Christian Approach," 40). The author in this article attempts to show as a misunderstanding the opinion that the members of Orthodox Christianity do not read it critically. She does this by showing the role of tradition in interpretation of the Bible, and discussing the role of the method used.

The concept that binds contemplation and science, as well as the historical and eschatological, is the patristic principle of *theōria*. What does that word mean? The Greek noun *theōria*, corresponding to the Latin *spectaculum*, has as a primary meaning seeing, beholding, and its origins lie in the verb *theōrein* (to look at, to observe, to consider).[39] In the Early church the main meaning of the term *theōria* was a vision and contemplation, while in the biblical context it means especially the vision by which the prophet sees the future, as well as its messianic and eschatological reality. When the church Fathers employed the concept, they related its meaning back to encounters with God as testified in the Bible, in particular in the prophets in whom they found the figurative examples of what a vision of the messianically transformed future might mean. The term *theōria* was known in both theological schools from this period. In the Alexandrian school they used it as an equivalent to allegorical interpretation, a meaning which was discovered through allegorical exegesis and connected with contemplation. This was opposite to Antiochene exegesis, where it referred to a higher meaning, but still based on the letter and history. *Theōria*, although used also in Alexandria, was rooted in Antiochene understanding, which affirmed that the spiritual meaning cannot be separated from the literal one and connected *theōria* with typology, rather than allegory.

The School of Antioch stood against allegory from Alexandria, and stressed the literal and spiritual sense of the text, with literal as intended by the sacred author and spiritual as the significance of the event for later interpreters. While allegory saw two different significances in the text, literal and spiritual, but only the latter was important, for *theōria* based on typology there is no separation between the spiritual and literal sense, as the antitype is already present in the type. The contribution and relevancy of *theōria* lies in several areas: (i) it helps to avoid fundamentalist tendencies, (ii) it accepts the historical grounding of the *kerygma*, (iii) its holistic character legitimizes and embraces a biblical method, (iv) it does not limit the revelation only to the Scripture, but expands it also to the Tradition and (v), *theōria* restores the doxological quality of the biblical texts.[40]

This concept that maintains balance in the spiritual revelation as well historical mediation arrived in modern Orthodox hermeneutics through the rehabilitation of non-Orthodox authors who focused on fulfilment in a human community. I especially have in mind the work of Bertrand de Margerie (1923–2003), who has already been mentioned in the section

---

39. One of the best works on the problem of *theōria* is Nassif, "Spiritual Exegesis," 343–77; see also Breck, "*Theoria* and Orthodox Hermeneutics," 195–219.

40. Cf. Breck, "Orthodoxy and the Bible Today," 155–57.

about alternative work with sources. In his *An Introduction to the History of Exegesis,* he speaks about the shift from a prophetic intention to a prophetic fulfilment. He claims that *theōria* "was intended rather to allude to a twofold objective realization of a prophecy than to a subjective awareness of a two-stage prophecy,"[41] and that fulfilment does not occur in chronological history, but within the liturgical life of the church. In this sense the *theōria* also becomes a vision of a post-biblical exegete and not only the vision of a prophet or New Testament author.

John Breck was inspired by this account of the aspect of prophetic fulfilment in the typological relationship, and for that reason he created a hermeneutical model that makes use of the historical element of the typological relationship, which is converted into the liturgical life of the interpretative community.[42] For Breck, *Theōria* discerns between a spiritual meaning and the biblical event, where the application and fulfilment of the event can be inner-biblical or eschatological.[43] Breck distinguishes among three levels of *theōria*: (i) the vision of the prophet, (ii) the reception of the text in the New Testament and (iii), the interpretation of the post-biblical reader. Of these three, the most important for Breck is the third level, which is the church represented in and by the liturgical life of the church.[44] He would argue that this appropriation of meaning in the worshiping community is the primary one, while its intended meaning is secondary. *Theōria* thus does not deal explicitly with the relation between past and present, as it contains a self-actualizing quality and fulfilment, which is the role of the Holy Spirit. A hermeneutical bridge is created between the literal meaning of the original context and the people in a current context. He underscores that this hermeneutical gap is only overcome by the person of the Holy Spirit, who reactualizes the biblical events in the church across the centuries.[45] It was the Holy Spirit that inspired Jewish authors and apostles during the writing and who inspired the church Fathers during their interpretation. It is the Holy

---

41. Margerie, *Introduction,* 180.

42. See Margerie, *Introduction,* 180. Breck sees that there are two fundamental presuppositions for *theōria* as a hermeneutical method: that Scripture is inspired by God, and that typology is the key to the right interpretation. Typology is a double movement, from past into the future, and from the future into the past. Historical events need to be considered in their much wider context, as signs, *typoi,* prophecies that reveal antitypes. Breck, *Power of the Word,* 95.

43. See Breck, *Power of the Word,* 102–5. "*Theoria* represents two constitutive elements in the *history of salvation,* a history in which we find ourselves directly and personally involved. . . . To Orthodox Christians, however, this experience becomes actual within the *liturgical life of the Church*" (Breck, *Power of the Word,* 104).

44. See Breck, *Power of the Word,* 93–113.

45. See Breck, *Power of the Word,* 31–32.

Spirit who in all generations inspires people during their interpretation and reveals to them the true meaning of *theōria*.

Inspired by these thoughts, Mihoc calls the Holy Spirit the hermeneutic bridge[46] and Osborne calls it the *"hermeneutical force."*[47] A pneumatological dimension means two things: first, that there is the Spirit's activity in the formation of the Scripture and, second, there the Spirit also has another role in the interpretation. Just as the Holy Spirit illumined the authors of Scripture, Holy Spirit inspired the believers to believe, love and guard the Word. The Holy Spirit is the illuminating agent who works in the church and enables human readers to apprehend the Bible correctly. This also points to the unfinished process of formation of the Scripture that, without the readers and interpreters, is not finished, "No canon of Scripture is able to be formed without interpretation."[48]

In this connection with *theōria* as a contemplative reading which grows from the literal meaning of the text but transcends in recognizing the one who contemplates to participate in the eschatological messianic reality, it is important to mention the mysteriological and poetic-mystical expressions of the salvific events by God in the liturgical celebration.[49] In order to avoid the possibility of recreating and rewriting anew the original salvific events, this trans-historical celebration is useful, for it does not neglect or ignore the importance of the historical events that still remain valid and places the emphasis on the present worship of "God in the event as on the event itself."[50]

An often-neglected fact of typology is that *typos* is not just a sign pointing to the future or to the transcendent reality, but is also a historical place where the future already *is* present. For example, the Apostle Paul in the The first epistle to Corinthians 10 presents the interpretation of the body of Christ as the Eucharistic community *ekklesia*. He introduces these thoughts with reference to the Israelites on their travel through the desert. The Israelites were baptized in the cloud and in the sea and all ate the same spiritual food and drank the same spiritual drink from the spiritual rock and that rock was Christ. This is an image of the rock from Exodus 17 and Numbers 20, which mentions only the rock and not Christ.

---

46. Mihoc, "Principles of Orthodox Hermeneutics," 311–14.
47. Osborne, "Many and the One," 286.
48. Prokurat, "Pneumatological Dimension," 105.
49. See Prokurat, "Orthodox Interpretation of Scripture," 63.
50. Osborne, "Many and the One," 298. Florovsky also asserts the importance of history, and writes: "historic events are the source and basis of all Christian faith and hope" (Florovsky, *Bible, Church, Tradition*, 24–25).

Nevertheless, according to the Apostle Paul, Jesus was already present in their midst in a pre-incarnated form. Here we have a virtual identification of rock and Jesus, between the prototype and antitype, where the eschatological antitype is already perceived as present, i.e., existing in the historical prototype. Thus, the historical prototype already participates in the eschatological antitype. The rock in the text is a type in a double sense. First, it points to the life and work of Jesus and second, it points to the place where Jesus' deeds are already present in the history of the Israelites. Similar typological interpretations can also be used with the manna in the desert or the sacrificial lamb. Both of these are a *prototype* of the incoming Christ and both already contained the future reality. Therefore, the church can see in manna and the lamb the activity of *logos*. The analysis of double-interpretation is very important in order to prove that God acts within history and that eschatological reality is present and is manifested in history, as well as that in order to prove that we can mediate not only the content of understanding of who we are in relation to each other, to the world in which we live and to God. Yet also to understand across various historical periods and different cultures.

The principle of *theōria* as a hermeneutical key for uniting historical and trans-historical aspects of Scripture is also asserted by Bradley Nassif in his articles. Similarly to Breck, he proposed *theōria* as a hermeneutic link and both agree that the *theōria* within itself brings together literal and contemplative elements. Further, they agree that the activity of the Holy Spirit is behind the process and that its final aim is the perceived life of believers. While for Breck the *theōria* is defined as an intuitive perception of a sacred author by a later interpreter, which links the literal and spiritual sense, Nassif sees three models of how Antiochenes utilized *theōria*, while Breck sees only one interpretative model. According to this, *theōria* was once a literal method of messianic exegesis, sometimes a mystical method of textual meaning, sometimes it was the historical sense, but "sometimes it *was not*."[51]

Chapter 9 discussed Orthodox hermeneutics from the perspective achieved in the previous chapters. The first part, dealing with Gadamerian hermeneutics, compelled us to have a section where the reception of Gadamer's work is closely analyzed in Orthodoxy from the perspective of modern Orthodox hermeneutics. The receptions of Gadamer by Andrew Louth, Assaad Kattan and Nicolae Turcan were presented. The continuation of the chapter was based on hermeneutical themes arising from this discussion and identified as important for Orthodoxy, first the role of Tradition and Scripture as classics as well as the bearers of meaning and second, the

---

51. Nassif, "The 'Spiritual Exegesis' of Scripture," 468.

discussion concerning contemplation and science. The hermeneutical circle between Scripture and Tradition was in the central focus, which means that the two are not in contrast or in too close cooperation, but in the form of a hermeneutical circle. Tradition and Scripture form the core of Orthodox hermeneutics with another concept, which is a community of believers and this is the theme of the next chapter.

10

The Role of Interpretative Community

PREVIOUS ideas create the basis for another concept, which is a community of believers, often called ecclesial reading. This reassesses the radical clash between the divine and human in our perception of the revelation of transcendence and includes the elements of participation and historicity of the interpretative community. In this case, they reside within the church, which leads to the liturgical dimension of current Orthodox hermeneutics.

Ecclesial Reading and the Community

The role of the interpretative community was strongly accentuated by Gadamer, who in his concept of a conversation between the *I* and *Thou* shows the role of community, conversation and *being with the other* as a necessity for a true revelation of meaning. Interpretation must be understood as not only one with Tradition, as previously, but also with the community. It is accepted, that the Bible is:

> the scripture of the Church, that it has proper meaning only within the life and experience of the People of God . . . cannot be isolated from its organic context within the churchly community in which and from which it exists.[1]

This definition enables one to include in the concept of the church the interpretation of the Bible because the place of the Bible, its *Sitz im Leben*,

---

1. Hopko, "Bible in the Orthodox Church," 66. The church is not to be understood here as a human organization, but as a "theandric life of progressive union with God through Christ, in the Holy spirit" (Hopko, "Bible in the Orthodox Church," 80).

is the church. This relationship is double: (i) Christians *receive* Scripture through the church that canonized it and (ii), Christians also *interpret* the Bible in and through the church.[2] The hermeneutical circle is in place here. In order that the church *is* church, it must be wholly expressive of the Bible, is used in the liturgy and all symbols are taken from the canonical writings. It is also used in the lectionary, as many hymns use the words of the Bible and it is used in sermons, as well as in religious education in schools.

The ecclesial reading of Scripture is a unique distinction of Orthodox churches and a unique suggestion for the hermeneutical debate in biblical scholarship.[3] The words of current Orthodox hermeneutical theologians are very clear: "the Church is the proper locus for the interpretation,"[4] and the "faith community is the final interpretative authority."[5] The implication of this statement is very straightforward. The Bible is not given for people to grasp theological truths or to receive ethical commands and norms, but to experience the life of communion that exists in God. It also means that Scripture and church cannot be separated and presuppose each other, thus Bible passages should be placed and understood within the context of the church.[6] The life of communion is addressed to each person individually, therefore reading of Scripture is personal, but cannot be separated from the community. The *book* and the *community* are inseparable. Without the church and Tradition, the believers are as the eunuch from Acts 8. Vasile Mihoc declares that believers need someone to guide them and, according to the Orthodox understanding, this guidance is provided by the church, which has authority to interpret God's word.[7] McGuckin uses the principle of consonance to explain how the church interprets Scripture: consonance with the ecclesial tradition, with the saints as the primary requirement for the Orthodox interpreter, as well as consonance with the Holy Spirit, who inspired the text. Consonance does not mean the "monotonous repetition of past utterance" warns McGuckin, but rather means the new application of text or narrative within the community.[8]

2. See Vassiliadis, "Canon and Authority," 29.
3. See Crisp, "Orthodox Biblical Scholarship," 130–33.
4. Breck, "Orthodox Principles of Biblical Interpretation," 88.
5. Stylianopoulos, *New Testament*, 36 n. 24.
6. Does it mean that the church cannot be wrong? Alexander Negrov quotes Russian authors who say this, "The Church cannot be wrong," but are they correct? See Negrov, "Three Hermeneutical Horizons," 88. Negrov lists the quotes from Russian scholars of the nineteenth century who stress the church as the final authority of interpretation.
7. See also Mihoc, "Principles of Orthodox Hermeneutics," 318.
8. See McGuckin, "Recent Biblical Hermeneutics," 311–16.

Pessimism is also appropriate in this regard. The Bible is used for the daily worship of Christians, in personal piety, but "only a small minority seeks daily nourishment." Breck summarizes the current situation as *we kiss it but do not read it, expository preaching is missing*.[9] A similar situation in Russia is as described by Alfeyev, who says that for Russian Orthodox Christians, the Bible is not part of their life and they are disinterested in it. He sees this as wrong and calls for a new translation based on the contemporary critical biblical text. He strongly urges that the achievements of biblical scholarship from the West should be made available to Russian Church circles. Besides the new translation, there should also be a Bible commentary that reflects several layers of comments that include the textual, historical-archaeological, exegetical, and ecclesial-theological.[10]

Wide diversity arises when Orthodox theologians try to answer how the individual reading of the Bible is contrasted with the interpretative community. For example, Mihoc states that we are encouraged to read the Scripture individually, "but not as isolated individuals. We read it as embedded in the Orthodox church."[11] Anton Ugolnik is very critical toward a movement that finds a biblical piety in harmony with Orthodox faith. He accepts private devotion and private reading of the Bible as important but, at the same time, only as a supplement to the proper liturgical and sacramental community that has the primary position in any encounter with the Word.[12]

Generally, it can be alleged that, in Orthodox biblical interpretation, there is little room for the individuality and self-sufficiency of the exegete. There is logic in this, because if authority is derived from an individual, or even from a group of individuals, then there is a certain possibility that mistakes and errors will occur. But there also exists a concept of *personalist ecclesiology*, according to which the freedom from the Holy Spirit is personal, just as responsibility is personal. All phases of church life, from catechetical instruction up to communion practices are a personal commitment of the Christian. Meyendorff posits that the word *melos* (1 Cor 6:15) that designates a *member* (Eph 4:25) is always applied to individuals and never to corporate entities. But, he continues, this is a dangerous thought because it can lead to pietism or emotional mysticism, as can be seen in many revival churches. Therefore, the task of Orthodoxy is to *recognize* the

---

9. See Breck, *Scripture in Tradition*, 17–18.

10. See Alfeyev, "Orthodox Theology in the Twenty-First," 131–32.

11. Mihoc, "Principles of Orthodox Hermeneutics," 319.

12. The axioms that Ugolnik sets regarding interpretation and private reading are: (i) the act of interpretation is not private but social in its nature, (ii) response to the Gospel is a collective act, (iii) the environment for proclamation of the Gospel is oral and public rather than private and written. Ugolnik, "Orthodox Hermeneutic in the West," 109.

communal, corporate entities, where the church is a sacrament and a community. Personal experience receives its *authenticity* from the sacrament and is *given* to the community.[13]

Therefore, prioritizing the communal aspect over the individual has its opponents, among which the most important is the recent work of John Galanis. He accepts that Holy Scripture is realized in the sacramental life of the church, but the private use of the Bible is still not prohibited and was already present in the Early church. There are many testimonies about private use in the Bible itself that lead to the significance of private use of scripture. When Christ showed opposition to accusations that he and his disciples ate corn on the Sabbath, He asked them if they never read the story about David (Mark 12:25; Matt 21:42). There are also examples for the private use of Scripture in the post-apostolic era and its writings, such as the Barnabas epistle, Ignatius of Antioch, the first epistle of Clement to Corinth, Polycarp, and others.[14] Private Bible study reached its final form in the fourth century, but then it coincided with the public, ecclesiastic use in the Holy liturgy. Galanis warns that the reason for this was that, at that time, many apocryphal texts appeared and were gaining popularity among the people. Therefore Cyril of Jerusalem writes, "Don't read privately any book which is not read in the Church," and Basil the Great confirms "Read only the books which are read in the Church."[15]

Liturgical Dimension of Hermeneutics

A specific category of ecclesial reading inspired by Gadamer's concepts is that Scripture should be celebrated in corporate worship, more precisely in a liturgy as the framework within which Orthodox Christians encounter the Gospel, where the Bible is more celebrated than interpreted.[16] The basic presuppositions that must be taken into account when talking about Orthodox liturgical hermeneutics are (i), Scripture was and is liturgical, what was once a liturgy became Scripture and (ii), Eastern Christians experience the Bible and its interpretation primarily as a liturgical celebration.[17]

13. See Meyendorff, *Living Tradition*, 179–81.
14. For more examples Galanis, "Use of the Holy Scripture," 115–16.
15. Galanis, "Use of the Holy Scripture," 115–16.
16. This is the main thesis also of Prokurat, that the place of Scripture and its interpretation is the liturgical celebration. See his study: Prokurat, "Orthodox Interpretation of Scripture," 60–61.
17. Florovsky describes this with *ut legem credendi statuat lex orandi* (so that the rule of worship should establish the rule of faith). Florovsky, *Bible, Church, Tradition*, 84.

Here, Breck sees a difference from Roman Catholics and Protestants. While they center on magisterium or word, the Orthodox unite word and liturgy in the church. He says that Protestant charismatic pneumatology is famous because it insists on the "spiritual illumination of an individual in his personal reading of the Bible."[18] Breck sees in it the loss of an ecclesial dimension—Protestants have dogma situated in the Scripture, but there is no interpretative body within which the interpretation occurs. He further mentions two dimensions of the Orthodox understanding of the liturgy. The first is horizontal, historical, paschal, or anamnetic, which participates in a liturgical worship as the *past* (salvific events of the Bible), *present* (reliving those events in worship) and *future* (anticipation of events to come). The second is pentecostal, epicletic, vertical, or transcendent and occurs as the Holy Spirit, which draws the believers into experiencing these redemptive acts in the liturgical and Eucharistic celebration.[19]

When talking about the liturgy, one of the ways to approach and understand it is as a Christian duty and to consider it as a real theology. This liturgical participation in the Tradition as well as in the *eschaton* prevents disconnecting the study of liturgy from the study of theology.[20] Philip Zymaris insists that the divorce of theology from liturgy is a development in Western Christianity and is not rooted in Orthodox teaching. This differentiation between theology and liturgy was not perceived even at the very beginnings, where theory was not an intellectual exercise, but considered as liturgical participation. As he says, not only the mind, but *all* the senses somehow participate in worship and experience it, because icons can be touched, incense smelled, communion tasted and sermon heard. These examples serve to confirm that *lex orandi est lex credendi*, i.e., what we pray is what we believe and what we do in church is exactly what we teach in theology. The relation between the two elements is explained by two approaches: the one who *prays* is a theologian, and the one who is a theologian *prays*. This illustrates the balance between theological thought and the inner movement of the prayer, while also insisting that *prayer* is the priority, where the one who prays is the deepest theologian. Prayer in the Spirit is genuine theology beyond words, concepts and theories.[21]

18. Breck, *Power of the Word*, 31.
19. Breck, *Power of the Word*, 131.
20. See the very important study by Zymaris, "The Forgotten Connection."
21. "To speak about God is to speak about abyss, mystery, sacred" (Bobrinskoy, *Compassion of the Father*, 126). Boris Bobrinskoy here gives four basic requirements for what he calls a living theology, a spiritual understanding renewed in spirit. Beside the *metanoia*, renewal of self, feeding on the Scriptures and knowledge and love, there is then also being in the communion of the church. Bobrinskoy, *Compassion of the Father*, 127–30.

Breck's discernment between these two dimensions of the Orthodox understanding of liturgy is an appropriate starting place from which to point out the vertical dimension of the liturgy, which has the form of icon and Holy Spirit, namely it is the symbolic participation in icons. While in English the word icon (*eikon*, image) refers mainly to a painting on a prepared wooden panel, the Orthodox meaning of the concept of icon is much wider than a pictorial representation of a religious object and includes decorations on walls, mosaics and frescoes. Icons were present in Christianity from the very beginning.

A very early story is handed down of when Christ wiped his image on the white cloth that healed King Abgar of Edessa from leprosy. Christians from the very beginning accepted the Old Testament critique of making images of God taken from the Decalogue (cf. Exod 20:4–5; Exod 33:20) yet, at the same time, believed that Christ is the *eikon* of an invisible God (cf. Col 1:15). When God binds with time and space, only then are we led into a new perspective, since the person of Christ is the *revealed* form of the face of God.

This tension between the forbidden idolatry and the practice of the church to use images in spreading the Gospel never disappeared, and was a matter of enormous discord. This controversy culminated in the period of iconoclasm (resistance, literally: smashing the images) from 726 to 843, where any practice that presented God in a visible form was called *idolatry* and blasphemy.[22] This iconoclast movement combined several outlooks such as longing for a pure spirituality, teaching of monophysites on one nature and including Judaic and Islamic prohibitions of images. There were several arguments at hand, the most widespread of which was that God was against icons, as was especially visible due to the military success of non-iconic Arabs over iconic Christians. This was understood as a sign of God's anger over the Christians for honoring icons. As a result of their opposition to icons, Emperors Leo III and Constantine V had a degree of military success, which only confirmed the correctness of their iconoclasm. The dogmatic basis for the existence of icons was laid at the Council of Trullo (691–692, also called Quinisext), where its eighty-second rule reacted against the common practice of replacing the human image of God with a symbol. It also asserted the connection of the icon with the Incarnation—depictions of God in material and animal symbols (even as a lamb) were not allowed, but only in the form of man. One consequence of

---

22. The opposition to the veneration of icons came from two successive emperors Leo III (717–741) and Constantine V (741–775), this crisis lasted for more than a century. In the first phase Emperor Leo III Isaurus issued a decree in 726 forbidding the veneration of icons.

the eighty-second rule is that the meaning of the symbol lies not in *what* is being represented, but in the *method* by which it is represented. This led in the following centuries to the creation of art not only in content, but also in form.[23]

Icons offer a unique artistic experience and can easily attract even the non-Orthodox, as they invite one for meditation and silence while observing them. However, they are much more than that, as they re-present something greater than is possible to be perceived by one's physical capabilities. The reason is that the icon is not merely an object used in worship, or an adornment that people kiss and treat as a sacred object, but icons are windows to another world and they help one over the doorstep to that other world. According to Mariamna Fortounatto, an icon is a microcosm that links the created world with the divine.[24]

Further, an icon used in worship cannot be reduced to an aesthetic object and lose its mediating function, which is connected with the symbolic function with two elements of the hermeneutical circle, portrait (type) and model (prototype). This symbolic function can be understood in various ways. We could say that an icon can represent the reality outside the actual image based on the *homoioma* likeness and argue with St Theodore the Studite for the relation between type and prototype with the one between a seal and the print—they show the same thing, only in different forms. But this still does not answer if a portrait has the power to carry the divine within itself, or only reveals (points to) the divine. In this connection, the one who paints the icon in his act offers matter back to its creator by creating God's image in the icon and the depicted subject matter also gives sacred meaning to the icon.

Theologically, the theology of icons connects the notion of revelation with its expression as an image, as it accepts that revelation and Tradition can be passed on via various ways and not only through the Bible as the privileged character of God's message. Theologically, an icon is connected as well with the interpretative community mentioned in the previous section. That is to say, as Solrunn Nes writes in his *Mystical Language of Icons*, an icon is always a part of a particular religious practice. It is never complete and can never stand as an autonomous work, especially because the icon uses a language that can hardly be understood if the interpreter is not at home with Orthodox spirituality and theology. The icon is always a result

---

23. On the nature of icons see also Noble, "Vztah člověka k prostoru," 97–98.
24. Fortounatto and Cunningham, "Theology of the Icon," 136–37.

of the community, "community's faith, a faith which is shaped within 'the fellowship of the saints.'"[25]

There are several Orthodox and non-Orthodox authors who show the limits of this approach and move the discussion further, including Ivana Noble, Assaad Kattan, Tudor Rebengiuc and Richard Schneider, some whom were already mentioned.

According to Charles University professor Ivana Noble, one of the main characteristics of icons is a symbolic participation, according to which they allow humans to change, thanks to the light of God in which these icons are immersed.[26] She points out that this approach is also seen by Alexander Schmemann, where symbols do not create a new reality, but unlock the eschatological dimension of what is *already there* and lead the observer into a deeper level, where the Light is reflected and in whose reflection all things receive new meaning. This symbolic participatory notion results in two problems, to which Noble points. The first is the anti-West self-identification and the negative approach toward Western religious art. Noble argues the opposite on the example of three non-Orthodox paintings (from Vincent van Gogh, Marc Chagall and Pranas Domšaitis), who still bring the relation between the imagined and the indistinguishable, the concept of a person that encompasses and transcends what the modern West can know about it. For example, Evdokimov says in his *Orthodoxy* that the crisis of sacral art appeared when the "sacral" was exchanged for the "aesthetic" and beautiful, so there remained only forms and colors without any meaning.[27] Another venue of argument might follow Gadamer's critique of Kant's subjective aestheticism, focusing on *"how it happens"* rather than *"what it is."* The second problem with this theory of the icon to which Noble points is that, if one takes his invention from the icon creator, as well as his right to have freedom and understanding, this transforms him into a mere craftsman. This leads to the result that the very idea of synergy, based on the positive encounter of the divine and human, is actually broken.

---

25. Nes, *Mystical Language of Icons*, 12. The icon writer cannot incorporate its dogmatic interpretations, quite the contrary, as there is an obligation to work with the authorized models. This is a dogmatic function of the icon, there are also liturgical and didactic functions: the liturgical is because in the liturgy a celestial reality is revealed and the icon depicts the salvific events and helps to re-create the past in the present; the didactic is because the icon illustrates the events and the people of the Bible, and makes it easier to grasp them. See Nes, *Mystical Language of Icons*, 13–14.

26. See Noble, "Vztah člověka k prostoru," 95. Noble uses the approach of Leonid Ouspensky, that the icons are here to give answers to problems of life, not to reflect them. See on this his books *Theology of the Icons* and *The Meaning of Icons*.

27. Evdokimov, *Orthodoxy*, 108.

Assaad Kattan makes a second contribution to this discussion when he focuses on the application of Gadamer's hermeneutics in the iconology and liturgy of the Orthodox Church.[28] In order to achieve this, he takes icons as an example, where the main struggle is whether believers kiss the piece of wood or kiss Christ. Traditionally, it has been argued that the honor paid to the icon (image) passes to the archetype and is not intended for the paint and wood. But Kattan argues that this might not be enough and claims that the icon is "endowed with the divine character."[29] This approach has few proponents and therefore Kattan argues with the help of Maximus the Confessor, according to whom Christ became a symbol *himself* and the visible was united with the divine as an "unbreakable unity."[30]

There is a reciprocal relationship where the symbolized dwells in the symbolizing and the symbolizing accomplishes the presence of the symbolized, but without confusion or change. This christological argumentation of a symbol is very close to Gadamer's concept of the symbol from *Relevance of Beautiful*, according to which the work of art is not simply a symbol that points to something existing outside, but rather makes the object *present*. The hermeneutical task is therefore not to refer to a reality or to search for the reality that is beyond, but to create a new reality. It is interesting that Gadamer supports his argument with Martin Luther's teaching on the real presence of Christ in the Eucharist developed in the struggle with Huldrych Zwingli. Kattan thus does not apply to Orthodox theology only Gadamer's concept of artwork, but also Luther's Eucharistic teaching. Icons and art works are in this regard real symbols in the sense that they carry out the presence of the symbolized object. In order to support his argument more strongly, Kattan could also have used the concept of religious symbol of another Protestant thinker, Paul Tillich, according to whom the symbol opens a hidden reality and takes part in its meaning.[31]

Something similar is seen when we ask how the events of salvation history can become a part of the liturgy. For Orthodoxy, the celebration of liturgy is always a participation in the event itself—every Eucharist is a direct participation in the Last Supper, each celebration of Easter is a participation in the resurrection, etc.[32] These thoughts directly correlate with Gadamer's concept of the festival that interrupts the pragmatic experience

---

28. See his Kattan, "Byzantinische Ikone," 287–97, and Kattan, "Byzantine Icon," 165–77.

29. One of the followers mentioned is Louth, *St. John Damascene*, 209. See Kattan, "Byzantine Icon," 171.

30. Kattan, "Byzantine Icon," 172.

31. See especially his book *Dynamics of Faith*.

32. See Prokurat, "Orthodox Interpretation of Scripture," 63.

of time and embeds an experience of mystery into the festival. Gadamer illustrates this with the example of Christmas that occurred a long time ago, but is repeated every year, because the festival, the celebration of Christmas, creates its own time that interrupts our daily perception of time. The category of "trans-historical" that involves salvation events and re-presents them in the liturgy reflects the same hermeneutical experience that Kattan describes with Gadamer's assistance. An icon is therefore a symbol in the very meaning of its word, it connects and links the visible to the invisible.

Next is Tudor Rebengiuc, a young Romanian Orthodox scholar who in his study draws a very strong line between Gadamer's hermeneutics and Orthodox theology and architecture in a way similar to how Kattan positions Gadamer's concept of symbol in the center. Rebengiuc claims that a better understanding of iconic language of the Orthodox Church is achieved when we draw on Gadamer's hermeneutics, that offers the opportunity to grasp the icon on its own terms, while using a technique true to its nature and thus "bypassing the instrumental framework of Western metaphysics, and restoring the basis on which liturgical arts can attain their full potential once again."[33]

A hermeneutical insight into the theology of icons can improve the horizon of Orthodox liturgical arts, so that the icon not only *presents* divinity, but also makes divinity *present*. This view of an icon is similar to Gadamer's description of an image that is never separated from the object represented. An image is the emanation of the original, and exists as a part of it. For Gadamer the relationship between the original and its copy is one-sided, from original to copy, having the form of the emanation and is never an opposition. This ontology helps to explain the question of the sacredness and irreplaceability of an icon. Therefore, Rebengiuc introduces Gadamer's concepts of picture, sign, symbol and icon.

The Canadian Orthodox theologian, Richard Schneider, with his synergistic understanding of icons is the last author to identify the problem of being possibly identical and different at the same time, and he moves the discussion further. The problem he reacts to is that the perspective of the *viewer* is not taken into account. This indicates that the meaning of symbols does not lie in the *relationship* between the image and portrait, but between the *viewer* and the subject matter of the symbol. For Schneider, iconology is not a theology of icons, but a theology of the relationship between God and us.[34] In other words, the crucial relationship is not between the portrait

---

33. Rebengiuc, "Nature of Language," iv.

34. See his published presentation: Schneider, "Orthodox Iconography as Liturgical Art," 33–36.

and the model, but between the subject of the icon (model portrayed) and the viewer. This is a relation mediated and created by the physical object, a physical icon. Schneider in his lecture in Prague calls his iconography a "hermeneutic interpretation of icons."[35] Therefore, besides the standard terminology of iconology, he suggests also using the hermeneutical vocabulary such as *signum–res*, sign–the signified, *significant–signifié*.[36] Schneider points out that an icon cannot just copy the Byzantine pattern, but must be alive, contextual and consider the viewer. He says that seeing is interpretation, but this interpretation is that of a particular viewer, as the icon actually requires understanding and shows a need for interpretation. In his lectures at St Vladimir's Theological Seminary, Schneider opposed the Orthodox triumphalism that refuses to take into account a plurality of interpretations but which, at the same time, also closes the possibility of a true dialogue.

Schneider talks rather about the *transcendent path* and one of the reasons for his opposition is the influence of the theological method of Bernard Lonergan, a Jesuit who allows the possibility of the critical evaluation of interpretations. He actually shares several basic convictions with Gadamer. Both Gadamer and Lonergan reject the primacy of science and the starting point of epistemology, as well as the concept of objectivity. The reason Schneider brings a transcendent path into iconology is its human perspective, more precisely, its dubious hold over the human perspective that doubts the absolute validity of human interpretations.

Let me offer a short summary of the second part of this book. In chapter 6, we drew an analysis of the various ways hermeneutic theory emerged in the Orthodox world. Modern and postmodern Orthodox theological hermeneutics have been developing in various directions, as patristic hermeneutics, biblical hermeneutics and hermeneutical theology. We began with the paradigm shift in neo-patristic synthesis, although the return to the critical thinking of the Fathers was missing in this concept. Then we continued with neo-Orthodoxy, characterized by its interest in apophatic theology and hesychasm. Even so, this also resulted in an antithesis between the East and West. In the next step, we continued with the reestablishment of the relation between patristics and biblical studies in the seventies. Finally, we finished in the current period, where hermeneutics is distinct as a discipline

---

35. He called it so in his lecture in Prague entitled "Symbols of the Divine and Created Wholeness in the Icons of the Orthodox Iconographers in the West," presented at the International Scientific Conference organized by The Protestant Theological faculty of Charles University, *Symbolic Mediation of Wholeness in Western Orthodoxy*, delivered on May 22, 2014.

36. See Schneider, "Orthodox Iconography as Liturgical Art," 34.

that examines the premises that stipulate understanding, rather than a mere return to the Fathers.

Further, chapter 7 presented the representatives of two movements and waves in the twentieth century, followed by identifying the problems that arose from them, which we call captivities, following Tim Noble. We concentrated on two captivities: a patristic captivity and captivity in an anti-Western attitude.

Chapter 8 further included a critique of patristic captivity and the captivity in anti-Westernism. It is the move beyond a neo-patristic synthesis, both its critical reception and alternative work with the sources, which achieves a perspective from which it is possible to see the strengths and weaknesses of its positions.

Chapter 9 discussed Orthodox hermeneutics in terms of the belonging to a community as the result of the interaction between people and history and simultaneously in terms of seeing the divine as something that mainly arrives into this relationship from outside. The balance of the chapter was based on topics addressed by the reception of Gadamer in Orthodox hermeneutics, such as the role of Tradition and Scripture as classics and the discussion concerning two types of knowledge.

In chapter 10 we continued addressing Gadamer's ideas from the perspective of modern Orthodox hermeneutics, namely the role of the interpretative community and the liturgical and iconic dimension of Orthodox hermeneutics. These reassess the radical clash between the divine and human in our perception of revelation of transcendence and include both the element of participation and the historicity of the interpretative community.

Conclusion

The main question explored in this work was how to express and describe the relationship between the horizontal and vertical dimensions of understanding, where the content of what is understood in relation to the word and to God was mediated in historically conditioned situations. We aimed to compare the Gadamerian hermeneutical project and Orthodox hermeneutics and taking the concept of *transcendence* as a starting point, we used this notion in two different nuances.

Whereas for Hans-Georg, Gadamer's transcendence is experienced horizontally through history and language as a limit of human knowledge, for Orthodox theology transcendence is rather vertical and presupposes faith in a transcendent being. This extension of the sense of transcendence led us to examine how *what is transcendent* can be asserted within and across the horizons of human understanding, without it becoming created by people. Reflection was paid not only to how what is transcendent can be mediated as the transcendent, but also as to what the authority was of the mediation and of those who mediate the transcendent.

In the hermeneutical school, represented by the German thinker Hans-Georg, Gadamer was shown to have had a decisive impact on Western hermeneutics, especially through discussions with Jürgen Habermas and Paul Ricoeur. The discussion he initiated included some of the main discussions in Western philosophy of the last third of the twentieth century and continue to include new impulses up till now, hence we spoke about a shift from Gadamer's to Gadamerian hermeneutics.[1] In a similar manner, Orthodox hermeneutics was exemplified by specific voices. It was made known that modern Orthodox hermeneutics was less concentrated around any person, but yet demonstrated common distinctive features. We followed its modern phase that lay in the struggles around the return to the sources.

---

1. Something similar also is visible in the Protestant theology with a move from Luther's to Lutheran theology.

The postmodern phase of Orthodox hermeneutics shows a revalidation of its relationship to the foundations, as is currently explored and revised by numerous authors.

Let me now conclude with what each of the chapters has contributed to my argument. The first chapter, entitled "*Sources of Gadamer's Hermeneutics*," had as an aim to answer the following two queries: what lies in the background of Gadamer's concepts and what is the context of Gadamer's thinking? Therefore, ancient and modern sources of Gadamer's hermeneutics were brought together, which inspired his views of holism, dialectics, historicity, linguisticality and universality. These also showed which, how and why some of the aspects underlined by his predecessors were overtaken into his own hermeneutics. Gadamer's interest in Greek philosophy originated in his early years and was crucial for his hermeneutics. Plato was mentioned because, through his dialogues, Gadamerian hermeneutics developed as dialectical with an emphasis on dialogue and conversation. Aristotle's articulation of practical knowledge *phronēsis*, illustrated the actual nature of the process of understanding, not from the perspective of a subject that grasps the object, but as an experience through which prejudice or habits passed on in tradition, encounter the strange and new.

Further it was pointed out why and how Gadamer was aware of the various modern thoughts he discussed. Only those who contributed to the discussion of the horizons of human understanding and transcendence were thoroughly mentioned, while others were omitted. The character of our being in language was developed through the discussion with Friedrich Schleiermacher, according to whom everything presupposed in hermeneutics is but language. Wilhelm Dilthey claimed that man is a historical being and developed the project of historical reason that influenced Gadamer. Lived experience is, according to Dilthey, associated with a hermeneutical circle, which he understood in the sense that human persons are permanently historical. Therefore, our understanding at the stage of lived experience is always connected with interpretations in the past and this builds the platform upon which understanding happens. Martin Heidegger was mentioned because he re-oriented understanding into the way in which humans exist and relate with the world. Gadamer accepted Heidegger's analysis of the human understanding that every interpretation is grounded on a fore-understanding and expanded on Heidegger's structure of understanding by making prejudice a part of the horizon of the reader. When doing this, Gadamer gave his theme a historical perspective, since prejudice is not something that the interpreter owns, but builds our horizon and constitutes our relation with the world and past traditions.

After showing how the concepts of dialogue, history, universality, language and prejudice cross the threshold into the Gadamerian hermeneutical school, the second chapter "*Development of Gadamer's Hermeneutical Project*" drew on the organization of Gadamer's work into three relevant periods (1921–1959, 1960–1965, 1966–2001), which is common for a so-called *new interpretation of Gadamer*. Here it was shown that his idea of the horizons of human understanding and transcendence developed as a "*religious turn*," which means that Gadamer struggled to free the area of human responsibility for people, recover human finitude and underline the methodical principle that "*the Other might be right*."

The thread we follow continues with "*Reception and Critical Evaluation*," the third chapter that discusses how Gadamer's thoughts have been accepted and how they were changed through this reception in both philosophical and theological areas. Gadamer's hermeneutics has been acknowledged by colleagues but, at the same time, has also been subject to various critiques, such as in discussions with Jürgen Habermas and Paul Ricoeur. Habermas noted Gadamer's reluctance to engage in methodological conversation, opposition between truth and method and absolutization of hermeneutic understanding at the expense of the critique. At the same time, he also argued that Gadamer failed to do justice to the power of reflection and therefore could not grasp the opposition between reason on one hand and prejudice on the other. Through dialogue with Habermas, Gadamer revisited his notion of authority and language.

Further, Gadamer with Ricoeur offered two paradigms for contemporary hermeneutics, while Gadamer developed a dialogical model of interpretation, in which the text is a *Thou* with whom one engages in conversation, Ricoeur insisted upon the reflective distance of the text as a linguistic object and stated that the moment of distance is the very primary stance of historical efficacy. This helped Gadamer return to the text as a center of reference, which characterized his writing in the last third of the twentieth century. Further yet in the third chapter the main voice was given to theological thinkers who critically received Gadamer's hermeneutics in various fields of their interests. These were divided according to the character of their analysis and elements they discussed, such as transcendental elements in Gadamer's hermeneutics, its traditional character, concept of history and notion of conversation. Several theologians who were mentioned include Kevin Vanhoozer, who talked about the miracle of understanding. Peter Stuhlmacher, a Protestant theologian who emphasized interpretative theology, defined understanding of faith as the process of fusion of horizons occurring in the history of effects. Francis Schüssler Fiorenza added to this that understanding is not placing oneself into the shoes of others, but entails the fusion of horizons. A universal-historical understanding was developed by Wolfhart Pannenberg, according to whom wider life settings and epochs had their meaning only as parts of an even more comprehensive continuity of events within the horizon of human understanding. David Tracy pushed the importance of interpretation in theology and the need to reflect and interpret the very process of interpretation. The fourth chapter, "*Horizons of Human Understanding and Transcendence in Gadamer's Hermeneutical School*," introduces some of the key passages for the topic under discussion here. Some areas are again omitted and special attention is paid to the historical character of our understanding and its elements, such as history, prejudice, authority and tradition. Further, it points to the forms of understanding that are born out of merging of horizons, as was illustrated in concepts of dialogue, application and play. After that, transcendence was presented as an aspect of our *being in language*, as was illustrated in the concepts of language, incarnation and aesthetic experience. In this regard, we talked about the transcendental rather than transcendent hermeneutics, since we do not deal with the *knowledge* of objects, but with how it is possible for us to *experience* those objects as objects. Namely, Gadamer's hermeneutics does not work with the transcendence in the sense of a polarity between the transcendent and immanent.

When the term *transcendence* is understood in connection between transcendence and immanence, it refers to God as something existing *outside* and contrasted with the *notion* of world. Immanent principles (within the limits of possible experience) are distinguished from transcendent principles (beyond the limits of possible experience). Immanuel Kant uses the term *transcendent* to describe those principles that pass beyond the limits of experience and are opposed to immanent principles as simply empty chat about things we cannot know because they lie beyond what our capacity to know. The transcendent realm of thought consists of objects that cannot be presented to us in intuition, such as those objects we can never experience with our senses. The closest we can come to gaining knowledge of the transcendent realm is to think about it by means of ideas.[2]

Transcendental, on the other hand, is used for all knowledge "if it is occupied, not with objects, but with the way that we can possibly know objects even before we experience them."[3] Kant understands and sees the use of transcendental in the meaning of the application of a "*concept in some principle*" to things in themselves, which need to be discerned from the

2. For the distinction between transcendent and immanent see Kant, *Kritik der reinen Vernunft*, A 308/B 365.

3. Kant, *Kritik der reinen Vernunft*, A 12. For distinction between transcendental and transcendent see Kant, *Kritik der reinen Vernunft*, A 296/B 352-3.

notion of appearance.[4] Everyday knowledge is the knowledge of objects, but something is transcendental if it plays a role in the way in which the mind establishes objects and makes it possible for us to experience those objects as objects in the first place.

Gadamer's hermeneutics is not transcendental in the Kantian sense, but can be termed transcendental insofar as it seeks to disclose the conditions of the possibility of understanding, thus being reminiscent of Kant's *apriori* question. The concept of *transcendental*, as Gadamer uses it, is therefore connected with the question how are objects possible apriori, how to know objects as objects in the first place even before we experience them and what makes it possible for us to experience objects as objects. Transcendental is every knowledge that does not deal with objects, but rather with our faculty for *knowing* these objects. In a certain way it means to give up the concept that objects exist in space and time as things in themselves, as absolute but relative, as they are related to the inevitable condition and context of our experience.

The transcendental element of Gadamer's hermeneutics was already visible in the motto of his main book taken from Rilke's poem, where Gadamer claimed that one experiences the limits of one's own experience by experiencing something that calls one to go *beyond the limits* of their own experience. Understanding begins when something addresses us and one is drawn out of one's constructions and is caught by something, drawn into one's way and game. This kind of experience was an event that one undergoes as one participates in a process that is more continuous than one is and in the context of which one always has a sense that there is much more to be said than one communicates. Hermeneutical experience happens in language, but this experience cannot be separated from language and its transcendence is always mediated historically. Therefore, there is a circular movement within tradition between prejudice and the process of understanding, which is defined as the fusion of horizons.

This fusion was described as a dialogue between application and play. Gadamer elaborated this discussion with the example of theological hermeneutics, which served for him as the model of interpretation. He pointed out that the text cannot speak without attaching onto the one who speaks. This was illustrated as the *hermeneutics of dialogue*, where the dialogue was characterized by an openness. First it is an openness toward our position, as the preconceptions we bring in the dialogue are part of history and tradition. Second, it means to be open to the position of the other, to what one has to say to us. The success of the dialogue is not measured by the level of

---

4. Kant, *Kritik der reinen Vernunft*, A 238–9/B 297–8.

new things we learn, but by the level of how one encounters the other and is transformed by this encounter. By insisting that in understanding, a subject participates in events with which one could never claim to be the source and cannot take up transcendental status, Gadamer gave an alternative medial path to this discussion, where the subject must forget one's self without losing one's self, as one's active role adds to the meaning of what is revealed and so enriches the experience. This concept was explained in Gadamer's discussion of truth in the notion of play.

The third stage of this analysis put its emphasis on how transcendence has been approached in the Gadamerian hermeneutical school. It was important here that, according to Gadamer, the whole process of understanding occurs as an event of language and that the experience of people with the world has always been linguistic. A parallel was given between the hermeneutical model and incarnation in order to show the proper relation between word and thought. The main argument here was the opening words from the prologue to John's Gospel, which holds that *Jesus is the Word*, present at the creation and will be in eternity with God. When God manifested His image to people in human form, this form was not a mere manifestation or appearance, a change into something else or separation of one thing from another. In this sense the transcendence was not simply *believing* in God, but its foundation is a religiously *experienced* limit of human knowledge, *ignoramus*, of admitting our not-knowing.

In this context, the universality of hermeneutics based on language was transformed into the universality of the hidden God and into the universality of not-knowing. A very important mark of new interpretations of Gadamer was a focus on the relationship between the aesthetic and religious experience, when the religious experience is exemplified with the limited human experience in aesthetics.

Since we have looked in detail at the development of Gadamer's project and its wider influence, in chapter 5 "*Contribution of Gadamerian Hermeneutics*," we summarized the Gadamerian contribution to the understanding of the relationship between horizons of human understanding and transcendence. Gadamerian hermeneutics is not theological hermeneutics but can still be considered hermeneutics of transcendence. Therefore, it has opened areas upon which theologians continued to build. One moment of transcendence is connected with the focus on the relation between the aesthetic and religious experience, when the religious experience is exemplified with the human experience in aesthetics.

In the second part of this book, an analysis was offered of modern and postmodern Orthodox hermeneutics and its representatives. In order to hermeneutically comprehend the question of human understanding and transcendence, in chapter 6 "*Emergence of Modern Orthodox Hermeneutics*" we drew a historical overview of various directions concerning how modern and postmodern Orthodox theological hermeneutics has been developing as patristic hermeneutics, biblical hermeneutics, and hermeneutical theology.

Although the major interest in this book is in hermeneutical theology and its attributes, it was necessary to provide a historical overview as the background upon which hermeneutics developed. We began with the paradigm shift in neo-patristic synthesis and the return to the Fathers, where the authority of the Fathers was underscored as a hermeneutical principle. Further, the teaching of the Fathers was asserted by Florovsky as a category of Christian existence and an ultimate criterion of correct faith. Nonetheless, a return to the critical thinking of the Fathers was missing.

Then we continued with neo-Orthodoxy, a movement in the sixties in Greece, characterized by interest in Byzantine iconography, apophatic theology, monasticism and the Eucharistic community, as well as hesychasm and especially Gregory Palamas. Nevertheless, it also conveyed the antithesis between the East and West, because the East refused the positive achievements of Western culture. In the next step, we continued with the restoration of the relationship between patristics and biblical studies in the seventies, when the moment of critical thinking was empathized, fundaments for patristic exegetical study were set and the discussion about biblical interpretation in the Orthodox world was initiated.

Finally, we finished in the current era, where a certain redefinition of the relation between exegesis and hermeneutics appeared. Two short examples of current hermeneutical theologians were offered in order to show the turn to the role of the reader, the plurality of interpretations and the importance of interpretation.

This historical overview offered three different understandings of the concept of hermeneutics. First is patristic hermeneutics that relies mostly in the results of the efforts of the church Fathers and the look at the Fathers as the main principle. Second is biblical hermeneutics, which relies on the methodology developed mostly in the West that enables a correct understanding of the words of Scripture. Third is hermeneutical theology that overcomes methodology and includes both interpretation and exploration of our own situation, as well as the relationship with the subject matter of the text. Since we concentrated on the relationship between human understanding and transcendence in this book, modern and postmodern Orthodox hermeneutical theology answers how what is transcendent can be testified within the horizons of human understanding without being created so much *by* the people as what reaches *beyond* them.

CONCLUSION 185

Further, chapter 7 "*Sources of Orthodox Hermeneutics Revisited*" presented the representatives of two dominant movements and waves in the twentieth century in order to present how modern Orthodox hermeneutics developed within these contexts. First, modern hermeneutics among Russian émigrés was presented, represented by Georges Florovsky and Vladimir Lossky, who were the founders of the neo-patristic movement. Florovsky's concept of a Christian Hellenism was shown as becoming a hermeneutical principle. To explain the mode of being of Orthodox Greek identity, Christos Yannaras, a representative of modern Orthodox Greek hermeneutics was introduced, especially as he brought a new hermeneutical key, which is the Greek culture. The main condition for this structure of Greek hermeneutics is a structural anti-Westernism and a radical contrast between Orthodoxy and the West.

These two expositions of representatives were followed by naming the problems that arose out of them, which we call here the captivities. We concentrated on two captivities, patristic captivity and captivity in an anti-Western attitude. According to my opinion, these captivities are the most dominant hermeneutical criteria that rule contemporary Orthodox theology. By developing the concepts of Western and Babylonian captivity, Orthodoxy aimed to find the unique Orthodox elements, but it lead to another extreme. The return to the Fathers turned into a patristic captivity in the moment when "*closer to the Fathers*" was acknowledged as "*further from the Bible.*" While in Western Christianity the authority of the Fathers has been subjected to the return to the Bible, in Orthodoxy the affirmation of authority in effect downplayed the authority of the Bible.

The captivity in anti-Westernism, which further contributed to expressions of Orthodox identity occurred when "*closer to Orthodox identity*" was identified with "*further from the West.*" We saw this hermeneutical approach in the Greek generation of the sixties. My aim is to relativize these differences and expose such a black and white clash as false, as well as to show that patristic criteria are not so anti-scientific as has seemed. Therefore, it was argued that critical thinking was not strange, unknown and rejected in the Early church, but quite the contrary as, along with spirituality, it built a strong holistic understanding of Christianity. This broken connection can be restored with a focus on the homiletic character of hermeneutics and on the connection of theology and spirituality. This discussion was very important for the theme of this book, because the positions presented show the weakness of the Orthodox approach.

Chapter 8 "*The Move Beyond Neo-Patristic Synthesis*" further included the critical reception of the way the neo-patristic school in its Russian and Greek forms worked with the sources and, more precisely, the critique of the patristic captivity and the captivity in anti-Westernism that arose as the result of the facts presented in the previous chapters. As written above, one of the questions is *how can the participatory relationship between the immanent and the transcendent as we find it in Orthodox theology be preserved without divinizing the world*? Orthodox hermeneutics, with its attributes of negative self-identification and antithesis between East and West, fails to achieve this. Only the move beyond neo-patristic synthesis, both its critical reception and alternative work with the sources, achieves a position from which it is possible to see the strengths and weaknesses of Orthodox positions.

The move beyond neo-patristic synthesis is required to see the strength of Orthodox hermeneutics identified in terms of a strong sense of belonging to a community. This is true as well in terms of seeing transcendence as something that comes mainly to this relationship from outside, as the Holy Spirit and not as an outcome of the interaction between humans and history.

Therefore, critical reception was introduced as the first step by Pantelis Kalaitzidis, who warned that the return to the Fathers was an introversion and conservatism, leading to polarization. Brandon Gallaher complements the problem of Orthodoxy by upholding what *is not* rather than what *is*, with a hermeneutical perspective of time that revises a neo-patristic synthesis. Aristotle Papanikolaou refused the strict division between the Orthodox theology of a neo-patristic perspective and Western theology, demonstrated in the self-identification of East against West, against Western liberal democracy, human rights, and individualism. I have also included one voice from outside the Orthodox tradition, yet who comments on it and brings another important point. Ivana Noble expands the concept of living tradition with the moment of innovation that will enable its delivery as living to other generations. Finally, Assaad Kattan assumes (as inspired by Gadamer) that Orthodoxy needs hermeneutics as it needs discipline about understanding and its premises in order to focus on the plurality of the reader's dimension.

Alternative work with the sources was a second step. John Breck offered an Orthodox answer, which is based on the return to patristics, but at the same time is also based on scientific exegesis of Scripture. He created a hermeneutical model that utilizes the historical element of the typological relationship, which is converted into the liturgical life of the interpretative community and enables one to preserve the balance between the past, present and future. The approach of Theodore Stylianopoulos is anchored upon a high regard for Scripture, the importance of prayer in the study of the Bible, primary meaning as historical and the purpose of exegesis to illuminate the theological truths and ethical values in Scripture. Stylianopoulos calls for a "*neo-biblical synthesis*." The purpose of this chapter was to achieve a re-reading of Orthodox hermeneutics and prepare the ground for the following chapter, where a presentation of the forms of modern Orthodox liturgical hermeneutics based on the Gadamerian basics was discussed.

Hence, chapter 9 *"Human Understanding and Transcendence in Current Orthodox Hermeneutics"* discussed Orthodox hermeneutics from the perspective covered in previous chapters. The structure of this book, where the first part deals with Gadamerian hermeneutics and the second with modern and postmodern Orthodox theological hermeneutics compelled us to have a section where we more closely approached the reception of Gadamer's work in Orthodoxy to identify the most important areas they use as themes and address them from the perspective of modern Orthodox hermeneutics.

Receptions of Gadamer by Andrew Louth, Assaad Kattan and Nicolae Turcan were presented. Themes addressed in this section were the basis for the rest of the chapter, namely that in Gadamer there is a focus that the reconstruction of the historical context includes the personality of the one who understands, which is the church. His work therefore expands upon the recovery of tradition, understood as the continuity of a human communication of an experience, rather than something that limits, yet is the context within which one is allowed to be free. His concept of genuine conversation showed that the church must accept the validity of tradition not simply in the sense of acknowledging it, but to *listen* to what it says to us. Gadamer also addressed the fact that interpreting is not an attempt to reconstruct the original historical context, but rather a matter of listening across a historical gulf that is filled with traditions that bring the interpreted object to the interpretative community.

Especially inspiring is Gadamer's concept of temporal distance, which presupposes that the act of understanding is not achievable without *fore-understanding* and that the interpreter is part of the *act* of interpretation. At the same time, the fusion of horizons that underlines an interpreter's involvement in the interpretative act might contribute to a healthy and fruitful discussion among the Orthodoxy over the limits of tradition. These thoughts of Gadamer's complement modern Orthodox hermeneutics and will form the basis for its discussion on Scripture and Tradition and contemplation over science. The hermeneutical circle between Scripture and Tradition will be in the center, which means that the two are not in contrast or in too close cooperation but, in the form of a circle, influence one another and cannot be divided.

The interpreter's involvement in the process of interpretation might well contribute to a fruitful discussion among the Orthodox over the limits of tradition. His notion of understanding as an agreement, where the reader does not engage with the writer himself but with the subject matter of the text, is in favor of understanding as an *engagement* with tradition, rather than an attempt to escape from it. The recovery of traditions is achieved in this case, not as something that limits, but is understood as the continuity of human communication of an experience.

Chapter 10 *"The Role of Interpretative Community"* discussed Orthodox hermeneutics in terms of a strong sense of belonging to a community while, at the same time, discussed seeing transcendence as something that principally comes into the relationship from outside. This theme reassesses the radical clash between the divine and the human in our perception of revelation of the transcendence and includes elements of the participation and historicity of the interpretative community as well as its liturgical and iconic dimension. The discussion of fulfilment in the community is closely related with the role of the interpretative community, in this case with the church.

The role of the interpretative community was strongly accentuated by Gadamer who, in his concept of conversation between the *I* and *Thou*, showed the role of community, conversation and *being with the other* as a necessity for true revelation of the meaning. Interpretation must be understood as one, not only with Tradition as previously, but also with the community. A specific category of ecclesial reading inspired by Gadamer's concepts is that Scripture should be celebrated in *corporate* worship, more precisely in a liturgy as the framework within which Orthodox Christians encounter the Gospel and where the Bible is more celebrated than interpreted.

Approaching a conclusion, let me spell out the areas in which both schools, the Gadamerian hermeneutical school and modern Orthodox hermeneutics, can enrich one another. Previous chapters considered the contribution of Gadamer's hermeneutical school to the relationship between horizons of human understanding, as well as the contribution of modern Orthodox hermeneutics to the Western audience and its limits. Throughout the book it was pointed out that a conversation between these two partners cannot be based only upon the parallels and similarities between two conceptions (although there are plenty) and their comparison. The method used in the book consists of a critical presentation of strengths and weaknesses of each concept, presenting the restrictions of each contribution and identifying the areas where mutual agreement is needed.

During the analysis of Gadamerian hermeneutics, the first part pointed out its strengths, especially in investigating transcendence as it appears in historically conditioned situations and simultaneously included new and evolving situations. This helped prevent understanding Christianity as a purely divine and un-interpreted matter, detached from the manifestation and reception by believers. Gadamer contributed to this with the relational character of understanding, which means that the hermeneutical process is described as a dialogue, in which *what is beyond* appeared within the human debate horizon as the result of human involvement. The weakness was noted in that he did not investigate it in relation to the *divine*. Therefore, Gadamer's hermeneutics is not transcendent as something existing outside and contrasted with the immanent notion of world, nor is it knowledge that goes beyond the categories of human reason. His hermeneutics is *transcendental*, as it provides an explanation of the required conditions of possible experience. Obviously, as a non-theologian and within his hermeneutical framework, Gadamer is fully justified to bracket purely theological queries. But, at the same time, this is one of the reasons why Gadamer's intentions need to be further advanced by theologians, as they would profit from the participatory relationship between the immanent and the transcendent, as we have it for example in Orthodox theology.

When examining some of the representative voices of Orthodox hermeneutics, its strong sense of belonging to community came to the fore, as well as seeing transcendence as something that generally comes to this relationship from outside, such as the Holy Spirit, rather than the result of cooperation between people and history. *What is beyond* is here more revealed than created and always transcends this world and human nature. This approach prevents transcendence from being misused by power structures. At the same time, the problem connected with it is that vertically understood transcendence might divinize too much and may not leave sufficient space for the human element, for suspicion and otherness. One of the consequences might be to turn Christianity into ideology. Further, there is a lack of criterion of validity to evaluate these elements and to discern between tradition and customs, between the voices of people and the call of the Holy Spirit. This distinction seems to be necessary in order to preserve the balance between the human and the divine.

This presentation of strengths and weaknesses follows in a conversation that is dialectical and results in a genuine openness toward the surprising and unexpected encounters with the Other, rather than resulting in synthesis. This means that this conversation ends in identifying areas where each side can learn something from the partner. First it must be shown that Gadamer's hermeneutical school can *enrich* Orthodox hermeneutics by strengthening the historical dimension of tradition rooted in language as a complement to the eschatological tradition. Further, by giving alternative criteria for discernment of what is a good interpretation of the classics, helping to move beyond the polarity of tradition and innovation and for the relational character of understanding where the hermeneutical process is described as a dialogue, as well as for accepting the plurality of the mediations of transcendent in historically conditioned situations.

Then it must be shown that Orthodox hermeneutics can enrich Western Gadamerian hermeneutics by the emphasis Orthodoxy places on the eschatology, mediation of the transcendent as transcendent, balance between communitarian and personal understanding, supremacy of active and revealed mystery and participation of the community through liturgy. The main argument contends that preserving *both* approaches and specifying *how* they supplement each other helps to show the limits of encountering the transcendent reality that can be testified by human language, yet not reduced to it.

In conclusion, I will to return to the book's opening quotation, that *"the conversation that we are is the one that never ends."* Indeed, this book is neither the final word nor the closing solution in this area.

Quite the contrary, it rather opens the conversation and sketches directions for further dialogue, as well as initiating deeper dialogue between Western and Eastern thinking on the ground of hermeneutics. Apparently, it is the conversation that leads *us*, not *we* who lead the conversion. The second line of the opening quotation, *"no word is the last word, just as there is no first word"* further illustrates the necessity of analyzing the themes in dialogue and in a conversation, rather than in isolation.

We did a similar thing in this book by analyzing Gadamer solely in relation to his predecessors, his followers and his critics. We analyzed Orthodox hermeneutics in relation to its roots, social and political contexts, weaknesses of its representative voices and representative voices who move and develop it further.

In due course, acknowledging that no word is either the first or the last shows that themes, questions, and answers do not exist as separate and disjointed, but always exist only in the conversation, history of effects and the traditions that were neither opened nor closed by them. It is actually the conversation itself that proves the existence of a relationship between the horizontal human dimension rooted in history and the transcendental vertical dimension rooted in revelation as a mystery, be it the mystery of language, incarnation, a hidden god, or the mystery of the Holy Spirit.

Bibliography

Agourides, Savvas. "Biblical Studies in Orthodox Theology." *Greek Orthodox Theological Review* 17 (1972) 51–62.

———. "The Orthodox Church and Contemporary Biblical Research." In *Auslegung der Bibel*, edited by James Douglas Grant Dunn et al., 139–56. Tübingen: Mohr Siebeck, 2000.

Albert, Hans. *Traktat über kritische Vernunft*. Tübingen: Mohr Siebeck, 1968.

Alfeyev, Hilarion. "Orthodox Theology in the Twenty-First Century." In *Orthodox Witness Today*, 125–45. Geneva: WCC, 2006.

———. "Orthodox Theology on the Threshold of the 21st Century." *Ecumenical Review* 3 (2000) 309–25.

———. "Orthodoxy in the Twentieth Century: The Persecution of Faith in Russia." In *Orthodox Christianity, The History and Canonical Structure of the Orthodox Church*, 1:257–322. Crestwood, NY: St Vladimir's Seminary, 2011.

———. "The Patristic Heritage and Modernity." In *Orthodox Witness Today*, 146–72. Geneva: WCC, 2006.

Andreopoulos Andreas. "The Gospel as an Image of the Kingdom: A Eucharistic Reading of the Bible in the Orthodox Tradition." In *Theologians on Scripture*, edited by Angus Paddison, 7–22. Bloomsbury: T. & T. Clark, 2018.

Arthos, John. "Gadamer's Dialogical Imperative: Linking Socratic Dialogue to Aristotle's Phronesis." In *Gadamer's Hermeneutics and the Art of Conversation*, edited by Andrzej Wierciński, 169–76. Berlin: Lit, 2011.

———. *The Inner Word in Gadamer's Hermeneutics*. Notre Dame: University of Notre Dame Press, 2009.

Audi, Elias. "First Conference of Orthodox Theologians in America." *St Vladimir's Theological Quarterly* 14 (1970) 219–21.

Aylesworth, Gary E. "Dialogue, Text, Narrative: Confronting Gadamer and Ricoeur." In *Gadamer and Hermeneutics*, edited by Hugo Silverman, 63–81. London: Routledge, 1991.

Baker, Matthew. "Bibliography of Literature on the Life and Work of Father Georges V. Florovsky." *Teologikon: The Annual of the Center for Systematic Theology University of Veliko Turnovo* 2 (2013) 253–331.

———. "Theology Reasons—in History: Neo-Patristic Synthesis and the Renewal of Theological Rationality." *Theologia* 4 (2010) 81–118.

Baker, Matthew, and Nikolaos Asproulis. "Second Bibliography of Scholarly Literature and Conferences on Florovsky." *Theologia* 4 (2010) 357–96.

Baker, Matthew, and Seraphim Danckaert. "Georges Florovsky." In *Orthodox Handbook on Ecumenism: Resources for Theological Education*, edited by Pantelis Kalaitzidis et al., 211–15. Oxford: Regnum, 2014.

Barrois, Georges Augustin. "Orthodox Conference on Hermeneutics, May 1972." *St Vladimir's Theological Quarterly* 16 (1972) 153–57.

Barthold, Lauren Swayne. *Gadamer's Dialectical Hermeneutics*. Plymouth: Lexington, 2010.

Behr, John "Returning to First Principles Articulating Orthodox Theology in a Postmodern Context." In *Thinking Modernity: Towards a Reconfiguration of the Relationship between Orthodox Theology and Modern Culture*, edited by Assaad Elias Kattan and Fadi Georgi, 21–35. Tripoli: St. John of Damascus Institute of Theology, 2010.

———. *The Way to Nicaea*. The Formation of Christian Theology 1. Crestwood, NY: St Vladimir's Seminary, 2001.

Bernasconi, Robert, ed. *Hans-Georg Gadamer: The Relevance of the Beautiful and Other Essays*. Cambridge: Cambridge University Press, 1986.

Bernstein, Richard Jacob. *Beyond Objectivism and Relativism*. Philadelphia: University of Pennsylvania Press, 1983.

———. "What Is the Difference That Makes a Difference? Gadamer, Habermas, and Rorty." In *Hermeneutics and Modern Philosophy*, edited by Brice Wachterhouser, 343–76. Albany: State University of New York Press, 1986.

Betti, Emilio. *Allgemeine Auslegungslehre als Methodik der Wissenschaften*. Tübingen: Mohr Siebeck, 1967.

———. *Die Hermeneutik als allgemeine Methodik der Geisteswissenschaften*. Tübingen: Mohr Siebeck, 1962.

Bigović, Radovan. *The Orthodox Church in 21st Century*. Belgrade: Ekopres, 2009.

Blane, Andrew, ed. *Georges Florovsky: Russian Intellectual and Orthodox Churchman*. Crestwood, NY: St Vladimir's Seminary, 1993.

Bleicher, Josef. *Contemporary Hermeneutics: Hermeneutics as Method, Philosophy and Critique*. London: Routledge, 1980.

Bobrinskoy, Boris. *The Compassion of the Father*. Crestwood, NY: St Vladimir's Seminary, 2003.

Bollnow, Otto Friedrich. "Waß heißt einen Schriftsteller besser verstehen als er sich selber verstanden hat?" *Deutsche Vierteljahresschrift* 18 (1940) 117–38.

Bouteneff, Peter, and Dagmar Heller, eds. *Interpreting Together: Essays in Hermeneutics*. Geneva: WCC, 2001.

Breck, John. "Orthodox Principles of Biblical Interpretation." *St Vladimir's Theological Quarterly* 40 (1996) 77–93.

———. "Orthodoxy and the Bible Today." In *The Legacy of St Vladimir*. edited by John Meyendorff and Eleana Silk, 141–57. Crestwood, NY: St Vladimir's Seminary, 1990.

———. *Power of the Word in the Worshiping Church*. Crestwood, NY: St Vladimir's Seminary, 1986.

———. *Scripture in Tradition: The Bible and Its Interpretation in the Orthodox Church*. Crestwood, NY: St Vladimir's Seminary, 2001.

———. "Theoria and Orthodox Hermeneutics." *St Vladimir's Theological Quarterly* 20 (1976) 195–219.

Brüning, Alfons."'Tradition and Traditions'—Relating Gadamer's 'Truth and Method' to Russian Orthodox Theology." *Journal of Eastern Christian Studies* 66 (2014) 73–90.
Bubner, Rüdiger, ed. *'Sein, das verstanden werden kann, ist Sprache'. Hommage an Hans-Georg Gadamer.* Frankfurt am Main: Suhrkamp, 2001.
Bulgakov, Sergius. *The Orthodox Church.* Crestwood, NY: St Vladimir's Seminary, 1988.
Bultmann, Rudolf. "Is Presuppositionless Exegesis Possible?" In *Existence and Faith*, edited by S. Ogden, 342–52. London: Collins, 1961.
Butcher, Brian A. *Liturgical Theology after Schmemann: An Orthodox Reading of Paul Ricoeur.* New York: Fordham University Press, 2018.
Calivas, Alkiviadis C. "Science, Technology and Faith: Overcoming False Barriers." In *Essays in Theology and Liturgy*, 2:27–40. Brookline, MA: Holy Cross Orthodox, 2001.
Caputo, John D. "Gadamer's Closet Essentialism: A Derridean Critique." In *Dialogue and Deconstruction: The Gadamer Derrida Encounter*, edited by Diane Michelfelder and Richard Palmer, 254–64. Albany: State University of New York Press, 1989.
Carr, Thomas K. *Newman and Gadamer: Toward a Hermeneutics of Religious Knowledge.* American Academy of Religion Reflection and Theory in the Study of Religion 10. Atlanta: Scholars, 1996.
Casiday, Augustine. "Church Fathers and the Shaping of Orthodox Theology." In *The Cambridge Companion to Orthodox Christian Theology*, edited by Mary B. Cunningham and Elisabeth Theokritoff, 167–87. Cambridge: Cambridge University Press, 2009.
Cavafy, Constantine Peter. "Waiting for the Barbarians." In *The Collected Poems*, 15–17. Translated by Evangelos Sach-peroglou. Oxford: Oxford University Press, 2007.
Clark, Timothy. "Recent Eastern Orthodox Interpretation of the New Testament." *Currents in Biblical Research* 5 (2007) 322–40.
Crisp, Simon. "Orthodox Biblical Scholarship between Patristics and Postmodernity: A View from the West." In *Auslegung der Bibel*, edited by James Douglas Grant Dunn et al., 123–38. Tübingen: Mohr Siebeck, 2000.
Crowley, Paul G. "Dogmatic Development after Newman: The Search for a Hermeneutical Principle in Newman, Marin-Sola, Rahner and Gadamer." PhD diss., Graduate Theological Union, 1983.
Culpepper, James Edward. "The Value of Hans-Georg Gadamer's Hermeneutic Philosophy for Christian Thought." PhD diss., Southern Baptist Theological Seminary, 1987.
Cunningham, Mary B., and Elisabeth Theokritoff. "Who are the Orthodox Christians? A Historical Introduction." In *The Cambridge Companion to Orthodox Christian Theology*, 1–18. Cambridge: Cambridge University Press, 2009.
Davey, Nicholas. "Doubled Reflection: Gadamer's Aesthetics and the Question of Spiritual Experience." In *Transcendence and Phenomenology*, edited by Conor Cunningham and Peter M. Candler, 151–73. London: SCM, 2007.
———. "Hermeneutics, Aesthetics and Transcendence." In *Imaging the Bible: An Introduction to Biblical Art*, edited by Martin O'Kane, 191–209. London: SPCK, 2008.
———. "Hermeneutics, Art and Transcendence." In *Gadamer's Hermeneutics and the Art of Conversation*, edited by Andrzej Wierciński, 371–82. Berlin: Lit, 2011.

———. "Truth, Method and Transcendence." In *Consequences of Hermeneutics*, edited by Jeff Malpas, 25–44. Evanston, IL: Northwestern University Press, 2010.
Demacopoulos, George E., and Aristotle Papanikolaou, eds. *Orthodox Constructions of the West*. New York: Fordham University Press, 2013.
Demetrios, Archbishop of America. "The Orthodox Churches in a Pluralistic World: Ecumenical Conversation." In *The Orthodox Churches in a Pluralistic World*, edited by Emmanuel Clapsis, 1–10. Geneva: WCC, 2004.
Demirezen, Ismail. "Gadamer's Hermeneutics as a Possibility for Interreligious Dialogue." *Ekev Academic Review* 15 (2011) 113–30.
Derrida, Jacques, and Gianni Vattimo, eds. *Die Religion*. Frankfurt: Suhrkamp, 2001.
Dostal, Robert J. "Gadamer's Platonism: His Recovery of Mimesis and Anamnesis." In *Consequences of Hermeneutics*, edited by Jeff Malpas, 45–65. Evanston, IL: Northwestern University Press, 2010.
———. "Introduction." In *The Cambridge Companion to Gadamer*, edited by Robert Dostal, 1–12. Cambridge: Cambridge University Press, 2003.
Dottori, Riccardo, ed. *A Century of Philosophy: Hans-Georg Gadamer in Conversation with Riccardo Dottori*. Translated by Rod Coltman and Sigrid Koepke. London: Bloomsbury, 2006.
———. *Die Lektion des Jahrhunderts: Ein philosophischer Dialog mit Riccardo Dottori*. Münster: Lit, 2002.
Dutt, Carsten, ed. *Hermeneutik—Ästhetik—Praktische Philosophie: Hans-Georg Gadamer im Gespräch*. Heidelberg: Universitätsverlag C. Winter, 1993.
D-Vasilescu, Elena Ene. "Orthodox Christian Approach to the Bible." *Transformation* 26 (2009) 40–44.
Eberhard, Philippe. "Gadamer and Theology." *International Journal of Systematic Theology* 9 (2007) 283–300.
———. "The Mediality of Our Condition: A Christian Interpretation." *Journal of the American Academy of Religion* 67 (1999) 411–34.
———. *The Middle Voice in Gadamer's Hermeneutics*. Tübingen: Mohr Siebeck, 2004.
Ebertz, Roger P. "Beyond Worldview Analysis: Insights from Hans-Georg Gadamer on Christian Scholarship." *Christian Scholar's Review* 36 (2006) 13–28.
Evdokimov, Paul. *L'Orthodoxie*. Paris: Delachaux et Niestlé, 1959.
———. "Principes de l'hemeneutique Orthodoxe." *Contacts: revue française de l'orthodoxie* 135 (1987) 127–35.
Figal, Günter. "Phronesis as Understanding: Situating Philosophical Hermeneutics." In *The Scepter of Relativism. Truth, Dialogue and Phronesis in Philosophical Hermeneutics*, edited by Lawrence Schmidt, 236–48. Evanston, IL: Northwestern University Press, 1995.
Figal, Günter, et al. *Hermeneutische Wege: Hans-Georg Gadamer zum Hundersten*. Tübingen: Mohr Siebeck, 2000.
Fiorenza, Francis Schüssler. "Theory and Practice: Theological Education as a Reconstructive, Hermeneutical, and Practical Task." *Theological Education* 23 (1987) 113–41.
Fischer, Mark F. "Catholic Hermeneutics: The Theology of Tradition and the Philosophy of Gadamer." PhD diss., Graduate Theological Union, 1983.
Florovsky, Georges. *Aspects of Church History*. Collected Works 4. Belmont, MA: Nordland, 1975.

———. *Bible, Church, Tradition: An Eastern Orthodox View.* Collected Works 1. Belmont, MA: Norland, 1972.

———. *The Collected Works of Georges Florovsky.* Belmont, MA: Nordland, 1972–1989.

———. "Elements of Liturgy." In *The Orthodox Church in the Ecumenical Movement*, edited by Constantin Patelos, 172–82. Geneva, WCC, 1978.

———. "The Legacy and the Task of Orthodox Theology." *Anglican Theological Review* 31 (1949) 65–71.

———. "The Mystical Theology of the Eastern Church." *Journal of Religion* 38 (1958) 207–8.

———. *Patristics and Modern Theology.* Athens: Pyrsos, 1938.

———. *Ways of Russian Theology: Part I.* Collected Works 5. Belmont, MA: Nordland, 1979.

———. *Ways of Russian Theology: Part II.* Collected Works 6. Belmont, MA: Nordland, 1987.

———. "Western Influences in Russian Theology." In *Collected Works of Georges Florovsky*, 4:157–82. Vaduz: Büchervertriebsanstalt, 1987.

———. "Westliche Einflüsse in der russischen Theologie." In *Procès-Verbaux du Premier Congrès de Théologie Orthodoxe à Athènes, 29 novembre–6 décembre 1936*, edited by Amilkas Alizivatos, 212–31. Athens: Pyrsos, 1939.

Fortounatto, Mariamna, and Mary B. Cunningham. "Theology of the Icon." In *The Cambridge Companion to Orthodox Christian Theology*, edited by Mary B. Cunningham and Elisabeth Theokritoff, 136–49. Cambridge: Cambridge University Press, 2009.

Frank, Manfred, ed. *F. D. E. Schleiermacher—Hermeneutik und Kritik.* Frankfurt am Main: Suhrkamp, 1977.

Gadamer, Hans-Georg. *Der Anfang der Philosophie.* Stuttgart: Reclam, 1997.

———. *The Beginning of Knowledge.* London: Bloomsbury, 2016.

———. *The Beginning of Philosophy.* London: Bloomsbury, 2016.

———. *A Century of Philosophy: Hans-Georg Gadamer in Conversation with Riccardo Dottori.* Translated by Rod Coltman and Sigrid Koepke. London: Bloomsbury, 2006.

———. "Danken und Gedenken." In *Hermeneutische Entwürfe*, 208–13. Tübingen: Mohr Siebeck, 2000.

———. *Dialektik und Sophistik im siebenten platonischen Brief.* Heidelberg: Carl Winter Universitätsverlag, 1964.

———. *Dialogue and Dialectic: Eight Hermeneutical Studies on Plato.* Translated by P. Christopher Smith. New Haven, CT: Yale University Press, 1980.

———. *The Enigma of Health.* Translated by Jason Gaiger and Nicholas Walker. Stanford: Stanford University Press, 1996.

———. *Das Erbe Europas: Beiträge.* Frankfurt am Main: Suhrkamp, 1989.

———. *Gesammelte Werke.* 10 vols. Tübingen: Mohr Siebeck, 1985–1995.

———. *Hegels Dialektik.* Tübingen: Mohr Siebeck, 1971.

———. *Heidegger's Ways.* Translated by John W. Stanley. Albany: State University of New York Press, 1994.

———. "Herméneutique et Théologie." *Revue des sciences religieuses* 51 (1977) 385–97. Strasbourg: Palais Universitaire. 1977.

———. *Hermeneutische Entwürfe.* Tübingen: Mohr Siebeck, 2000.

———. *The Idea of the Good in Platonic-Aristotelian Philosophy*. New Haven, CT: Yale University Press, 1986.
———. *Kleine Schriften*. 4 vols. Tübingen: Mohr, 1967–1977.
———. *Lob der Theorie: Reden und Aufsätze*. Frankfurt am Main: Suhrkamp, 1983.
———. *Philosophical Apprenticeships*. Translated by Robert R. Sullivan. Cambridge, MA: MIT, 1985.
———. *Philosophische Lehrjahre*. Frankfurt: Klostermann, 1977.
———. *Plato's Dialectical Ethics: Phenomenological Interpretations Relating to the Philebus*. New Haven, CT: Yale University Press, 1991.
———. *Poetica*. Frankfurt am Main: Insel, 1977.
———. *Le problème de la conscience historique*. Paris: Beatrice-Nauwelaerts, 1963.
———. *Reason in the Age of Science*. Translated by Frederick G. Lawrence. Cambridge, MA: MIT, 1983.
———. "The Relevance of the Beautiful." In *Hans-Georg Gadamer: The Relevance of the Beautiful and Other Essays*, edited by Robert Bernasconi, 3–53. Cambridge: Cambridge University Press, 1986.
———. "Rhetorik, Hermeneutik und Ideologiekritik." In *Hermeneutik und Ideologiekritik*, edited by Jürgen Habermas et al., 57–82. Frankfurt am Main: Suhrkamp, 1971.
———. "Temoignage et Affirmation". In *La Testimonianza*, edited by E. Casteli, 161–65. Rome: Instituto de Studi Filosofici, 1972.
———. "Text and Interpretation." In *Dialogue and Deconstruction: The Gadamer-Derrida Encounter*, edited by Diane Michelfelder and Richard Palmer, 21–51. Albany: State University of New York Press, 1989.
———. *Truth and Method*. 2nd rev. ed. Translation revised by Joel Weinsheimer and Donald G. Marshall. London: Continuum, 2004.
———. "The Truth of the Work of Art." In *Heidegger's Ways*, 95–110. Albany: State University of New York Press, 1994.
———. *Über die Veborgenheit der Gesundheit: Aufsätze und Vorträge*. Frankfurt am Main: Suhrkamp, 1993.
———. *Die Vernunft im Zeitalter der Wissenschaft*. Frankfurt am Main: Suhrkamp, 1976.
———. *Die Vielfalt Europas. Erbe und Zukunft*. Vortragsreihe: Ein Jahrhundert wird besichtigt. Stuttgart: Robert Bosch Stiftung, 1985.
———. *Wahrheit und Methode*. 6th ed. Tübingen: Mohr Siebeck, 1990.
———. "Wahrheit und Methode. Der Anfang der Urfassung (ca. 1956)." *Dilthey Jahrbuch* 8 (1993) 131–42.
———. *Wer bin ich, und wer bist du?* Frankfurt am Main: Suhrkamp, 1973.
———. "Zur Systemidee in der Philosophie." In *Festschrift für Paul Natorp zum siebzigsten Geburtstage, gewidmet von Schülern und Freunden*, edited by Ernst Cassirer, 55–75. Berlin: Walter de Gruyter, 1924.
Galanis, John. "The Use (Private or Ecclesiastic) of the Holy Scripture in the Orthodox Church According to the Fathers of the Church." In *Orthodoxe Theologie zwischen Ost und West*, edited by Konstantin Nikolakopoulos, 115–21. Frankfurt am Main: Otto Lembeck, 2002.
Galitis, Georg, et al. *Glauben aus dem Herzen*. München: TR–Verlagsunion, 1987.
Gallaher, Brandon. "Georges Florovsky on Reading the Life of St Seraphim." *Sobornost* 27 (2005) 58–70.

———. "Waiting for the Barbarians: Identity and Polemicism in the Neo-patristic Synthesis of Georges Florovsky." *Modern Theology* 27 (2011) 660–92.

Gavrilyuk, Paul L. "Florovsky's Neopatristic Synthesis and the Future Ways of Orthodox Theology." In *Orthodox Constructions of the West*, edited by George Demacopoulos and Aristotle Papanikolaou, 102–24. New York: Fordham University Press, 2013.

———. "Vladimir Lossky's Reception of Georges Florovsky's Neo-Patristic Theology." In *A Celebration of Living Theology: A Festschrift in Honour of Andrew Louth*, edited by Justin A. Mihoc and Leonardo Aldea, 191–202. London: T. & T. Clark, 2014.

George, K. M. "An Oriental Orthodox Approach to Hermeneutics." *Indian Journal of Theology* 31 (1982) 203–11.

Grondin, Jean. "Do Gadamer and Ricoeur Have the Same Understanding of Hermeneutics?" In *The Agon of Interpretations: Towards a Critical Intercultural Hermeneutics*, edited by Ming Xie, 43–64. Toronto: Toronto University Press, 2014.

———. *Einführung zu Gadamer*. Tübingen: Mohr Siebeck, 2000.

———. "Gadamer and Bultmann." In *Philosophical Hermeneutics and Biblical Exegesis*, edited by Petr Pokorný, 121–43. Tübingen: Mohr Siebeck, 2002.

———. *Gadamer Lesebuch*. Tübingen: Mohr Siebeck, 1997.

———. *Hans-Georg Gadamer—eine Biographie*. Tübingen: Mohr Siebeck, 2000.

———. "Hans-Georg Gadamer, Paul Ricoeur: Correspondance/Briefwechsel 1964–2000." *Studia phaenomenologica* 13 (2013) 51–93.

———. *The Philosophy of Gadamer*. Ithaca, NY: McGill-Queen's University Press, 2003.

———. "Ricoeur's Long Way of Hermeneutics." In *The Routledge Companion to Philosophical Hermeneutics*, edited by Jeff Malpas and Hans-Helmuth Gander, 149–59. London, Routledge, 2015.

———. *Der Sinn der Hermeneutik*. Darmstadt: Wissenschaftliche Buchgesellschaft, 1994.

———. "Zur Komposition von Wahrheit und Methode." *Dilthey Jahrbuch* 8 (1993) 57–74.

Guarino, Thomas. "Revelation and Foundationalism: Toward Hermeneutical and Ontological Appropriateness." *Modern Theology* 6 (1990) 221–35.

Habermas, Jürgen. "Zu Gadamers Wahrheit und Methode." In *Hermeneutik und Ideologiekritik*, edited by Jürgen Habermas et al., 45–56. Frankfurt am Main: Suhrkamp, 1971.

———. "Der Universalitätsanspruch der Hermeneutik." In *Hermeneutik und Ideologiekritik*, edited by Jürgen Habermas et al., 120–59. Frankfurt am Main: Suhrkamp, 1971.

———. "Zur Logik der Sozialwissenschaften." *Philosophische Rundschau* 14 (1967) issue 5. Tubingen, Mohr Siebeck, 1967.

Habermas, Jürgen, et al. *Hermeneutik und Ideologiekritik*. Frankfurt am Main: Suhrkamp, 1971.

Halsey, Jim S. "History, Language, and Hermeneutic: The Synthesis of Wolfhart Pannenberg." *Westminster Theological Journal* 41 (1979) 269–90.

Hammermeister, Kai. *Hans-Georg Gadamer*. München: C. H. Beck, 1999.

Hampton, Alexander J. B. "The Conquest of Mythos by Logos: Countering Religion without Faith in Irenaeus, Coleridge and Gadamer." *Forum Philosophicum International Journal for Philosophy* 12 (2007) 57–70.

Hedges, Paul. "Gadamer, Play, and Interreligious Dialogue as the Opening of Horizons." *Journal of Dialogue Studies* 4 (2016) 5–27.
Heidegger, Martin, "Language." In *Poetry, Language, Thought*, 189–210. Translated by Albert Hofstadter. New York: Harper & Row, 1971.
——. "Letter on Humanism" In *Basic Writings*, edited by David Farrell Krell, 193–242. New York: Harper & Row, 1977.
——. "Natorp-Bericht." *Dilthey Jahrbuch* 6 (1989) 235–74.
——. "Phenomenological Interpretations with Respect to Aristotle: Indications of the Hermeneutical Situation." Translated by Michael Baur. *Man and the World* 25 (1992) 355–93.
——. *Platons Lehre von der Wahrheit*. Bern: Francke, 1954.
——. *Sein und Zeit*. 18th ed. Tübingen: Max Niemeyer, 2001.
——. *Der Ursprung des Kunstwerkes*. Frankfurt: Klostermann, 1935.
Helmholtz, Hermann von. "Ueber das Verhältniss der Naturwissenschaften zur Gesamtheit der Wissenschaft." In *Vorträge und Reden, erster Band*, 159–85. Braunschweig: Friedrich Vieweg und Sohn, 1903.
Hilberath, Bernd Jochen. *Theologie zwischen Tradition und Kritik: Die philosophische Hermeneutik Hans-Georg Gadamers als Herausforderung des theologischen Selbstverständnisses*. Düsseldorf: Patmos, 1978.
Hirsch, E. D., Jr. *The Aims of Interpretation*. Chicago: University of Chicago Press, 1976.
——. *Validity in Interpretation*. New Haven, CT: Yale University Press, 1967.
Hopko, Thomas. "The Bible in the Orthodox Church." *St Vladimir's Theological Quarterly* 14 (1970) 66–99.
Hovorun, Cyril. "Patristics after Neo-Patristics." In *A Celebration of Living Theology: A Festschrift in Honour of Andrew Louth*, edited by Justin A. Mihoc and Leonardo Aldea, 205–13. London: T. & T. Clark, 2014.
Hoy, David Cousens. *The Critical Circle: Literature, History and Philosophical Hermeneutics*. Berkeley: University of California Press, 1982.
Jeanrond, Werner G. "Biblical Criticism and Theology: Toward a New Biblical Theology." *Journal of Literature and Theology* 6 (1992) 218–27.
——. *Theological Hermeneutics: Development and Significance*. London: SCM, 1991.
Kalaitzidis, Pantelis. "Challenges of Renewal and Reformation Facing the Orthodox Church." *Ecumenical Review* 61 (2009) 136–64.
——. "From the 'Return to the Fathers' to the Need for a Modern Orthodox Theology." *St Vladimir's Theological Quarterly* 54 (2010) 5–36.
——. "The Image of the West in Contemporary Greek Theology." In *Orthodox Constructions of the West*, edited by George E. Demacopoulos and Aristotle Papanikolaou, 142–60. New York: Fordham University Press, 2013.
——. "Orthodox Theology and the Challenges of a Post-Secular Age: Questioning the Public Relevance of the Current Orthodox Theological 'Paradigm.'" In *Proceedings of the International Academic Theology in a Post-Secular Age*, 4–25. Lviv: Institute of Ecumenical Studies, 2013.
——. "Theological, Historical and Cultural Reasons for Anti-Ecumenical Movements in Eastern Orthodoxy." In *Orthodox Handbook on Ecumenism: Resources for Theological Education*, edited by Pantelis Kalaitzidis et al., 134–52. Oxford: Regnum, 2014.
Kant, Immanuel. *Kritik der reinen Vernunft*. Nach der ersten und zweiten Originalausgabe herausgegeben von Jens Timmermann. Hamburg: Meiner, 1998.

Karavidopoulos, Ioaniss. "Offenbarung und Inspiration der Schrift—Interpretation des Neuen Testaments in der Orthodoxen Kirche." In *Auslegung der Bibel*, edited by James Douglas Grant Dunn et al., 157–68. Tübingen: Mohr Siebeck, 2000.

Karuvelil, George. "Pragmatism, Existentialism, and Media Theory as Approaches to Religion and Science." *Zygon* 47 (2012) 415–37.

Kattan, Assaad Elias. "The Byzantine Icon: A Bridge Between Theology and Modern Culture?" In *Thinking Modernity: Towards a Reconfiguration of the Relationship between Orthodox Theology and Modern Culture*, edited by Assaad Elias Kattan and Fadi Georgi, 165–77. Tripoli: St. John of Damascus Institute of Theology, 2010.

———. "Die Byzantinische Ikone: Ort des Dialogs zwischen Theologie und moderner Kultur?" *Catholica* 60 (2006) 287–97.

———. "Essentialism Reconsidered: The Myth of a Non Hermeneutical Approach to Orthodox Tradition." Presentation at the conference Neo-Patristic Synthesis or Post-Patristic Theology: Can Orthodox Theology Be Contextual? Volos, 2010.

———. "Die Freiheit des theologischen Denkens: Das Abenteuer eines Dialogs?" In *Ostkirchen und Reformation 2017: Begegnungen und Tagungen im Jubiläumsjahr*, edited by Irena Zeltner Pavlović and Martin Illert, 2:181–90. Leipzig: Evangelische Verlagsanstalt, 2018.

———. "Gadamer 'Ad Portas': The Orthodox Understanding of Tradition Challenged by Hermeneutics." *Journal of Eastern Christian Studies* 66 (2014) 63–71.

———. "Hermeneutics: A Protestant Discipline for an Orthodox Context?" *The Near East School of Theology Theological Review* 23 (2002) 47–57.

———. "Les lignes directrices de la pensée théologique antiochienne contemporaine." *Istina* 56 (2011) 379–91.

———. "Orthodoxe Theologie und moderne Hermeneutik." *Catholica* 95 (2005) 67–86.

———. "Revisiting the Question about an Absolute Theological Criterion: Orthodox Theology Challenged by Modern Hermeneutics." In *Accents and Perspectives of Orthodox Dogmatic Theology as Part of Church Mission in Today's World*, edited by Ioan Tulcan and Cristinel Ioja, 128–43. Arad: Aurel Vlaicu University of Arad, 2008.

———. "La théologie orthodoxe interpelée par l'herméneutique moderne: La question d'un critère théologique absolu revisitée." *Contacts: revue française de l'orthodoxie* 234 (2011) 180–96.

Kelly, Michael. "The Gadamer–Habermas Debate Revisited: The Question of Ethics." *Philosophy and Social Criticism* 14 (1988) 369–90.

Khodr, Georges. *The Ways of Childhood*. Crestwood, NY: St Vladimir's University Press, 2016.

Kimmerle, Heinz, ed. *Fr.D.E. Schleiermacher. Hermeneutik*. Heidelberg: Carl Winter Universitätsverlag, 1974.

———. *Hermeneutics: The Handwritten Manuscripts*. Translated by James Duke and Jack Forstman. Missoula, MT: Scholars, 1977.

Kishkovsky, Leonid. "Russian Theology after Totalitarianism." In *The Cambridge Companion to Orthodox Christian Theology*, edited by Mary B. Cunningham and Elisabeth Theokritoff, 261–75. Cambridge, MA: Cambridge University Press, 2009.

Kisiel, Theodore. "The Happening of Tradition: The Hermeneutics of Gadamer and Heidegger." *Man and World* 2 (1969) 358–85.
Knotts, Mathew W. "Readers, Texts, and the Fusion of Horizons: Theology and Gadamer's Hermeneutics." *AUC Theologica* 4 (2014) 233–46.
Konstantinow, Dimitry. *Die Kirche in der Sowjetunion nach dem Kriege*. New York: All-Slavic, 1967.
Körner, Felix. "Gadamer Receptions Among Turkish Theologians Movements in Muslim Koran Hermeneutics." *Igreja e missão* 67 (2014) 205–24.
Lammi, Walter. *Gadamer and the Question of the Divine*. London: Continuum, 2008.
Lawlor, Leonard. "The Dialectical Unity of Hermeneutics: On Ricoeur and Gadamer." In *Gadamer and Hermeneutics*, edited by Hugo Silverman, 82–92. London: Routledge, 1991.
Lawn, Chris. *Gadamer: A Guide for the Perplexed*. London: Continuum, 2006.
Lawn, Chris, and Niall Keane. *The Gadamer Dictionary*. London: Continuum, 2011.
Lawrence, Fred. "Gadamer, Hermeneutic Revolution, and Theology." In *The Cambridge Companion to Gadamer*, edited by Robert Dostal, 167–200. Cambridge, MA: Cambridge University Press, 2002.
Linge, David E., ed. *Hans-Georg Gadamer Philosophical Hermeneutics*. Los Angeles: University of California Press, 1977.
Lonergan, Bernard. *Method in Theology*. New York: Herder and Herder, 1972.
Lossky, Vladimir. *The Mystical Theology of the Eastern Church*. Crestwood, NY: St Vladimir's Seminary, 1944.
———. *Orthodox Theology: An Introduction*. Crestwood, NY: St Vladimir's Seminary, 1978.
———. "Tradition and Traditions." In *The Meaning of Icons*, edited by Leonid Ouspensky and Vladimir Lossky, 10–22. Crestwood, NY: St Vladimir's Seminary, 1982.
Louth, Andrew. *Discerning the Mystery: An Essay on the Nature of Theology*. Oxford: Oxford University Press, 1983.
———. "Foreword." In *The Way to Nicaea*, edited by John Behr, ix–xii. Crestwood, NY: St Vladimir's Seminary, 2001.
———. *Introducing Eastern Orthodox Theology*. London: SPCK, 2013.
———. "Introduction." In *On the Absence and Unknowability of God*, edited by Christos Yannaras, 1–14. London: T. & T. Clark, 2005.
———. *Modern Orthodox Thinkers*. Downers Grove, IL: InterVarsity, 2015.
———. *St. John Damascene: Tradition and Originality in Byzantine Theology*. Oxford, Oxford University Press, 2002.
Malpas, Jeff, and Hans-Helmuth Gander, eds. *The Routledge Companion to Philosophical Hermeneutics*. London, Routledge, 2015.
Malpas, Jeff, and Santiago Zabala, eds. *Consequences of Hermeneutics: Fifty Years after Gadamer's Truth and Method*. Evanston, IL: Northwestern University Press, 2010.
Manoussakis, John Panteleimon. "Hermeneutics and Theology." In *Blackwell Companion to Hermeneutics*, edited by Niall Keane and Chris Lawn, 530–38. Chichester: Wiley Blackwell, 2016.
Margerie, Bertrand de. *An Introduction to the History of Exegesis: Greek Fathers*. Petersham: Saint Bede's, 1993.

McGrath, Patrick. "Gadamer and the Hermeneutic Problem of Biblical Revelation." In *Gadamer's Hermeneutics and the Art of Conversation*, edited by Andrzej Wierciński, 323–38. Berlin Lit, 2011.

McGuckin, John Anthony, ed. *The Concise Encyclopedia of Orthodox Christianity*. Chichester: John Wiley, 2014.

———. "Recent Biblical Hermeneutics in Patristic Perspective: The Tradition of Orthodoxy." *Greek Orthodox Theological Review* 47 (2002) 295–325.

———. Review of *The Way of Christ*, by Theodore Stylianopoulos. *Ecumenical Review* 56 (2004) 268–69.

Meek, Russell. "Hans-Georg Gadamer: His Philosophical Hermeneutics and Its Importance for Evangelical Biblical Hermeneutics." *Eleutheria* 1 (2011) 97–106.

Merras, Merja. "Do We Meet Modernity with Out-Of-Date Questions? Some Hermeneutical Reflections." In *Thinking Modernity: Towards a Reconfiguration of the Relationship between Orthodox Theology and Modern Culture*, edited by Assaad Elias Kattan and Fadi Georgi, 11–19. Tripoli: St. John of Damascus Institute of Theology, 2010.

Meyendorff, John. "Light from the East? 'Doing Theology' in an Eastern Orthodox Perspective." In *Doing Theology in Today's World*, edited by John D. Woodbridge and Thomas Edward McComiskey, 339–58. Grand Rapids: Zondervan, 1991.

———. *Living Tradition: Orthodox Witness in the Contemporary World*. Crestwood, NY: St Vladimir's Seminary, 1978.

———. "Orthodox Theology Today." *St Vladimir's Theological Quarterly* 13 (1969) 77–92.

Misgeld, Dieter, and Graeme Nicholson, eds. *Hans-Georg Gadamer on Education, Poetry, and History: Applied Hermeneutics*. Translated by Lawrence Schmidt and Monica Reuss. Albany: State University of New York Press, 1992.

Mihoc, Vasile. "The Actuality of Church Fathers' Biblical Exegesis. In *Auslegung der Bibel*, edited by James Douglas Grant Dunn et al., 3–28. Tübingen: Mohr Siebeck, 2000.

———. "Principles of Orthodox Hermeneutics." In *Congress Volume Ljubljana 2007*, edited by André Lemaire, 293–320. Leiden: Brill, 2010.

Mootz, J. Francis, III, and George H. Taylor, eds. *Gadamer and Ricoeur: Critical Horizons for Contemporary Hermeneutics*. London: Bloomsbury, 2012.

Mueller-Vollmer, Kurt. *Hermeneutics Reader: Texts of the German Tradition from the Enlightenment to the Present*. London: Bloomsbury, 1988.

Munteanu, Daniel. "Culture of Love and Hermeneutics of Truth: The Relevance of an Ecumenical Anthropology for a Pluralistic Society." In *Thinking Modernity: Towards a Reconfiguration of the Relationship between Orthodox Theology and Modern Culture*, edited by Assaad Elias Kattan and Fadi Georgi, 201–12. Tripoli: St. John of Damascus Institute of Theology, 2010.

Nassif, Bradley. "'Spiritual Exegesis' in the School of Antioch." In *New Perspectives on Historical Theology: Essays in Memory of John Meyendorff*, 343–77. Grand Rapids: Eerdmans, 1996.

———. "The 'Spiritual Exegesis' of Scripture: The School of Antioch Revisited." *Anglican Theological Review* 75 (1993) 437–70.

Negrov, Alexander. *Biblical Interpretation in the Russian Orthodox Church*. Tübingen: Mohr Siebeck, 2008.

---. "Biblical Interpretation in the Russian Orthodox Church: An Historical and Hermeneutical Perspective." *Verbum et Ecclesia* 22 (2001) 352–65.

---. "Three Hermeneutical Horizons of Slavic Evangelicals." *International Congregational Journal* 6 (2006) 83–104.

Nes, Solrunn. *The Mystical Language of Icons*. Grand Rapids: Eerdmans, 2004.

Nikolakopoulos, Konstantin. *Das Neue Testament in der Orthodoxen Kirche*. Münster: Lit, 2012.

---. "An Orthodox Critique of Some Radical Approaches in New Testament Studies." *Greek Orthodox Theological Review* 47 (2002) 339–55.

---. "Die Orthodoxe Hermeneutik in ihrem Selbstverständnis gegenüber der historisch-kritischen Methode." *Revista Ecumenica Sibiu/Review of Ecumenical Studies Sibiu* 6 (2014) 473–86.

---. *Die 'unbekannten Hymnen' des Neuen Testaments: Die orthodoxe Hermeneutik und die historisch-kritische Methode*. Aachen: Shaker, 2000.

Nissiotis, Nikos A. "The Unity of Scripture and Tradition: An Eastern Contribution to the Prolegomena of Hermeneutics." *Greek Orthodox Theological Review* 11 (1965) 183–208.

Nixon, Jon. *Hans-Georg Gadamer: The Hermeneutical Imagination*. New York: Springer, 2017.

Noble, Ivana. "History Tied Down by the Normativity of Tradition? Inversion of Perspective in Orthodox Theology: Challenges and Problems." In *The Shaping of Tradition: Context and Normativity*, edited by Golby Dickinson, 283–96. Leuven: Peeters, 2013.

---. "Vztah člověka k prostoru a k transcendence na ikonách a obrazech." In *Sensorium Dei*, edited by Karl Rechlík et al., 67–78. Brno: CDK, 2013.

---. "'Your Word Is a Lamp to my Feet and a Light to my Path': Critical Work with Pre-Critical Methods in the Hermeneutics of John Breck." *Communio Viatorum* 53 (2011) 51–62.

Noble, Ivana, and Tim Noble. "A Latin Appropriation of Christian Hellenism: Florovsky's Marginal Note to Patristic and Modern Theology and Its Possible Addressee." *St Vladimir's Theological Quarterly* 55 (2012) 269–88.

---. "Orthodox Theology in Western Europe in the 20th Century." *EGO-European History Online*. Mainz: Leibniz Institute of European History, 2013. http://www.ieg-ego.eu/noblei-noblet-2013-en.

Noble, Ivana, et al. *The Ways of Orthodox Theology in the West*. Yonkers, NY: St Vladimir's Seminary, 2015.

Noble, Ivana, et al. *Wrestling with the Mind of the Fathers*. Yonkers, NY: St Vladimir's Seminary, 2015.

Noble, Tim. "Rights of the Indigenous People and the Orthodox Mission to Alaska." *Communio Viatorum* 54 (2012) 164–73.

Obielosi, Dominik, and Ani Donpedro. "Gadamer's Hermeneutics and Its Relevance to Biblical Interpretation." *Preorc Journal of Arts and Humanities* 2 (2017) 1–15.

Odenstedt, Anders. *Gadamer on Tradition—Historical Context and the Limits of Reflection*. Berlin: Springer, 2017.

Oikonomos, Elias. *Bibel und Bibelwissenschaft in der Orthodoxen Kirche*. Stuttgart: KBW, 1976.

Ommen, Thomas B. "Bultmann and Gadamer: The Role of Faith in Theological Hermeneutics." *Thought* 59 (1984) 348–59.

Osborne, Grant R. "The Many and the One: The Interface between Orthodox and Evangelical Protestant Hermeneutics." *St Vladimir's Theological Quarterly* 39 (1995) 281–304.
Ouspensky, Leonid. *Theology of the Icons*. Crestwood, NY: St Vladimir's Seminary, 1978.
Ouspensky, Leonid, and Vladimir Lossky. *The Meaning of Icons*. Crestwood, NY: St Vladimir's Seminary, 1982.
Palmer, Richard E. *Hermeneutics: Interpretation Theory in Schleiermacher, Dilthey, Heidegger and Gadamer*. Evanston, IL: Northwestern University Press, 1969.
Pannenberg, Wolfhart. "Hermeneutics and Universal History." In *Basic Questions in Theology: Collected Essays*, 1:96–136. Minneapolis: Fortress, 2008.
———. "Hermeneutik und Universalgeschichte." *Zeitschrift für Theologie und Kirche* 60 (1963) 90–121.
Papanikolaou, Aristotle. "Contemporary Orthodox Theology." In *The Concise Encyclopedia of Orthodox Christianity*, edited by John Anthony McGuckin, 114–17. Chichester: John Wiley, 2014.
———. "Eastern Orthodox Theology." In *Routledge Companion to Modern Christian Thought*, edited by Chad Meister and James Beilby, 538–48. London: Routledge, 2013.
———. "Tradition as Reason and Practice: Amplifying Contemporary Orthodox Theology in Conversation with Alasdair MacIntyre." *St Vladimir's Theological Quarterly* 59 (2015) 91–104.
———. "Tradition or Identity Politics: The Role of the 'West' in Contemporary Orthodox Theology." *Teologia* 3–4 (2010) 18–25.
Papathanasiou, Athanasios N. "Some Key Themes and Figures in Greek Theological Thought." In *The Cambridge Companion to Orthodox Christian Theology*, edited by Mary B. Cunningham and Elisabeth Theokritoff, 218–31. Cambridge: Cambridge University Press, 2009.
Pentiuc, Eugen J., et al. *Studies in Orthodox Hermeneutics: A Festschrift in Honor of Theodore G. Stylianopoulos*. Brookline, MA: Holy Cross Orthodox Press, 2016.
Peters, Carmichael C. *A Gadamerian Reading of Karl Rahner's Theology of Grace and Freedom*. Lanham, MD: Catholic Scholars, 2000.
Pöggeler, Otto. *Heidegger und die hermeneutische Philosophie*. Freiburg: Karl Alber, 1983.
———. "Hermeneutik und Dekonstruktion." In *Verstehen und Geschehen*, 63–86. Heidelberg: Martin Heidegger-Gesellschaft, 1991.
Prokurat, Michael. "Orthodox Interpretation of Scripture." In *The Bible in the Churches: How Various Christians Interpret the Scriptures*, edited by Kenneth Hagen, 61–100. Milwaukee, WI: Marquette University Press, 1998.
———. "The Pneumatological Dimension in the Hermeneutical Task." In *Interpreting Together*, edited by Peter Bouteneff and Dagmar Heller, 102–10. Geneva: WCC, 2001.
Przylebski, Andrzej. "Gadamer's Critique of the Instrumental Philosophy of Language." In *Gadamer's Hermeneutics and the Art of Conversation*, edited by Andrzej Wierciński, 231–42. Berlin: Lit, 2011.
Rebengiuc, Tudor. "The Nature of Language in Orthodox Church Architecture: A Hermeneutical Approach." PhD diss., University of Cincinnati, 2010. https://etd.ohiolink.edu/!etd.send_file?accession=ucin1282169753&disposition=inline.

Rese, Friederike. "*Phronesis* als Modell der Hermeneutik: Die hermeneutische Aktualität des Aristoteles." In *Hans-Georg Gadamer: Wahrheit und Methode*, edited by Günter Figal, 127–50. Berlin: Akademie, 2007.

Ricoeur, Paul. "Ethics and Culture Habermas and Gadamer in Dialogue." *Philosophy Today* 17 (1973) 153–65.

———. "The Hermeneutical Function of Distanciation." *Philosophy Today* 17 (1973) 129–41.

———. "Hermeneutics and the Critique of Ideology." In *Hermeneutics and the Modern Philosophy*, edited by Brice Wachterhauser, 300–339. Albany: State University of New York Press, 1986.

———. *Hermeneutics and the Human Science: Essays on Language, Action and Interpretation*. Cambridge: Cambridge University Press, 1981.

———. "Philosophical Hermeneutics and Theological Hermeneutics." *Studies in Religion/Sciences Religieuses* 5 (1975–76) 14–33.

Ringma, Charles Richard. *Gadamer's Dialogical Hermeneutic*. Heidelberg: Universitätsverlag C. Winter, 1999.

Rossen, H. Stanley. "Horizontverschmelzung." In *The Philosophy of Hans-Georg Gadamer*, edited by Lewis Edwin Hahn, 207–15. Chicago: Open Court, 1997.

Sauvé, Ross Joseph. "Florovsky's Tradition." *Greek Orthodox Theological Review* 55 (2010) 213–42.

Schillebeeckx, Edward. "Towards a Catholic Use of Hermeneutics." In *God the Future of Man*, 1–50. New York: Sheed & Ward, 1968.

———. *The Understanding of Faith: Interpretation and Criticism*. New York: Seabury, 1974.

Schleiermacher, Friedrich Daniel Ernst. *The Christian Faith*. London: T. & T. Clark, 2016.

Schmemann, Alexander. "Inter-Orthodox Symposium of Thessalonica." *St Vladimir's Theological Quarterly* 16 (1972) 150–53.

Schneider, Richard. "Orthodox Iconography as Liturgical Art: Call and Response between the Painted Icon and the Living Icon." *Proceedings of the North American Academy of Liturgy* (2007) 33–36.

———. "Symbols of the Divine and Created Wholeness in the Icons of the Orthodox Iconographers in the West." Presentation at the International Scientific Conference "Symbolic Mediation of Wholeness in Western Orthodoxy," 2014.

Schuchman, P. "Aristotle's Phronesis and Gadamer's Hermeneutics." *Philosophy Today* 23 (1979) 41–50.

Schweiker, William. "Sacrifice, Interpretation, and the Sacred: The Import of Gadamer and Girard for Religious Studies." *Journal of the American Academy of Religion* 55 (1987) 791–810.

Sheridan, Mark. Review of *The New Testament: An Orthodox Perspective*, by Theodore Stylianopoulos. *The Catholic Biblical Quarterly* 61 (1999) 606–7.

Stenger, Mary Ann. "Gadamer's Hermeneutics as a Model for Cross-Cultural Understanding and Truth in Religion." In *Religious Pluralism and Truth*, edited by Thomas Dean, 151–68. Albany: State University of New York Press, 1995.

Stobbe, Heinz-Günther. *Hermeneutik—ein ökumenisches Problem: Eine Kritik der Katholischen Gadamer-Rezeption*. Gütersloh: Benzinger, 1981.

Stolzenberg, Jürgen. "Hermeneutik der praktischen Vernunft: Hans-Georg Gadamer interpretiert Martin Heideggers Aristoteles–Interpretation." In *Dimensionen des*

Hermeneutischen: Heidegger und Gadamer, edited by Günter Figal and Hans-Helmuth Gander, 133–52. Frankfurt: Klostermann, 2005.

Stover, Dale. "Linguisticality and Theology. Applying the Hermeneutics of Hans-Georg Gadamer." *Studies in Religion/Sciences Religieuses* 5 (1975–76) 34–44.

Stuhlmacher, Peter. *Vom Verstehen des Neuen Testaments: eine Hermeneutik*. Göttingen: Vandenhoeck & Ruprecht, 1979.

Sturm, Thomas. "Rituale sind wichtig: Hans-Georg Gadamer über Chancen und Grenzen der Philosophie." *Der Spiegel*, February 21, 2000 (8/2000) 305.

Stylianopoulos, Theodore G. "Biblical Studies in Orthodox Theology: A Response." *Greek Orthodox Theological Review* 17 (1972) 69–85.

———. "Comments on Chrysostom, Patristic Interpretation, and Contemporary Biblical Scholarship." *Greek Orthodox Theological Review* 54 (2009) 189–204.

———. *The Good News of Christ*. Brookline, MA: Holy Cross Orthodox Press, 1991.

———. "Holy Scripture, Interpretation and Spiritual Cognition in St Symeon the New Theologian." *Greek Orthodox Theological Review* 46 (2001) 3–34.

———. *The New Testament: An Orthodox Perspective*. Vol. 1, *Scripture, Tradition, Hermeneutics*. Brookline, MA: Holy Cross Orthodox Press, 1997.

———. "Orthodox Biblical Interpretation." In *Dictionary of Theological Interpretation of the Bible*, edited by Kevin J. Vanhoozer, 554–58. Grand Rapids: Baker Academic, 2005.

———. "Perspectives in Orthodox Biblical Interpretation." *Greek Orthodox Theological Review* 47 (2002) 327–38.

———. "Scripture and Tradition in the Church." In *The Cambridge Companion to Orthodox Christian Theology*, edited by Mary B. Cunningham and Elisabeth Theokritoff, 21–34. Cambridge: Cambridge University Press, 2009.

Širka, Zdenko. "Experience with Hermeneutics in Modern Orthodox Theology." *International Journal of Orthodox Theology* 9 (2018) 58–89.

———. "Gadamer's Concept of Aesthetic Experience as a Possibility for the Orthodox Biblical Theology." *Revista Ecumenica Sibiu/Review of Ecumenical Studies Sibiu* 6 (2014) 378–407.

Tarazi, Paul Nadim. *Galatians: A Commentary*. Crestwood, NY: St Vladimir's Seminary, 1994.

———. *The Old Testament Introduction*. Crestwood, NY: St Vladimir's Seminary, 1991.

Taylor, Charles. "Understanding the Other: A Gadamerian View on Conceptual Schemes." In *Gadamer's Century: Essays in Honor of Hans-Georg Gadamer*, edited by Jeff Malpas et al., 279–81. London: MIT, 2002.

Thiselton, Anthony. *The Two Horizons New Testament Hermeneutics and Philosophical Description with Special Reference to Heidegger, Bultmann, Gadamer and Wittgenstein*. Exeter: Paternoster, 1980.

Tietz, Udo. *Hans-Georg Gadamer zur Einführung*. Hamburg: Junius, 1999.

Tillich, Paul. *Dynamics of Faith*. New York: Harper, 1957.

Tingley, Edward. "Gadamer and Light of the Word." *First Things* 139 (2004) 38–45.

Tracy, David. "Is There Hope for the Public Realm? Conversation as Interpretation." *Social Research* 65 (1998) 597–609.

———. *Plurality and Ambiguity: Hermeneutics, Religion, Hope*. San Francisco: Harper & Row, 1987.

———. "Western Hermeneutics and Interreligious Dialogue." In *Interreligious Hermeneutics*, edited by C. Cornile and Christopher Conway, 1–43. Eugene, OR: Cascade, 2010.

Tsirpanlis, Constantine. *Introduction to Eastern Patristic Thought and Orthodox Theology*. Collegeville, MN: Liturgical, 1991.

Turcan, Nicolae. "Tradiția bisericii sau despre hermeneutică și sfințenie (Church tradition. Reflection on hermeneutics and holiness)." *Studia Universitatis Babes-Bolyai Theologia Orthodoxa* 1 (2010) 227–37.

Ugolnik, Anton. "An Orthodox Hermeneutic in the West." *St Vladimir's Theological Quarterly* 27 (1983) 93–118.

Valliere, Paul. *Modern Russian Theology: Bukharev, Soloviev, Bulgakov: Orthodox Theology in a New Key*. Grand Rapids: Eerdmans, 2000.

Vanhoozer, Kevin J. "Discourse on Matter: Hermeneutics and the 'Miracle' of Understanding." *International Journal of Systematic Theology* 7 (2005) 5–37.

———. "Scripture and Tradition." In *The Cambridge Companion to Postmodern Theology*, 149–69. Cambridge: Cambridge University Press, 2003.

Vanhoozer, Kevin, et al., eds. *Hermeneutics at the Crossroads*. Bloomington: Indiana University Press, 2006.

Vassiliadis, Petros. "Canon and Authority of Scripture: An Orthodox Hermeneutical Perspective." In *Orthodox and Wesleyan Scriptural Understanding and Practice*, edited by S. T. Kimbrough Jr., 21–35. Crestwood, NY: St Vladimir's Seminary, 2005.

Vessey, David. "Hans-Georg Gadamer and the Philosophy of Religion." *Philosophy Compass* 5 (2010) 645–55.

Vilhauer, Monica. *Gadamer's Ethics of Play: Hermeneutics and the Other*. Plymouth, UK: Lexington, 2010.

Ware, Kallistos. *The Orthodox Way*. Crestwood, NY: St Vladimir's Seminary, 1979.

———. "The Unity of Scripture and Tradition: An Orthodox Approach." In *What Is It that the Scripture Says? Essays on Biblical Interpretation, Translation and Reception in Honour of Henry Wansbrough OSB*, edited by Philip McCosker, 231–46. London: T. & T. Clark, 2006.

Warnke, Georgia. *Gadamer: Hermeneutics, Tradition and Reason*. Cambridge: Polity, 1987.

Weinsheimer, Joel C. *Gadamer's Hermeneutics: A Reading of Truth and Method*. New Haven, CT: Yale University Press, 1985.

Weiss, James R. Review of *Scripture in Tradition*, by John Breck. *Greek Orthodox Theological Review* 49 (2004) 143–48.

Wierciński, Andrzej. "The Hermeneutic Retrieval of a Theological Insight: Verbum Interius." In *Between the Human and the Divine: Philosophical and Theological Hermeneutics*, 1–23. Toronto: Hermeneutics, 2002.

———. "'Sprache ist Gespräch': Gadamer's Understanding of Language." In *Gadamer's Hermeneutics and the Art of Conversation*, 37–58. Berlin: Lit, 2011.

Wilhelm Dilthey. *Gesammelte Schriften*. 12 vols. Leipzig: Teubner, 1922–36.

Williams, George H. "The Neo-Patristic Synthesis of Georges Florovsky." In *Georges Florovsky: Russian Intellectual, Orthodox Churchman*, edited by Andrew Blane, 289–340. Crestwood, NY: St Vladimir's Seminary, 1993.

Yannaras, Christos. *Elements of Faith: An Introduction to Orthodox Theology*. London: T. & T. Clark, 1991.

———. "Orthodoxy and the West." *Greek Orthodox Theological Review* 17 (1972) 115–31.

———. *Orthodoxy and the West*. Brookline, MA: Holy Cross Orthodox Press, 2006.

———. "Theology in Present-day Greece." *St Vladimir's Theological Quarterly* 16 (1972) 195–214.

Young, Frances M. *Biblical Exegesis and the Formation of Christian Culture*. Cambridge: Cambridge University Press, 1997.

Zimmermann, Jens. "Confusion of Horizons: Gadamer and the Christian Logos." *Journal of Beliefs and Values: Studies in Religion and Education* 22 (2001) 87–98.

———. "The Ethics of Philosophical Hermeneutics and the Challenge of Religious Transcendence." *Philosophy Today* 51 (2007) 50–69.

———. "*Ignoramus*: Gadamer's 'Religious Turn.'" *Symposium: Journal for Hermeneutics and Postmodern Thought* 6 (2006) 204–17.

———. *Recovering Theological Hermeneutics: An Incarnational-Trinitarian Theory of Interpretation*. Grand Rapids: Baker, 2004.

Zizioulas, John D. *Being as Communion: Studies in Personhood and the Church*. Crestwood, NY: St Vladimir's Seminary, 1985.

———. "Doctrine as the Teaching of the Church." In *Lectures in Christian Dogmatics John D. Zizioulas*, edited by Douglas Knight, 1–39. London: T. & T. Clark, 2008.

———. "The Orthodox Church and the Third Millennium." http://theology.balamand.edu.lb/index.php/local-events/738-zizioulaslecture.

———. "Person and Nature in the Theology of St Maximus the Confessor." In *St Maximus the Confessor*, edited by Maxim Vasiljević, 85–113. Belgrade: Sebastian, 2013.

———. "The Task of Orthodox Theology in Today's Europa." *International Journal of Orthodox Theology* 6/3 (2015) 9–17.

Zymaris, Philip. "The Forgotten Connection between Liturgy and Theology." *Praxis* 12/1 (2012) n.p. https://www.academia.edu/5141448/The_Forgotten_Connection_Between_Liturgy_and_Theology.

Index of Names

Abgar (King of Edessa), 171
Agourides, Savvas, 99, 100, 100n22, 102n28, 121, 121n49
Albert, Hans, 36n1, 37, 37n5
Alfeyev, Hilarion, 111n5, 130, 130n8, 156, 156n27, 168, 168n10
Alivizatos, Hamilcar, 99
Andreopoulos, Andreas, 103, 141n44
Ani, Donpedro, 88n25
Antiochenes, 140, 164
Antoniadis, E., 101
Apostle Paul, 59, 122, 163, 164
Aquinas, Thomas, 79n99, 132
Aristotle, xvi, 3, 8, 8n33, 9, 10, 10n39, 10n40, 10n41, 11, 117n37
Arthos, John, 9n34
Asproulis, Nikolaos, 96n8
Audi, Elias, 102n30
Augustine, 77n94, 79, 79n99, 79n103, 113, 117, 118, 118n42
Aylesworth, Gary E., 45, 45n43

Baker, Matthew, 96n8, 112n14, 114, 114n24, 114n25, 115, 115n26, 115n27, 115n30, 136n29
Balthasar, Hans Ursvon, 112n8
Barrois, Georges Augustin, 103, 141n43
Barth, Karl, 7, 132
Barthold, Lauren Swayne, 51n65
Bartholomew I of Constantinople, 97n11
Basil the Great, 169
Bateman, Debbie, 112n11

Behr, John, 92, 105n39, 107, 107n47, 107n48, 107n49, 129, 129n2
Bernasconi, Robert, 30n35, 31n36, 37n8, 87n24, 91n37
Bernstein, Richard Jacob, 37, 37n7, 41, 41n28, 61n23
Betti, Emilio, 6, 37, 37n3
Blane, Andrew, 97n14, 114n25
Bobrinskoy, Boris, 170n21
Bollnow, Otto Friedrich, 15n58
Bonhoeffer, Dietrich, 132
Bratsiotis, Panayotis, 99, 99n20, 101
Breck, John, xv, xx, 92, 104n33, 128, 138–42, 139n34, 139n35, 139n36, 139n38, 140n39, 140n40, 140n41, 140n42, 140n43, 141n44, 141n45, 141n47, 143, 152, 154, 154n18, 154n19, 154n21, 155, 155n23, 161n39, 161n40, 162–63, 162n42, 162n43, 162n44, 162n45, 164, 167n4, 168, 168n9, 170, 170n18, 170n19, 171, 186
Brock, Sebastian, 112n8
Bröcker, Walter, 9n34
Brüning, Alfons, 111n6
Bubner, Rüdiger, 28n24
Bukharev, Alexander M., 110
Bulgakov, Sergius, 134, 135
Bultmann, Rudolf, 1, 2, 7, 7n30, 26n16, 62n27, 86, 104n33, 108, 123
Butcher, Brian A., 42n29

Calivas, Alkiviadis, 159, 159n33

INDEX OF NAMES

Caputo, John D., 86, 86n17
Carr, Thomas K., 46n47
Casiday, Augustine, 121n49
Cassian, John, 156
Cavafy, Constantine Peter, 132, 132n18
Celan, Paul, 6, 19n74, 29
Chagall, Marc, 173
Chrysostom, John, 120n47, 143
Clark, Timothy, 104n36, 140n43
Clement of Alexandria, 123, 169
Constantelos, Demetrios, 101
Constantine V, 171, 171n22
Crisp, Simon, 167n3
Crowley, Paul G., 47, 47n52
Cunningham, Mary B., 95n6, 172n24
Cyprian, Saint, 149n7
Cyril of Jerusalem, 169

Danckaert, Seraphim, 114n25
Daniélou, Jean, 112n8, 113
Davey, Nicholas, 33n44, 88n29, 89–90, 89n31, 89n32, 90n33, 90n34, 90n36
Demacopoulos, George E., 123n52
Demetrios, Archbishop of America, 105, 105n40
Demırezen, Ismael, 84, 84n10, 85n11
Derrida, Jacques, 1, 31, 36
Descartes, René, 1
Dilthey, Wilhelm, xvii, 15–17, 17n66, 19, 25, 44, 144n59, 148, 179
Domšaitis, Pranas, 173
Dostal, Robert J., 8n31, 26n17
Dottori, Riccardo, 31–32, 32n40, 33, 33n45, 33n46
Droysen, Johann, 25
Drozdov, Philaret, 110, 115
Dutt, Carsten, 21n85, 28n23
D-Vasilescu, Elena Ene, 160n38

Eberhard, Philippe, 7n27, 72n66
Ebertz, Roger, 81, 81n1, 82n2
Eckhart, Meister, 135
Evdokimov, Paul, 102n29, 104n33, 173, 173n27

Feyerabend, P., 36n1

Figal, Günter, 10n41
Fiorenza, Francis Schüssler, 48, 148n1, 180–81
Fischer, Mark F., 46n47, 50n60
Florensky, Pavel, 134, 135, 138, 144
Florovsky, Georges, xix, 96, 96n8, 96n9, 96n10, 97, 97n12, 97n13, 97n14, 98, 99, 103, 109, 111, 111n6, 111n7, 112–13, 112n9, 112n10, 112n12, 112n13, 113n16, 113n17, 113n19, 114, 114n20, 114n21, 114n22, 114n23, 114n24, 115, 115n28, 115n29, 115n30, 124n54, 126, 129, 130, 131, 132, 133, 136, 159, 163n50, 169n17, 184, 185
Fortounatto, Mariamna, 172, 172n24
Frank, Manfred, 13n49, 13n50, 13n52, 13n53, 14n53, 14n54, 15n58
Friedländer, Paul, 3n6

Gaiger, Jason, 30n30
Galanis, John, 169, 169n14, 169n15
Galitis, Georg, 155n26
Gallaher, Brandon, xx, 96n8, 114, 114n20, 128, 132–34, 132n15, 132n16, 132n17, 133n19, 133n20, 133n21, 134n22, 186
Gavrilyuk, Paul L., 96n10, 111n7
George, K. M., 29, 65n39, 104n33
Germanus, Saint, 156
Goethe, Johann Wolfgang von, 26n16
Gondikakis, Vasileos, 99n19
Gregory of Nyssa, 158
Grondin, Jean, 2n1, 2n2, 5n18, 5n21, 7n25, 15, 15n61, 18, 19n73, 22n1, 24n5, 24n7, 24n9, 24n10, 24n11, 25, 25n14, 26n16, 27n20, 28n23, 36n1, 42n29, 42n31, 57n3, 63n30
Guardini, Romano, 56n1
Guarino, Thomas, 52, 52n70

Habermas, Jürgen, xvii, 1, 6, 35, 38–41, 38n11, 38n12, 39n12, 39n13, 39n14, 39n15, 39n16,

INDEX OF NAMES

40n17, 40n21, 40n22, 40n23, 52,
  53–54, 178, 180
Halsey, Jim S., 51n68
Hammermeister, Kai, 58n6
Hampton, Alexander J. B., 85, 85n14,
  85n15
Hartmann, Nicolai, 1, 2, 3
Hedges, Paul, 84n10
Hegel, Georg, 1, 6, 9n35, 25, 45, 52,
  113n19
Heidegger, Martin, xvii, 1, 3, 3n4,
  3n6, 4, 4n12, 6, 6n24, 7, 8n32, 9,
  9n34, 9n35, 10, 10n40, 10n41,
  17–21, 18n69, 18n71, 18n72,
  19n74, 19n77, 20n78, 20n79,
  20n80, 20n81, 23n2, 25, 28n21,
  29n29, 34n51, 42n30, 45, 61n20,
  67n51, 99, 117, 117n37, 126,
  132, 179
Helmholtz, Hermann von, 25, 25n12
Heraclitus, 118n39
Hilberath, Bernd Jochen, 46–47,
  47n49, 47n50, 47n51, 148n1
Hirsch, Eric Donald, Jr., 37, 37n4
Hopko, Thomas, 158n31, 166n1
Horton, Robin, 134
Hovorun, Cyril, 120n46
Hoy, David Cousens, 59, 59n11
Humbolt, Alexander von, 75, 75n84
Husserl, Edmund, 1, 3, 69, 69n57

Ignatius of Antioch, 169
Ioannidis, A. C., 101

Jaeger, Werner, 112n8
Jasper, Karl, 4
Jeanrond, Werner, 52n71, 148n1
Jesus, 49n58, 51, 79, 87, 107,
  140–41n43, 154, 156, 157, 164,
  169, 171
Justin Martyr, 103

Kalaitzidis, Pantelis, xx, 96n8, 97,
  98n15, 100n21, 116n31, 116n32,
  116n33, 128, 129–32, 129n1,
  129n3, 130n5, 130n6, 130n7,
  131n9, 131n10, 131n11, 132n13,
  132n14, 135, 136, 136n28, 137,
  186
Kant, Immanuel, 1, 15, 27, 48, 57n3,
  59, 124, 132, 173, 181, 181n2,
  181n3, 182, 182n4
Karavidopoulos, Ioaniss, 155n24
Karuvelil, George, 83, 83n5, 83n6
Kasel, Odo, 114n24
Kattan, Assaad Elias, xv, xx, 92, 128,
  129n3, 134n23, 136–38, 136n30,
  137n31, 137n33, 141n43,
  144n59, 147, 150–51, 150n13,
  151n14, 164, 173, 174, 174n28,
  174n29, 174n30, 175, 186, 187
Keane, Niall, 7n27, 28n22
Kehm, George H., 50n62
Kelly, Michael, 41n25
Kesich, Veselin, 102n29, 141n43
Khodr, Georges, 136–37
Kierkegaard, Søren, 99, 104n33
Kimmerle, Heinz, 12n48, 13n51, 14,
  14n55, 14n57
Kishkovsky, Leonid, 111n5
Klein, Jakob, 3
Kniazeff, Father, 103
Knotts, Mathew W., 69n57
Koller, Erwin, 7n29
Konstantinou, Miltiadis, 100
Konstantinow, Dimitry, 111n3
Körner, Felix, 85n11
Krüger, Gerhard, 3, 9n34, 24

Lawlor, Leonard, 45n44
Lawn, Chris, 7n27, 28n22, 30n34
Lawrence, Fred, 86, 86n19, 87n21
Leibniz, Gottfried Wilhelm, 4n13
Leo III, 171, 171n22
Lévi-Strauss, Claude, 134
Linge, David E., 86n20
Lledó, Emilio, 4
Lonergan, Bernard, 148n1, 176
Lossky, Vladimir, 111, 111n6, 111n7,
  114, 115, 126, 134, 135, 135n25,
  153n16, 159, 159n35, 185
Louth, Andrew, xx, 92, 94n1, 95,
  95n6, 105, 116n34, 117n37, 147,
  148–50, 148n2, 148n3, 148n4,

149n6, 149n7, 150n9, 150n10, 150n12, 164, 174n29, 187
Louvaris, Nikolaos, 99
Löwith, Karl, 3
Lubac, Henri de, 112n8, 113
Lucaris, Cyril, 120
Lücke, Friedrich, 14n54
Luther, Martin, 59, 104n33, 132, 154n20, 174, 178n1

Macario of Corinth, Saint, 96
Malpas, Jeff, 36n2
Mann, Horace, 5
Manoussakis, John Panteleimon, 106, 107n46
Mantzaridis, Georgios, 99n19, 155n26
Margerie, Bertrand de, 139, 141, 141n46, 161–62, 162n41, 162n42
Marx, Karl, 132
Matsoukas, Nikos, 99n19
Maximus the Confessor, 96, 120, 120n47, 174
McGrath, Patrick, 86n18, 87, 88, 88n26, 88n27
McGuckin, John Anthony, 95, 95n7, 120n47, 125–26, 125n56, 126n60, 143n53, 152, 154–55, 155n22, 167, 167n8
Meek, Russell, 88n25
Merras, Merja, 104, 105n38
Metallinos, George, 116n32
Meyendorff, John, 95, 95n4, 95n5, 111, 111n5, 135, 168, 169n13
Mihoc, Vasile, 92, 104, 104n36, 121n50, 152, 154, 154n20, 154n21, 158, 158n32, 159–60, 163, 163n46, 167, 167n7, 168, 168n11
Misgeld, Dieter, 30n30, 30n31
Möhler, Johann Adam, 132
Mootz, J. Francis, III, 45n45
Mueller-Vollmer, Kurt, 19n77
Munteanu, Daniel, 105, 105n41

Nassif, Bradley, 164, 164n51
Natorp, Paul, 1, 2, 3, 18n69
Negrov, Alexander, 110n1, 110n2, 167n6

Nellas, Panayiotis, 99n19
Nes, Solrunn, 172, 173n25
Newman, John, 114
Nicholson, Graeme, 30n30, 30n31
Nietzsche, Friedrich, 117
Nikodimos of Holy Mountain, Saint, 96
Nikolakapoulos, Konstantin, 104n37, 123, 123n51, 125n58, 160, 160n36, 160n37
Nissiotis, Nikos A., 99, 101, 101n26
Noble, Ivana, xx, 92, 111n4, 113, 113n18, 114, 114n24, 128, 131n12, 135, 135n27, 136, 136n28, 136n29, 139n36, 172, 173, 173n26, 186
Noble, Timothy, xix, xixn2, 111n4, 113, 113n18, 114, 114n24, 119n45, 120n46, 125n57, 131n12, 136n29, 177

Obielosi, Dominik, 88n25
Odenstedt, Anders, 64n35
Oikonomos, Elias, 124n55
Ommen, Thomas B., 86n18, 86n19
Origen, 103, 122
Osborne, Grant R., 163, 163n47, 163n50
Ouspensky, Leonid, 173n26

Palamas, Gregory, 96, 99, 120n47, 184
Palmer, Richard, 73n70
Palmer, Richard E., 58n7
Pannenberg, Wolfhart, xv, 50, 50n62, 50n63, 50n64, 51, 51n66, 51n67, 51n69, 52, 148n1, 181
Papamichael, Gregorios, 99
Papanikolaou, Aristotle, xx, 123n52, 128, 134, 134n24, 135, 135n25, 135n26, 152, 156, 156n28, 156n29, 157, 157n30, 159n34, 159n35, 186
Papathanasiou, Athanasios N., 99, 99n18
Paul the Apostle, 59, 122, 163, 164
Pavskii, Gerasim, 110
Pearson, John, 114
Pentiuc, Eugen J., 142n48

INDEX OF NAMES

Peters, Carmichael C., 46n47
Petrou, Ioannis, 100
Philippides, Leonidas, 99
Photius the Great, 120
Picht, Georg, 9n34
Plato, xvi, 3, 8, 8–9n33, 8n32, 9, 9n35, 10, 10n41, 11, 23, 25, 59, 66, 66n43, 76, 76n89, 79, 82, 117, 117n37
Pöggeler, Otto, 18n72
Polycarp, 169
Popović, Justin, 112
Prokurat, Michael, 104, 104n35, 152, 163n48, 163n49, 169n16, 174n32
Przylebski, Andrzej, 76n87

Quasten, Johannes, 112n8

Rambach, Johann Jakob, 69
Rebengiuc, Tudor, 173, 175, 175n33
Rese, Friederike, 10n41
Ricoeur, Paul, xvii, 26n18, 35, 38, 41–45, 42n29, 43n32, 43n33, 43n34, 44n36, 44n37, 44n38, 44n39, 44n40, 44n41, 44n42, 52, 53–54, 60, 84, 108, 119, 125, 178, 180
Rilke, Rainer Maria, 29, 34, 56, 56n1, 57n3, 80, 182
Ringma, Charles Richard, 37n6, 41n26
Romanides, John, 99n19, 99n20, 116, 135n25
Rorty, Richard, 1, 36
Rossen, H. Stanley, 65n41

Sartre, Jean-Paul, 132
Sauvé, Ross Joseph, 113n15, 113n19
Scheller, Max, 1
Schelling, Friedrich, 132
Schillebeeckx, Edward, xv, 46, 46n47, 46n48
Schleiermacher, Friedrich, xvii, 1, 12–15, 13n50, 13n53, 14n54, 17, 25, 45, 108, 144n59, 179
Schmemann, Alexander, 100, 100n24, 101n25, 111, 111n5, 135, 173

Schneider, Richard, 173, 175–76, 175n34, 176n35, 176n36
Schuchman, P., 10n41
Schweiker, William, 83, 83n4
Sheller, Max, 2
Sheridan, Mark, 144n58
Simeon the New, 120
Socrates, 9, 23
Sokolowski, Robert, 90n36
Solovyov, Vladimir, 134
Sophocles, 48n54
Stăniloae, Dumitru, 112, 135
Stanley, John W., 18n70
Stenger, Mary Ann, 84n10
Stobbe, Heinz-Günther, 49, 50, 50n60, 50n61, 148n1
Stolzenberg, Jürgen, 10n41
Strauss, Leo, 3, 9n34
Stuhlmacher, Peter, 47, 47n53, 48, 148n1, 180
Sturm, Thomas, 29n28
Stylianopoulos, Theodore, xvi, xx, 92, 94n3, 102n29, 103, 104n33, 125, 125n59, 128, 138, 142–45, 142n49, 142n50, 142n51, 143n52, 143n53, 143n54, 143n55, 143n56, 144n57, 144n58, 144n59, 144n60, 144n61, 144n62, 145n63, 145n64, 158n31, 167n5, 186
Suhrkamp, 6n23
Symeon, Saint, 143

Tarazi, Paul Nadim, 94, 137, 137n32
Taubes, Jacob, 38n12
Taylor, Charles, 33n46, 45n45
Theodore the Studite, Saint, 172
Theokritoff, Elisabeth, 95n6
Thiselton, Anthony, 60n18, 148n1
Tillich, Paul, 119, 174, 174n31
Tracy, David, xv, 52, 52n71, 53, 53n72, 53n73, 53n74, 53n75, 53n76, 53n77, 84, 84n7, 84n8, 84n9, 104n33, 125, 148n1, 156, 157, 181
Trembelas, Panagiotis, 99n20
Tsirpanlis, Constantine, 120–21, 121n48

Turcan, Nicolae, xx, 147, 151–52, 152n15, 164, 187

Ugolnik, Anton, 104n33, 168, 168n12

Valliere, Paul, 132n17
van Gogh, Vincent, 173
Vanhoozer, Kevin, xv, xvin1, 46n46, 48, 48n55, 48n56, 49, 49n57, 49n59, 148n1, 180
Vassiliadis, Petros, 100, 154n19, 167n2
Vattimo, Gianni, 4, 31, 37
Vellas, Vasileos, 99, 101
Verra, Valerio, 4
Vessey, David, 32n41
Vico, Giambattista, 148
Vilhauer, Monika, 68n54, 73n70
Vorobiova, Masha, 114n25

Walker, Nicholas, 30n30
Wallace, Robert, 3n9
Ware, Kallistos, 94n1, 152, 153, 154n17, 155n25
Warnke, Georgia, 105n41
Weinsheimer, Joel C., 37, 37n9, 37n10, 58n7

Weiss, James R., 139n37
Whitehead, Alfred North, 105
Wierciński, Andrzej, 34n50, 66n44
Williams, George H., 96n10
Wittgenstein, Ludwig, 39

Yannaras, Christos, xix, 98, 98n16, 98n17, 99, 99n20, 109, 116, 116n34, 116n35, 117, 117n37, 117n38, 118, 118n39, 118n40, 118n41, 118n42, 118n43, 119, 119n44, 126, 131, 132, 132n14, 159, 185
Young, Frances, 139, 140n43, 141n43

Zabala, Santiago, 36n2
Zimmermann, Jens, 29n29, 33n47, 34n48, 34n49, 34n51, 34n52, 85, 85n12, 86n16
Zizioulas, John, 94, 94n2, 99, 106, 106n42, 106n43, 106n44, 106n45, 107, 124, 124n53, 135n25, 159, 159n35
Zolotas, E., 101
Zwingli, Huldrych, 174
Zymaris, Philip, 170, 170n20